THE
BOOK OF
CATHOLIC AUTHORS

(Fifth Series)

*Informal self-portraits of famous
modern Catholic writers, edited
with preface and notes*

by

WALTER ROMIG

fully illustrated by portraits

WALTER ROMIG—PUBLISHER
979 Lakepointe Road
GROSSE POINTE 30, MICHIGAN

WALTER ROMIG,—PUBLISHER

also issues

The Guide to Catholic Literature
The American Catholic Who's Who
American Catholic Convert Authors
Negro Catholic Writers

PRINTING, TYPOGRAPHY, AND BINDING BY KINGSPORT PRESS, INC.,
KINGSPORT, TENNESSEE

To

SISTER MELANIA GRACE, S.C.

Librarian of Seton Hill College
Greensburg, Pennsylvania

PREFACE

The increasing demand for this series can be regarded only as a command for its continuation. Hence, while this fifth series is going through the press the manuscript of the sixth is in preparation.

The secret of the popularity of the series evidently lies largely in the fact that being autobiographical it brings you both the personality of each author as well as a generous specimen of his writing style.

Also by now it has been proven that the principal purpose of the series is being achieved, namely, that these genial, informal and informative autobiographies of distinguished Catholic writers are leading more and more readers from an author's sketch to his books.

Those who desire greater detail in factual biographical data are referred to the volumes of *The American Catholic Who's Who,* each of which includes biographies of more than seven hundred notable living Catholic writers, and those who want more material on any or all of the author's books are referred to *The Guide to Catholic Literature.*

To all who have shared in the making of this series I express my thanks—a special thanks on this my Twenty-Fifth Anniversary in the Catholic reference field.

WALTER ROMIG

CONTENTS

of the first five series of *The Book of Catholic Authors*, with the number preceding the name indicating in which series the author's chapter is to be found.

AUSTIN JOSEPH APP

"IT IS A HARD AND NICE THING FOR A MAN TO WRITE OF himself," said Cowley. Considering how much authorship has dominated my life, yet how little I have actually written, I feel embarrassed though flattered to have been invited to write about my books. As one who suffers from what Juvenal called "the incurable itch for writing," I console myself reflecting that anyone who feels the Lord's call to be a missionary among cannibals is still more unfortunate! The worst thing about trying to be a writer is that one is always harried for time. It presses one to sacrifice everything, however pleasurable, which can no longer enrich one's knowledge or experience. I usually do not even read the daily papers, substituting for them the more-rewarding and less time-consuming news magazines. Though I could well wish to be married, I have never been able to adjust myself gracefully to the time-killing exigencies of courtship long enough to make it adequately re-

ciprocal! Lucky the people who have the time and the will
to do things just for the fun of it, but they are people
not stricken with the fever to write—or act, or paint, or
compose!

With the effort of writing so absorbing, the pay so meager
and fickle, the hope of glory so unrealistic, only the passion for some cause or truth would seem to justify authorship. Some conscious ideas that have motivated my writings are:

(1) that Christianity, especially Catholic Christianity, should be
accepted all over the world as life's first and greatest blessing;
(2) that literature is the best engine for carrying the ideals of
Christianity from the heads of men to their hearts;
(3) that profane and indecent speech, along with the greater sins
of violence, immorality, and dishonesty, must be vigorously
repressed;
(4) that world peace is God's reward for justice and that enforc-
ing an unjust peace is a criminal responsibility;
(5) and that, to advance Christian ideals, good people must not
only become informed but must also be trained to express
themselves persuasively.

The very titles of my published books suggest these
themes. Even to my doctoral dissertation, *Lancelot in English Literature: His role and Character* (1929), otherwise
favorably reviewed, some "moralizing" is imputed. From
1929 to 1935, as instructor in English at the Catholic University, and from 1935 to 1942, as head of the department
of English at the University of Scranton, I wrote and got
published only three short stories, ten poems, but thirty-
eight articles, some digested in the *Catholic Digest*, and
some hundred book reviews. While in the army (1942-43)
and while administrative assistant in personnel with the
Jaeger Machine Company, Columbus, Ohio, 1943-44, I wrote
more poems, two stories, many articles and reviews. Most
of the latter appeared anonymously in *Best Sellers*, The
bi-monthly magazine which librarian Eugene P. Willging,

Dr. Leonard Wolf and I, all then at the University of Scranton, started in 1941.

After I returned permanently to college teaching, during my professorship at the Incarnate Word College, San Antonio, Texas, from 1944 to 1948, three factors influenced my writing career. For the first time in my teaching life I was not burdened with extension courses so that I had more time. Secondly, the casual advice of one of my former professors, Dr. Peter Leo Johnson, St. Francis Seminary, Milwaukee. His warning that "Article writing gets you nowhere; you must write books if you want to be recognized," shocked me into realizing that in the forties I was getting long on years fast but staying short on books. Thirdly, and most compellingly, I saw with horror that the Yalta and Potsdam pacts were delivering much of Christian Europe to the Bolshevists, who were looting, killing, and ravishing their way into Eastern Germany, Austria, and Hungary. With the approval of American leftists and Morgenthauists, the Communists and Partisans were expelling twelve million ethnic Germans from their ancient homelands, which "forced migration of millions of people," another former professor of mine, now Archbishop Aloisius J. Muench, called "the greatest crime of this age."

When even many Catholic magazines feared to publish the painful truth about Morgenthauism and the Potsdam peace, I felt forced, no matter what the cost, to publish myself. Beginning with a reprint from the Brooklyn *Tablet* entitled "Propaganda 'To Hate All Germans' Is Debunked" (Feb. 16, 1946) by an army officer, upon which as a lucky afterthought I set a price, "One copy, a stamp; ten, 25 cents," I wrote and published in the next five months: "Ravishing the Women of Conquered Europe"; "The Big Three Deportation Crime"; and "Slave-laboring German Prisoners of War." I was overwhelmed by the response. With one swoop my ivory-tower teaching status was ended. Morgenthauistic attacks, angry letters, thank-you and help-seeking letters literally by the thousands, and orders, also by the thousands, flooded into my apartment. In a matter of months several of the pamphlets were out of print at 30,000 copies; one went to 80,000 in English and was translated into four foreign languages.

In December, 1946, collecting some of my articles on war and peace from the *Catholic World, Magnificat,* and *Our Sunday Visitor,* along with a Commencement Address at St. Mary's University and a few unpublished articles, I ventured on a small book, *History's Most Terrifying Peace.* By February a second printing was required. In 1950, Father E. J. Reichenberger's translation into German was published in Austria as *Der Erschreckendste Friede der Geschichte.* It was my first and so far my only book to appear in a foreign language.

Thus encouraged, and so as not to neglect my literature area too much, I collected some of my human interest articles previously published in the *Catholic Home Journal, Magnificat, Queen's Work,* and *The Victorian,* as well as a Commencement Address at Incarnate Word College, and published them as my third book, *Courtesy, Courtship and Marriage.* This too was well reviewed and sold well. However it was a personal failure: I sent an autographed copy to a young woman I hopefully admired; and after some months she sent me an enthusiastic note, saying that she had applied the hints in my book and they *worked*—for she was now happily engaged to be married!

Forming the Mission Press in April, 1948, I published *The True Concept of Literature,* more ambitiously in a cloth and in a paper edition. This consists of some of my critical articles from the *Catholic World, The Classical Bulletin, The Catholic Educational Review, College English, Magnificat,* and one long chapter on "How to Judge a Novel Artistically," which, with the republished one, "How to Judge a Novel Ethically," one reviewer, Father G. W.

Hafford in the *Salesianum*, called "well worth the price of admission." I myself fondly believed *The True Concept of Literature* to be an enduring contribution towards fixing the nature, function, and proper place of literature.

Since my becoming associate professor of English at La Salle College, Philadelphia, in 1948, the Mission Press is the Boniface Press.

After a summer in Europe in 1949 and another in 1951, I published other pamphlets and many journalistic articles, some in German, on conditions in Central Europe. Since 1952 I write a weekly column entitled "Here and Abroad" for the Nord-*Amerika*, of Philadelphia.

My most unified and successful book so far has been *Making Good Talk: How to Improve Your Conversation*, published in 1950. It went into a second printing, became the choice of the Catholic Literary Foundation for November, 1950, and led to my election in 1951 to the Gallery of Living Catholic Authors. As a first grader, during a catechism class in St. James Parish, Mequon, Wisconsin, after I had labored through the story of Jesus being lost in the Temple, Father Anthony Bertram, my first pastor, while warmly complimenting me, added in an aside to the parents in back, that of course I was to be excused for employing too many *ands*. This comment made me conscious ever after of over-coordination and of other faults and virtues in speech. By and by I collected instances on 4x6 cards and in 9x12 folders, my custom with all topics that interest me. In 1948-49, upon Father Clement J. Lambert's preference, I contributed three articles on conversation to the *Marianist*. When I showed them to Mr. Aloysius Croft, an editor of Bruce, he said "Why not recast and expand these into a book." By June 15, 1949, the twelve-chapter book was written.

In general, nearly everything I write has kicked around a comparatively long time in my mind and in my files, but when I once start the actual writing the first draft proceeds fast, at the rate of some two or three thousand words a day. The first draft, later carefully revised and shortened by thirty pages, of my latest book, *Way to Creative Writing*, was started on June 15, 1953, and finished 330 typed pages later on August 14. This text on how to become a writer is the only one to date that includes specific chapters on each creative genre: poetry, essay, short story, plays, and novel.

Several other subjects have now been agitating my mind and accumulating in my files long enough to encourage my hope that a seventh book will soon be under way.

EDITOR'S NOTE: *Making Good Talk* (1950) and *Way to Creative Writing* (1954) are both Bruce books. Dr. App's thesis on Lancelot is a Catholic University Press book and his other works are available from his own Boniface Press, 5353 Magnolia st., Phila. 44, Pa.

WILLIAM EDMUND BARRETT

THE INITIAL CREATIVE URGE IS MERELY TO WRITE, TO EX-
press thought and feeling in words, heedless of form. I
felt that urge early. While attending Manhattan Prep I
wrote a verse which was published in the New York *Evening Journal*. I wrote many more, but my lifetime total
of published verses stands at three. My teenage fiction was
not published. It was written with the hope that it would
be. I was not ready, even in a tentative, unsure way, to
write fiction until my mid-twenties. I did write articles
and essays, newspaper feature stories and advertising copy.
Unless a writer is endowed, and very few writers are, he
must support his own creative development.

My first fiction was published while I was southwestern
advertising manager for Westinghouse. My stories were
written at night, in hotel rooms, in oil camps, in the odd
corners of the seventeen states which comprised my territory. The avocation ultimately became my vocation. I

resigned from Westinghouse in 1929 to devote all my time
to creative writing.

I embarked on my freelancing career during the depression years. It was a difficult time. People were letting
their magazine subscriptions expire and buying few magazines on the newsstands. They were borrowing their books
from the libraries. Many book publishers went bankrupt
and the survivors published small lists. As advertising fell
off, magazines grew thin, using fewer stories. The writing of books became the luxury of the comparative few.

Many interviewers have tried to make a sob story out of
the experience of depression freelancing. It was not that.
The depression years had the grandeur of epic tragedy in
these United States, and tragedy is a spiritual experience.
The people who were an author's contemporaries, and the
people who were an author's models, had courage. An author did not have to seek for drama, for bravery, for compassion, for shining faith; it was all around him.

There was very little demand in the thirties for the so-
called "realistic novel," or the novel of social significance.
People wanted stories of hope and faith and gallantry. We
who wrote had trouble, because it was a time of trouble;
but we learned to keep our fear and our worry and our
personal disasters out of our writing. The reader had trouble of his own and we did not offer him more. That was
a great lesson to learn. I wrote adventure stories and detective stories. If they were not significant, neither were
they defeatist.

The novel which was a project when I started freelancing
had been dated by events before it was finished, and necessarily abandoned. A book on the American air squadrons
of the first world war, for which I had a contract and on
which I expended much work, was also abandoned when
the contracting publisher went into bankruptcy. I became dependent upon the popular magazines for a creative
outlet and I developed a respect for them that I have never

lost. Magazine readers are the most responsive of all audiences. They write letters and they provide the author
with his greatest reward for the toil of writing, the knowledge that he is touching lives.

The depression did not end in 1932; it continued through
most of the thirties. If there were grants, fellowships, or
foundations for the financing of worthy books in that period, I never heard of them. An author with a project, or
a hope, financed it himself or it never developed into a book.
My wife and I were living in Washington, where the ill-
fated air squadron book had taken us. I wanted to do the
joint biography of Francisco Lopez and Elisa Lynch of
Paraguay, which appealed to me as the most dramatic story
in all of Spanish America. My adventure and detective
stories supported the writing of it. For four and a half
years I worked on my shorter projects through the days,
and spent the nights, till closing time, at the Library of
Congress or the Lima Library of Catholic University.

My wife worked many nights with me. We searched
the daily newspapers of mid-nineteenth century Paris, the
newspapers of Buenos Aires and Asuncion from the same
period, in the Library of Congress catacombs. We examined original source material which the Library had bor-
rowed from the government archives of Brazil and the Ar-
gentine. We examined other documents and relics of the
Paraguayan War in Lima Library. The research notes
totaled a quarter of a million words; the finished book,
150,000 words.

Woman on Horseback, the Lopez-Lynch biography, was
published in 1938 and is still in print, the most often quoted
work on Paraguay and a standard volume in college courses
on Spanish-American history. It is dedicated: "To Christine, who rides a retreat as gallantly as she rides an advance."

There were other books, most of them out of print now,
and many magazine stories; serials, short stories and com-

plete novels. In the writing of them my own writing philosophy developed. I became deeply aware of the reader because he, or she, so often wrote to me. I became convinced that a reader reads fiction for an extension of his own experience. He reads to widen his horizons, to escape from time and place and circumstance, from the narrow confines of a single existence; to live, for a time, in other lives. The experience that I offered the reader, the people to whose lives I introduced him, became a personal responsibility. I could not offer him life stripped of humanity without being false to reason, nor life reduced to the physical without being false to Art. As I matured, I tried to present life through fiction in the three dimensions of body, mind and soul.

The Left Hand of God was my outstanding popular success. It was serialized in *Red Book Magazine,* with a circulation of more than two million. It sold over a million copies in the combined Doubleday and Pocket Book editions. It has been translated into nine languages, including Arabic. It was made into a motion picture. *The Left Hand of God* was an adventure story in which the spiritual adventure paralleled the physical. It was the story of a man engaged in sacrilege, of a layman measuring himself against the priesthood. Its suspense, its plausibility, the significance of its central theme of sacrilege, all hinged on the acceptance of the true meaning of the act of Consecration in the Mass, of the true presence of Jesus Christ in the Blessed Sacrament. *The Left Hand of God* has been called a Catholic novel. It received most of its critical and popular support from non-Catholics.

The success of that work made it possible for me to devote two entire years, with no other writing whatever, to the writing of a novel as I believed that a novel should be written. The result was *The Shadow of the Images.* It began as a fictional study of spiritual conflicts in American universities where the most ardent defenders of religious

faith often, inexplicably, lose that faith. It did not take
me long to discover that colleges and universities can be
understood only in terms of the larger communities which
contain them. *The Shadow of the Images,* then, became a
novel of sinners, a novel of the modern city, of good and
evil. The popular reception disappointed me but the book
did not, and does not. It still represents my concept of the
novel.

Another book died unborn between *The Shadows of the
Images* and *The Sudden Strangers.* I worked for a year on
the biography of J. K. Huysmans, French novelist and art
critic of the nineties, a reformed occultist who became a
great exponent of Catholic mysticism. Two English writers
published biographies of Huysmans within three months
of each other. I reluctantly discarded a year's work, de-
clining the doubtful honor of writing the third.

The Sudden Strangers was written around the conflict
between illusion and reality in modern life. The action
moved from back stage to a monastery. It was the August
1956 choice of the Catholic Digest Book Club and is proving
surprisingly popular in Europe where the number of translations may yet equal those of *The Left Hand of God.*

The novel in process is laid against the background of
French Canada. It, too, may be regarded as a Catholic
novel, but I do not consider myself a Catholic novelist. Any
adjective before the term "novelist," implies a subordina-
tion of art to propaganda. Any novel with a qualifying
adjective is less than a novel. I write in the three dimensions of body, mind and soul. For the third dimension
I am often compelled to draw upon the symbols and the
philosophies with which I am most familiar, but I respect
the prayers of any man who prays and I deny the realism
of any wide-scale novel in which no one prays.

I was born in New York City in 1900, attended Christian
Brothers schools and Manhattan College. My wife (née
Christine Rollman) was born in Texas and attended Mount

St. Joseph's on the Ohio. She writes and she is a part of all my writing. We live in Denver. Our daughter, Marjorie, a graduate of Loretto Heights College, is a feature writer and assistant to the drama editor of the *Rocky Mountain News*. Our son, Bill, a graduate of Georgetown University, is picture editor for N.C.W.C. News Service in Washington, D. C. He and his wife, Mary, live in Arlington, Virginia. We are a very fortunate family and the owners of many typewriters.

EDITOR'S NOTE: Doubleday published *The Left Hand of God* (1950) *The Shadow of the Images* (1953), and *The Sudden Strangers* (1952), and reprinted *Woman on Horseback* with additional bibliographical data in 1952. Mr. Barrett is a member of the Serra Club, the Nocturnal Adoration Society, and the First Friday Club.

HILAIRE BELLOC
(1870 - 1953)

JOSEPH HILAIRE PIERRE BELLOC, ONE OF THE TRUE LORDS
of the English language, was not an Englishman by birth.
His father was French, his mother was Irish; and when
he married, his bride was an American. But he looked
more like the traditional figure of John Bull than any Englishman could. He wore a stand-up collar several sizes too
large for him. His rotund head was crowned with a black
hat—sometimes tall, sometimes of the pancake variety. He
was big and stocky and red of face, and a typically British
great-coat draped his beefy form except in the warmest
weather.

Hilaire Belloc—he dropped the other appendages at an
early age—was born at La Celle, near Paris, on July 20,
1870. His father, Louis Swanton Belloc, was well known
as a barrister throughout France. Bessie Rayner Belloc,
his mother, was of Irish extraction. Somewhere in his immediate background was an infusion of Pennsylvania Dutch

blood. His mother, who lived into her nineties and died
in 1914, was a remarkably intellectual woman, noted as
one of the signers of the first petition ever presented for
women's suffrage.

Her son studied at the Oratory School at Edgebaston,
England, and at Balliol College, Oxford, where he matric-
ulated in 1893. In his third year he was Blackenbury History Scholar and an honor student in the history schools.

Between Oratory School and his matriculation at Oxford, Belloc served in the French Army, where as a driver
in the Eighth Regiment of Artillery, he was stationed at
Toul. It was from this spot that, years later, he was to set
forth on the pilgrimage afoot to St. Peter's that furnished
material for the book that many critics consider his best,—
The Path to Rome.

In 1903 Belloc became a British subject and in 1906 was
returned to Parliament by the South Salford constituency.
He was a member of the Liberal party in the brilliant House
of Commons created by the Tory debacle of the preceding
year. He made his maiden speech in the House early in
1906 and it won him an immediate reputation as a brilliant
orator. He had already attracted considerable attention
during his campaign. In the year of his return to Parliament he was also the nominee of the British Bishops to
the Catholic Education Council.

Belloc's literary career began immediately after Balliol.
He rapidly achieved success as a newspaper and magazine
writer and as a light versifier. His first book, published
in the year of his graduation, was *Verses and Sonnets,*
and this was followed within a year by *The Bad Child's
Book of Beasts,* in which his reputation as a master of
whimsy was fully established. One of the most famous
in this category starts out thus:

> The nicest child I ever knew
>   Was Charles Augustus Fortesque;
> He never lost his cap or tore
>   His stockings or his pinafore;

In eating bread he made no crumbs.
He was extremely fond of sums.

Another, more dire, ballad about an untruthful maiden
named Mathilde was a famous forerunner to the Ogden
Nash style of rhyming:

It happened that a few weeks later
Her aunt was off to the theatre
To see that entertaining play
The Second Mrs. Tanqueray.

Belloc sat in the House of Commons from 1906 to 1910,
but refused to serve a second term because, in his own
words, he was "weary of the party system," and thought
he could attack politics better from without Parliament
than from within. From that time on he devoted his entire efforts to writing and lecturing.

Belloc's wife, the former Elodie Agnes Hogan of Napa,
California, whom he married in 1896, died in 1914. He
never remarried. His eldest son, Louis, was killed while
serving as a flier in World War I, and his youngest, Peter,
a captain of the Royal Marines, died during World War II.
Belloc made his home with his elder daughter, Mrs. Eleanor
Jebb, wife of a member of Parliament, in Horsham, Sussex.
Besides Eleanor, he had another daughter, Elizabeth, a poet,
as well as another son, Hilary, who lives in Canada. Belloc's
sister, Mrs. Marie Belloc Lowndes, also a noted British
writer, died in 1947.

By Pope Pius XI, Belloc was decorated with the Grand
Cross of the Order of St. Gregory the Great in 1934 for his
services to Catholicism as a writer. In the same year, his
alma mater, Oxford, conferred upon him the honorary degree of Master of Arts. He shared with the then British
Prime Minister, Sir Winston Churchill, the distinction of
being the only persons to have their portraits hung in the
National Portrait Gallery while they were alive.

Mr. Belloc visited the United States on many occasions.
In 1937 he served as a visiting Professor of History at

the Graduate School of Fordham University in New York. From the matter of these lectures came his book, *The Crisis of Civilization*.

A prolific writer, he was the author of 153 books of essays, fiction, history, biography, poetry and light verse as well as a vast amount of periodical literature. He was largely responsible for G. K. Chesterton's conversion to Catholicism, and the two of them became ranked as not only among England's greatest writers but as the most brilliant lay expounders of Catholic doctrine. The two were also close friends and frequent collaborators, especially on the magazine which came to be known as *G. K's. Weekly*, and in which they came to wage many a valiant crusade together. As a critic noted: "To Hilaire Belloc this generation owes big glimpses of the Homeric spirit. His mission is to flay alive the humbugs and hypocrites and the pedants and to chant robust folk-songs to the naked stars of the English world to a rousing obligato of clinking flagons."

Because of his antagonism to many British sacred cows and his free and caustic criticism of them, he was not a wholly popular man in England. Nor did his espousal of the Franco cause against the Communists during the Spanish civil war add to his popularity there. But Belloc had never been a man to purchase popularity at the price of integrity.

Just four days before his eighty-third birthday, while dozing before the fireplace in his daughter's home, he fell into the flames and was so badly burned that he died in hospital at Guildford, Surrey, soon afterward on July 16, 1953.

Despite his own prediction to the contrary, his place in English letters is forever secure, primarily as a poet and as the author of *The Path to Rome*.

EDITOR'S NOTE: Among recent reprints of Belloc's works are *The Cruise of the Nona* (Newman, 1956), *The Path to Rome* (Regnery,

1954, and Image Books, Doubleday, 1956), *Joan of Arc* (McMullen, 1949), *Selected Cautionary Verses* (Penguin, 1950), *Stories, Essays and Poems* (Everyman's Library, Dutton, 1948), *The Servile State* (Holt, 1946), and *Sonnets and Verse* (Sheed, 1946).

Notable books on his life and works include *The Young Hilaire Belloc*, by Marie Belloc Lowndes (Kenedy, 1956), *Hilaire Belloc: a Memoir*, by John B. Morton (Sheed, 1955), *Hilaire Belloc, No Alienated Man*, by F. D. Wilhelmsen (Sheed, 1953), *Hilaire Belloc: an Introduction to His Spirit and Work*, by Robert Hamilton (Organ, 1945), and *Testimony to Hilaire Belloc*, by Reginald and Eleanor Jebb (Methuen, 1956). In 1953 Patrick C. Cahill of 20 Cavendish Gardens, London, S.W.4, compiled and published *The English First Editions of Hilaire Belloc*, a chronological catalogue of the 153 works attributed to our author.

EVA KELLY BETZ
(Mrs. Joseph P. Betz)

FALL RIVER, MASSACHUSETTS, WHERE I WAS BORN (ON A DATE preferably undisclosed) was a splendid place in which to grow up and my home there was a stimulating, warm, welcoming one, always full of life. I came from a family of readers and writers. Talk was good in our dining room where guests from all parts of the world and all walks of life were welcome if they brought interesting conversation. Irish Members of Parliament, bishops, boys and girls from school, authors, travelers,—the list was catholic, lengthy, and constant. My role was that of listener because my parents, brother, and sister were all intellectual, and I was not. I had a half-wild horse to ride and lovely Mount Hope Bay to swim in.

My first book, written when I was about nine, has fortunately been lost to posterity. It was about horses. They creep into everything I write.

I went to St. Mary's parochial school, the Dominican high school and then on to Kenwood in Albany.

I became a school teacher, first in various Rhode Island towns and then in Fall River. During that time I wrote a few things for teachers' magazines, some bits of verse and some one-act plays for children.

After my marriage in 1923 to Joseph P. Betz, City Attorney in Passaic, N. J., the writing slowed for a while but after our son, Peter, was born and needed a new story each night I began setting some of them down. They were later aired on radio station WOR where I had a program for a season.

Being an omniverous reader I was delighted when I discovered the world of book reviewing where you get all the new books free and are paid for saying what you think of them. I said—in the Providence *Journal,* two small Catholic magazines, on the lecture platform and on radio. Through this period, to my husband's amused amazement, I organized the Girl Scouts in the area and was the first Commissioner, was on the organizing board of the board of directors of the Community Chest, organized our parish unit of the National Council of Catholic Women, was president of the New Jersey Women's Press Club, housekeeper, family chauffeur, and mender of toys of increasing complexity as Peter grew.

In World War II, when Peter was on an LCT for the Normandy invasion (his father had been a mine layer in the North Sea in World War I), I added driving for the AWVS in New York to my schedule.

I stopped in our branch public library one day for some books and found the librarian disgruntled because teachers kept sending children for reading books about New Jersey during the Revolution and there were none. She suggested that I write some.

Having grown up in New England, I felt sure that the Revolution was a New England activity. Of course I was willing to give a nod to Patrick Henry in the Virginia House of Burgesses and a bow to Trenton—I remembered that bit because that was where, according to the painting, George Washington stood up in a rowboat, which had always seemed to be singularly unintelligent for the man who was to be the Father of his Country. But, on the whole, I felt that the Revolution belonged to New England.

I was interested, however, in trying the books because I was anxious to make a certain point—that the Revolution was not the effort of one single religious or racial group but the work of many people of many backgrounds; people similar only in their love of liberty.

As soon as I dipped into research, I discovered that New Jersey, lying as it did between the prize cities of New York and Philadelphia, was the cockpit of the Revolution. I dove into books, old papers, diaries and records and came up with material for a dozen books. I fell in love with the four young people about whom my stories revolve and carried them through four volumes from 1774 to 1781.

During the years in which they were being written, Peter came home from war, went to college, married, and has two sons of his own. I became a member of the Authors' League, the National Women's Book Association, the Mark Twain Association (honorary), and was given an honorary life membership in the New Jersey Historical Society.

My patient husband remained amused but unsurprised when I went to the St. Anthony Guild Press in Paterson first to do sales promotion and then advertising. The first books of my Revolutionary series had been under another imprint but now they have joined the later ones and all bear the Guild imprint, as does my latest, a life of Father Damien of Molokai for young people.

I am eager to go on with these teenage books because children nowaday seem to be offered such shoddy "heroes" in too many cases.

My father, a doctor who wrote poetry for John Boyle

O'Reilly's Boston *Pilot,* used to come upstairs after office hours were over, and read or tell us legends and stories of Irish saints and scholars. My mother, great-grand-niece of the famous Bishop Cantwell of Mullingar, had her own collection of tales. They were all dramatic and all, I realize now, inspirational. My tomboy youth cultivated in me a love of excitement and approval of people who get things done. Such people are fun to write about. I would like to help children realize that goodness and dullness are not necessarily synonymous.

EDITOR'S NOTE: St. Anthony Guild Press now publishes Mrs. Betz's four New Jersey in the Revolution stories for young readers, all illustrated by June Driscoll: *Young Eagles* (1947), *Desperate Drums* (1951), *Freedom Drums* (1953), and *Victory Drums* (1955), as well as her *Knight of Molokai* (1956).

REVEREND HYACINTH
BLOCKER, O.F.M.

IN LOOKING BACK, OFTEN AN AUTHOR IS CONFUSED WHEN HE tries to isolate the incidents or pinpoint the circumstances that led him to write. As far as I can recall, the first noticeable nudge to clothe ideas with paper and ink came from the Franciscan English teacher in my fifth year of the minor seminary. He coaxed me into writing poetry. That I consider an amazing achievement for any English teacher (having for a while been one myself).

Later, during my theological studies in the major seminary (Holy Family Friary, Oldenburg, Indiana), I discovered—and this is rather disconcerting—that I frequently had more time yo-yoing at my fingertips than I knew what to do with. Or was I deluding myself? Anyway, hours that otherwise would have been vacuous and vapid in this somnolent country village I turned to writing.

Being young at the time, brashly optimistic and utterly unacquainted with the ways and wiles of the world, I had that youthful color-blindness that sees everything through the sunset glow of poetry. For some time the first products of my neophytic pen were poems, simple and sugary little things that the editor of the *St. Anthony Messenger* condescended to publish. This was in 1926.

For the record, I should interpolate here that I was born on Lincoln's Birthday in 1904 in Louisville, Kentucky, the second youngest son of seven children of an old-fashioned but a moderately successful grocer and saloon-keeper. He had immigrated to the United States from Germany. My mother, a sliver of a woman who lived to be 86, came from a farm in Indiana. Some day I hope to write nostalgically of the 'good old days' in a book to be titled "Papa Was a Saloon-Keeper."

Ordained by Bishop Chartrand of Indianapolis in 1930, I was assigned to teach English literature and composition in Roger Bacon High School, Cincinnati, Ohio. During the summer vacations (what a misnomer for a teacher trying to get a degree!) I attended Catholic University, taking postgraduate courses in English and education. One of my campus companions was Theodore Maynard, getting his Ph.D. while teaching during the year at Georgetown; and one of my teachers in a course on the romantic poets of the nineteenth century was the accomplished author, George N. Shuster. It was here in Gibbons' Hall, that I also heard Sister Madeleva read her poems. Such chance contacts intensified my interest in literature and creative writing.

Naturally, my teaching assignments at Roger Bacon helped considerably too. I always believed that before I could actually teach my pupils the fundamentals of creative writing, I should be able to show them that I could do the very thing I expected of them. As a result, there were so many character sketches, descriptive pieces, informal essays and similar 'home-work' compositions that I wrote for and read in my classes that I seriously began to plan my own textbook.

During these years—and they were challenging, invigorating and consoling ones despite the drudgery and discouragement often associated with teaching—my extracurricular activities consisted in supervising the school's literary magazine, yearbook, poetry and debating clubs. With approximately 150 junior students every day in English, I had a program which, though heavy scholastically speaking, brought me into contact with much that was written, good, bad and indifferent, in the past and in the present.

Then suddenly—as often happens in religious life—after six years of teaching I awakened one morning to discover that I was an editor. The editor of the *St. Anthony Messenger* became gravely ill. I was told to take his place until he could return to duty. What for me was to have been a temporary assignment of a month or two lengthened into nearly ten years. How well I remember my introduction into the editorial chair! It was January 27, 1937, with the worst flood in the history of the Ohio valley inundating Cincinnati and throwing the city into panic and confusion. Deprived of both electricity and gas, using candles for light and additional layers of clothing for warmth, I put the February issue to bed, thanks to the help of the editor's secretary who managed somehow to drive by a round-about way from her home in the suburbs to the cold downtown office.

During these six years of teaching and ten of editing, I continued to write—poems, editorials, expository articles, even short stories, some under my own name, many more pseudonymously under bylines long since forgotten. My first book was a collection of poems, *Locust Bloom,* published in 1938. Its sale was mediocre, one thousand copies, but it did satisfy a desire to have what I considered my better poems a little more permanently packaged. Not that posterity really cared!

That decade of editing embraced the happiest and, in

many ways the most fruitful, years of my life. I came into contact with one of the finest fellowships in the professional field, the men and women of the Catholic press. There was a camaraderie in the national and regional conventions of the Catholic Press Association that would be difficult to duplicate in similar groups of individuals bound by a common cause. Even more, there was the inspiration and encouragement to be derived from association with men dedicated to an apostolate as essential for the salvation of souls as the pastoral tasks of preaching, catechising and administering the Sacraments.

I served one term on the executive board of the Catholic Press Association when the late and lovable Monsignor Peter Wynhoven of New Orleans was president; edited for one year the Association's monthly news bulletin; supervised the Association's annual short story contest; and appeared as speaker or discussion leader at various conventions. Busy years but happy ones because I was doing what I liked, and for which I considered myself qualified and equipped.

In the summer of 1946 my religious superiors transferred me to the Franciscan home mission band of the Cincinnati province of St. John the Baptist. During the next five years I preached parish missions, retreats to nuns, Forty Hours, triduums, and other courses of sermons wherever duty called me, traveling from Calumet in the north to San Antonio in the south, and from Lowell in the east to Gallup in the west. Living out of a suitcase, serving as the channel through which God poured His mercy upon sinners, I was able to see the United States more completely and intimately than if I had joined the army or navy. I have said more than once that this experience, in the rusty realm of dollars and cents, was worth a million, there being no better way to study the human heart and the sad results of original sin. No priestly work is so consoling and so spiritually rewarding, but it takes a rough constitution, a rugged nervous system and a relentless faith to hold up under the work for a long time.

For me those years on the mission band proved in many ways the proverbial blessing in disguise. Between consulting bus and train schedules, clicking off thousands of confessions in that tiny dark box which holds the history of the world, and selling salvation by tongue, I was able to write two books, *Good Morning, Good People,* and *Walk With the Wise.* The former, a collection of retreat conferences for religious, will soon appear in its fourth printing, and the latter, sermonettes based upon incidents in the lives of fifty saints, is selling well in its second.

Authorship has many compensations, not the smallest of which is the fan mail and the friendships that unexpectedly come the writer's way. I have had letters (as no doubt many other writers have had too) from such faraway places as New Zealand, India, England, Ireland, the Philippines, Australia, Germany, most of them, I must admit, from nuns who had read my *Good Morning, Good People.* Much unsolicited mail also reached my desk from readers in this country.

In mid-June, 1951, I returned to Louisville, Kentucky, where I was then stationed, from two consecutive retreats preached to nuns in Dubuque, Iowa, and I had not even unpacked when a telephone call from Cincinnati informed me that the chapter meeting of our province had elected me a definitor, or board member. That same summer chapter appointed me the rector of St. Francis Seminary, situated in the rolling hills of Mount Healthy, a town bordering Cincinnati. This double post of definitor and rector I served for one three-year term, the assignments terminating in 1954.

The next year I taught English and American literature in Duns Scotus College, Detroit, where I also had charge of the large nine-hundred-member Third Order of

St. Francis fraternity which meets monthly in the college chapel.

Since the summer of 1955 I have been the director of the Friarhurst Retreat House, Cincinnati, where every weekend the whole year round, excluding conflicts with national holidays, a closed retreat is held for lay men and lay women. During the winter and spring months four to five local high schools also send all of their senior girls to Friarhurst for a three-day closed retreat.

My future plans? I still have a book or two that I hope to write. These will evolve from the planning stage only when days have more than twenty-four hours or I can discover a method of going without sleep.

EDITOR'S NOTE: St. Anthony Guild Press published Fr. Blocker's *Locust Bloom and Other Poems* (1938), while *Good Morning, Good People*, and *Walk With the Wise* (both 1950) bear the imprint of St. Francis Bookshop, 1618 Vine st., Cincinnati 10, Ohio.

T(HOMAS) BOWYER
CAMPBELL

I AM, ONE MIGHT SAY, THE CLEAR EXAMPLE OF THE HAS-
been because my life has been of frequent change from one
thing to another. Or would it be paradox?

I was born and educated in Virginia. My forebears were
all Protestants, nothing extra, and no clergymen ever
amongst them. From my infancy, however, the trends to
religion were strong, ultimately motivating my whole life.
I loved going to church because of what served for the
Episcopalian liturgy, and I looked down upon other Protestants for their lack of a service-book.

But as I began my collegiate studies I receded from the
religion I had known. I hit on a sort of liberalism as the
ticket for me. Then, during my last year in college (William and Mary), I met a new student who had come to
begin his preparation for going to an Episcopal seminary
to become a minister. He was a good, sensible fellow. He
told me of the doctrine of Apostolic Succession, and I caught

my first notion of sacramentalism. It fascinated me: there might be something in Episcopal Christianity after all. In 1910, I entered the seminary with my friend.

But the Alexandria Seminary was evangelical, that is Low Church; only the bars were lowered for a dash of liberalism in tribute to the times. I quailed at the prospect of remaining in the to me stifling air of Virginia Episcopal Protestantism. A wild thought struck me: I would go to the ends of the earth: I would go to China. And off I sailed as soon as I had got my degree and been ordained.

In the Episcopalian mission at Shanghai the churchmanship was academic with heavy emphasis on do-goodism; it was Protestant and static. What to do? If I could form or better still join a monastic group, my personal problem as well as my ideal would be realized. As I was casting about, an offer came from the Cowley Fathers in America. Would I come home to serve a novitiate and then be returned to China? I accepted the offer. It all came to nothing, for in the end I left the novitiate, yet I had learned a lot of Catholic living. In two new respects I was now a has-been.

My ambitious scheme to combine missionary work in China with promoting the growth of the religious life in Anglicanism lay in ruins. And so circumstances forced me to a run of seven or eight years in one Anglo-Catholic parish after another. It was rather stultifying. An effort to bring the so-called Catholic Movement back on the road to Rome seemed to me essential. I found among my confreres a few of like conviction, disillusioned with the trend of the Movement, fearful of eclecticism and hating Modernism. Four of us organized the Confraternity of Unity to proclaim and promote our aims and point of view: return of the schismatic Anglican Communion to the center of Catholic authority and unity.

Modest as our efforts were, an uproar of dissent faced us from all the ranks of Episcopalianism, chiefly from

the High Church Party itself. We were regarded as traitors
within the fold, and our very livings were jeopardized.

It was then that I began to write in order to earn money
for a livelihood. I had formerly tried my hand at writing,
even when at college and soon after. I had written a play
(an unmitigated low comedy) and the college dramatic club
acted it. And I had written a sentimental novel shot
through with a religious thread. It was never submitted
to a publisher; and I tore up the manuscript in Shanghai.
In the late 1920s, I wrote several articles which were published in the (now defunct) Episcopalian *American Church
Monthly* whose editor was Dr. Selden Delany until he became a Catholic in 1929. I did book-reviews for the same
periodical. Everything I wrote had a pro-Roman slant.

At just about that time my brother and his wife had
each begun to write successful novels. Why shouldn't I
follow suit? Why not, indeed!

Late in 1927 I began to write *Black Sadie*. Imagine my
elation when the Houghton Mifflin Company of Boston re-
tained it when I had written only two paragraphs. It appeared in 1928. It was a story of Colored people in three
social and economic brackets: in Virginia some two decades
after the emancipation, in the north as house servants with
higher wages, and lastly entering into professional and
creative work. The publishers held out a carrot before the
donkey: they thought *Black Sadie* might be a Guild choice.
But Julia Peterkin's *Scarlet Sister Mary* supplanted *Black
Sadie*.

Houghton Mifflin had more carrots in their pharmaco-
poeia. They accepted my second novel, written fast on the
heels of *Black Sadie*. It was entitled *Old Miss* and was
the life of my great-grandmother who bridged all the times
and changes from 1808 to 1898. *Old Miss* appeared in
October 1929 and was a financial failure because of the
Wall Street crash at the same time.

In the meantime, in 1928, with my head turned by what

seemed unexpected success, I sailed off to England. I now
felt financially safe and free enough to carry our Confraternity to the very heart and head of Anglicanism. Soon there
was a coterie forming a branch of the Confraternity. We
published a leaflet of which I was co-editor and large contributor. And all that year I worked on a third novel.

My returning to the United States in the fall of 1929 was
not a wise move. I found myself merely a minister-at-large
in the Episcopal Church. *Old Miss* was not selling well
because of the depression; and Houghton Mifflin refused to
publish the new book I had sent them. I was not, however,
without prospects: *Old Miss* and *Black Sadie* were going
to be published by William Collins & Sons in England.

In February 1930 I returned to England. I was employed
as part-time assistant at St. Paul's Church, Oxford. Collins
had also accepted the novel Houghton Mifflin had rejected
on the grounds that it was a 'hot' subject and that the depression looked bad for the sale of new books. I had entitled the book *Sweet Chariot;* Collins changed it to *White
Nigger.* I didn't like that name. The story dealt with the
problem of the person in whose veins ran merely a few
drops of Negro blood. To which race could he belong?
Would the Negroes assimilate him, or could he 'pass' white?
The book was far from a success, for the English people
see no urgency in that question. A. M. Heath & Company,
my agents, sold *The Sketch* a couple of short stories.

I was existing on a considerably frayed shoe-string. I
set myself to write a pot-boiler. It took me a year to turn
out *Far Trouble,* a story of kidnapping and mystery in
the China of 1927. Collins published it in England in 1931
and McRae Smith in the United States in 1932. Monied reward was insubstantial, and I called a halt to writing. I
had to consider myself once more a has-been.

The Lambeth Conference consists of all the Anglican
bishops and their corporate voice is all the expression the
mind of Anglicanism has. The pronouncements of the Con-

ference meeting in London in the summer of 1930 finally and fully killed whatever confidence I had clung to in the Anglican Communion. Therefore, in August of 1931, at the Paulist Fathers' Church of Santa Susanna in Rome, I was received into the Catholic Church, having some months previously cast off from Anglicana.

At that moment when everything whereon I had stood was gone—profession, friends, dear ties and associations—a cable came offering me a post to teach history at the University of Notre Dame. Naturally, I accepted gladly, and at Notre Dame I remained for sixteen years. Then the War came and the accelerated program at Notre Dame to pressure-train officers for the Navy. I began to sink under the strain and just as the War ended I had a nervous breakdown. The only cure was retirement. I cut loose from Notre Dame, having developed a strong allergy for that institution.

For a year or more I was struggling back to my feet. In the meantime I tried to find a publisher for the book written years before which I had called *Sweet Chariot*. No luck, after many tries. I wrote a full-length book on the Virginia scene of the 1890s, calling it *Our Gentle Hills*. No publisher for that either. And I roughed out a novel with a dual locale: Virginia of the turn of the century and China of the Red conquest. Further, I partly completed a personal memoir: *The Pendant Years*.

All the while I cast about for another teaching job. At my age and lacking a Ph.D., one was hard to find. I really wanted a berth in a small college where the pressure of life would be less severe. At length I found it at St. Bede in Illinois, and here I came in September of 1949. Life is busy, pleasant and easy. The summers are free, and then I go to Virginia, to Bedford, the village where I was born and passed my boyhood. There I have been able to renew many early associations and friendships, though being a Catholic I am thought a rather queer fish far adrift from my spawning grounds. And I have had time to do a little writing, too; merely a few articles published in the English language edition of *Unitas,* and one short story and an article in *The Catholic World,* the one in the November 1949, the other in the September 1956 issue.

Such is the story of a has-been. I am nothing that I once was. My books have been out of print for many years. Time has certainly rolled away behind me.

Monsignor Joseph Cardijn

CANON JOSEPH CARDIJN
by
Reverend Eugene Langdale

JOSEPH CARDIJN, ELDEST SON OF HENRI CARDIJN AND LOUISE van Daelen, was born on November 13th, 1882, at Schaerbeck, a district of Brussels, where his parents were employed as caretakers of a small block of flats. Madame Cardijn's bad state of health did not allow her to nurse her child, and young Joseph was entrusted to the care of his grandparents, who lived at Hal, a small Flemish town to the south of Brussels, on the borders of Brabant and Hainault. His parents joined him there a few years later, and his father took up a coal merchant's business—a very modest affair, which gave to the family a relative degree of prosperity and independence.

The childhood and adolescence of Joseph Cardijn were spent in a typical Christian home of Flanders. Monsieur Cardijn, his father, could neither read nor write, but he was a man of high principle and deep religious conviction. His children were brought up strictly, and Monsignor Cardijn has told us how one long whistle up the stairs was a sufficient reveille when he was due to serve Mass at the parish Church. He does not tell us what happened if a second call was needed!

Joseph Cardijn began his education at the elementary school with the working-class boys of the little town. The impact of industrial development was making itself felt in Flanders, and Hal was fast becoming the centre of an industrial district. When Joseph was about to leave school, his parents naturally thought of placing him in a factory, but the lad had other ambitions. This is how he has told the story of his vocation:

"It was the eve of my entry into the factory. I went up to the bedroom with my brothers and sisters. When they were all in bed, I crept down barefoot to the kitchen, where my father and mother, in spite of the late hour, were talking by the fireside.

" 'Father,' said I, 'there's something I want to ask you. Please let me continue my studies!'

" 'But you know well enough,' answered my father, 'that you are the eldest, and that we rely on you to help us in bringing up your brothers and sisters.'

"But I insisted: 'Dad, I've felt within me a call from God. I want to be a priest.'

"I saw two great tears roll down my father's cheeks, and my mother became whiter than the kitchen wall. At last my father said to my mother:

" 'Woman, we have already worked hard, but to have that joy, we will work harder still.' "

And so Joseph Cardijn was sent to continue his studies at the College of Notre Dame de Hal. In September, 1903, he entered the Malines Seminary, and one day a message arrived that his father was dying:

"I left at once, and on entering the room where my poor father lay dying, I knelt beside him and received his blessing from his old, wrinkled hands, worn by ceaseless toil.

"Before that man who was so valiant, so great, I swore to give myself entirely, to die for the working class."

He now saw the purpose of his vocation; he was to become a priest to give Christ to the working masses, to reveal to the workers their temporal and eternal destiny. Ever since his boyhood the problem of the working classes had haunted him.

"When fifty years ago I entered the junior seminary," he told us recently, "my schoolmates went out to work. They were intelligent, decent, God-fearing. When I came back for my holidays they were coarse, corrupted and lapsed from the Church—whilst I was becoming a priest. I started to make enquiries, it became the obsession of my life. How did it come about that young lads brought up by Christian parents in Christian schools should be lost in a few months?"

To the solution of this enigma he was to devote the whole of his life, but it took him many years to discover the means of fulfilling his vocation.

Joseph Cardijn was ordained priest on September 22nd, 1906, and was sent to follow a course of sociology and political science at the University of Louvain. But the following year he was recalled to his diocese and appointed to teach at the junior seminary of Basse-Wavre. He had not forgotten the problems of the working class, and he devoted his summer holidays to traveling abroad, studying working conditions in Germany, France and England. He has given us an account of his travels in England, where he visited Manchester, London and Sheffield and made a close study of trade union organization, meeting Tom Mann and Ben Tillett. His impression of Ben Tillett is particularly interesting as it shows that, as far back as 1912, his mind was already working on the lines which were to result, some twenty years later, in the foundation of the Young Christian Workers:

"If we follow Ben Tillett during his twenty-four years

of social work, it seems that two ideas have crystallized his aspirations and, like two guiding stars, have directed his efforts towards a better future: first of all, he wishes to create the most powerful, strongest, most united organization possible, in which the workers of the world will feel the solidarity of their interests and the invincible power of their union; secondly, he sets out to enable each worker in particular to educate his own individuality, to uplift himself morally and intellectually, so that he may feel the pressing need of more well-being and more justice."

It was during one of his visits to England that he met Baden-Powell, then at the height of his fame as the founder of Scouting. Baden-Powell explained to him the Scout ideals and methods, and suggested to Father Cardijn that he should start the movement in Belgium. But though he felt an intense admiration for the educative value of Scout training, Cardijn realized that it did not hold the solution of his preoccupations: "I expounded to Baden-Powell," he tells us, "the concrete and practical problems of the life and work of the young workers. Baden-Powell admitted that he had never looked at the problem in that way, and that Scouting could not solve this concrete and practical problem."

In 1912, a very severe bout of illness put an end to his teaching career. Hardly convalescent, he was appointed curate at Laeken, on the outskirts of Brussels. The parish priest could hardly conceal his disappointment when he first met his new assistant: "All the parish organizations are topsy-turvy, and they send me a sick man!" It was not long before he formed a different opinion of Father Cardijn.

It was true that the parish organizations were in a bad way. The Working Men's Club boasted of a bowls team and little else; the Girls' Club, with a membership of thirty, offered innocent amusements to its members and a play at Christmas. No other working-class organizations existed in the parish. Father Cardijn was put in charge of the girls, and his first concern was to transform the club. Within a year he had raised the membership to 160 and had founded study-circles at which, for the first time, problems of work were discussed. This caused a mild revolution in the parish, where talk about these matters was considered dangerous and unsettling. But the young curate went still further. He founded for the young seamstresses a branch of the Needleworkers' Trade Union, and started for the adults a section of the League of Christian Women Workers, which in a few years achieved a membership of over a thousand. He also founded a study-circle of working lads. From this group were to come the first three leaders of the Young Christian Workers—Fernand Tonnet, Paul Garcet, Jacques Meert.*

Those years were a period of ceaseless activity and experiment. Father Cardijn was not a mere theorist; he did not start off with preconceived ideas and try to force them upon reality. He was always ready to try new methods over and over again until they achieved real formative results. The War did not interrupt his efforts. In 1915, whilst remaining curate at Laeken, he was appointed Director of Social Work for the district of Brussels by Cardinal Mercier. On two occasions he was imprisoned by the Germans for patriotic activities, and during several months spent in prison-cells he was able to meditate upon his experiences and to outline what was to become the method of the Young Christian Workers. In 1919 he left Laeken and was able to devote himself full-time to social work in Brussels.

A number of Trade Union leaders had come to realize the need for grouping together young workers. The pioneers trained by Father Cardijn formed the nucleus of this

* Fernand Tonnet and Paul Garcet died at Dachau Concentration Camp in February, 1945. See Marguerite Fieves: Fernand Tonnet, premier Jociste (1947, Editions Jocistes, Brussels).

new movement, which in 1919 took the name of La Jeunesse
Syndicaliste (the Young Trade-Unionists). For the next
few years it developed slowly, finding its way and establish-
ing its methods, and meeting with a great deal of opposition, even, it is said, from the Cardinal Archbishop of
Malines. Catholic Belgium possessed a strong network of
traditional organizations, and this movement of young
workers was looked upon as a dangerous and revolutionary
innovation. But it managed to break through every prejudice and misunderstanding. In 1924, the Jeunesse Syndicaliste became the Jeunesse Ouvriere Chretienne, the Young
Christian Workers, and Father Cardijn was appointed its
National Chaplain by the Belgian bishops. In March,
1925, Pope Pius XI received in audience the founder of
the Young Christian Workers, and gave to the movement
the final sanction of the Church. Msgr. Cardijn has often
told the story of this momentous interview. "Here at last,"
said the Pope, "is someone who comes to speak to me about
the masses! The greatest scandal of the nineteenth century
was the loss of the workers to the Church. The Church
needs the workers, and the workers need the Church."

It is not our purpose to tell in any detail the subsequent
history of the Young Christian Workers; its astonishing
development in Belgium, where it became in a very short
while the most powerful youth movement in the country;
its growth in France, its spread in other countries, including England and the English-speaking world. One writes
the history of something that is past, whereas the Young
Christian Worker is a living thing, one of the most vital
forces, perhaps, in contemporary Catholicism. It is at present established in more than sixty-two countries; it groups
more than a million and a half young workers of every
race, color and nationality. Its founder has become a
world famous personality, and his name is venerated by
young workers all over the world. Few men have been able
to achieve so much in their lifetime. When Father Cardijn

started his first small group of working lads more than thirty years ago, he said to them: "We are setting out to conquer the world." Today the Y. C. W. International has become a reality. It has taken its place among the great world organizations, it can speak for working youth with the prestige and authority of an international movement.

The writings collected in his books will, we hope, give a clear idea of the mind and spirit of the founder of the Young Christian Workers. The reader will be struck by the dynamism, enthusiasm, the freshness of vision of the man. His greatness does not lie in having discovered anything new; it consists essentially in having restated, with uncommon force and genius, truths as old as Christianity itself, truths which many of us had almost forgotten. In a period in the Church's life which is marked by a new development of the lay apostolate, he stands out as one of the most significant figures of modern Catholicism.

EDITOR'S NOTE: We thank Father Langdale and Fides Publishers for this chapter on the Very Rev. Leon Joseph Marie Cardijn which introduced his collection of stirring and significant addresses, *Challenge to Action*. Other recent works by the Canon include *The Church and the Young Worker*, and, *The Hour of the Working Class*, both published in England by the Young Christian Workers. Canon Cardijn was made a Domestic Prelate, with the title Right Reverend Monsignor, by Pope Pius XII, in July of 1956.

REVEREND JOHN
CARR, C.SS.R.

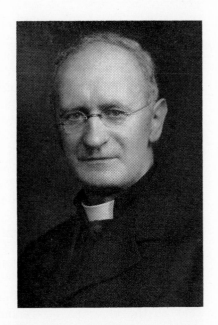

I SUPPOSE I HAD BETTER BEGIN IN THE ORTHODOX FASHION
by stating that I was born on the 9th of November, in the
year of grace 1878, in the City of Limerick, Ireland. I
was one of ten. I was a weakling (or was supposed to be)
and the despair of the doctor. One day my godfather—
an eminent ecclesiastic and a famous personage in his
day—met me in town in the nurse's arms. He looked at
me and then said: "Take the child home at once. Don't
let him die in the street." To make sure she would, he
hailed a jaunting-car, as it was then called, and paid our
passage. But the weakling managed to pull through. In
1917 he preached before that godfather; the godfather was
over seventy, the preacher in his fortieth year.

My last two years at school were spent at the Jesuit College in the city. Amongst our teachers was a scholastic
—who lived to a ripe old age as Father Whittaker and was
the idol of his class. Though sixty-five years have now

passed, I remember his singling out certain vivid words and phrases from the *Sketch Book* of Washington Irving and pointing out their force and beauty to us youngsters in a way I never forgot. The tempo of class hours is probably too fast today and programmes too crowded for much of that sort of thing. But I think we were the better for it.

At fourteen I entered the preparatory college of Mount St. Alphonsus, Limerick, with the intention of eventually becoming a Redemptorist. There I spent five years and finished my secondary education. In the August of 1897 I was sent to the French novitiate near Paris. At the end of the year I was recalled to be the first novice of the newly-constituted Irish Province of the Congregation. I made my profession on February 2nd, 1899, studied my philosophy in the house of studies, Devonshire, spent two years reading theology in Belgium, and was ordained in 1903.

After teaching in our college in Limerick for five years, I went on the missions in Ireland and for the next dozen years preached missions and retreats of all kinds up and down the land. In 1922, for reasons of health, I spent six months in Switzerland and then, towards the end of that year, went to Australia, where I spent five years teaching and giving occasional retreats to religious. In 1927 I returned to Ireland, where, apart from four years teaching French in our house of studies in Galway, I spent all the intervening years giving retreats. Some eight years ago my state of health called for a complete cessation of all external apostolic activity. Since then, besides hearing confessions, I have devoted myself chiefly to the apostolate of the pen.

But I had begun writing before this. If I am asked how I came to write, really I can scarcely say. Even as a small boy at school I seemed to have a sort of flair for what was then called—as it may still be called—composition. From early childhood my one hobby was reading. I also took up stamp collecting with youthful seriousness. On the field of sport I am afraid I was a complete wash-out.

I did not publish a line before I was a priest. Then I took up the writing of verse of a religious nature. Much of this was published in various magazines. But I soon recognized that poetry was not my métier and dropped it. I published no prose until I went to Australia, in 1927. There I began writing articles on the Little Flower. These appeared later in book form under the title of *The Lover of Lisieux* and saw several editions. I then took to translating from the French some rather long books, chiefly lives of Servants of God of the Redemptorist Congregation.

When in Australia, I preached a Lenten course on our Lord in the cathedral of Perth, at the request of Archbishop Clune. These were afterwards published in London under the title of *Christ is All*. This book went through several editions and was translated into several languages. It has been found particularly useful for sermons and Holy Hours.

On returning from Australia, I took to hagiography. My first effort in this line was the life of the Redemptorist St. Clement Hofbauer, Patron of Vienna. It was published by Sands of London and is in its fourth edition.

My largest book is the life of our St. Gerard Majella. I spent several years at it, and it is in its third edition. It has been translated into Malayanam and, quite recently, into Japanese. I took the title: *To Heaven Through a Window*, from an incident in the Saint's life. A rather amusing incident happened in connection with this book. To a very favorable review in a Canadian Catholic periodical the reviewer added this grim postscript: "The author, Father John Carr, has since passed away. May he rest in peace." Now as I felt very much alive at the time and by no means inclined to anticipate the decrees of Providence, I did not quite agree with this little piece of history. After all, though not of much importance to the world, it was supremely important for myself. So I wrote to my reviewer

somewhat in this strain. I thanked him of course for all
the nice things he had said about my book, but begged
leave to disagree with him in the little matter of my death.
I admitted that no man is a judge in his own cause, but
at the same time I felt I was in a position to call his statement about me into question. I asked him to reconsider
it in the light of the following facts. In the first place,
I said, I had not the faintest recollection of having died.
Secondly, I found myself still eating and drinking, getting
into bed and getting out of it, washing and shaving, just
as usual—in fact, doing things we don't associate with
life in the world to come. Thirdly, I found myself still
surrounded by humans, doing all these things with myself.
Fourthly, I told him, that my knowledge of the other world
was just as hazy as it ever was, which should not be the
case, had I died. Finally, to clinch matters, I enclosed a
recent snap of myself and signed it. The next issue of
the periodical carried my letter in full and the snap, with
apologies for having unwittingly shortened my life—on paper.

    I may also add in connection with this book, *To Heaven
Through a Window*, that it got my name on the list of
pilgrims from Ireland to the shrine of St. Gerard in Capo-
sele, Italy, when, twelve months ago we celebrated the
bicentenary of the Saint's death. This book is looked upon
as the most complete life of St. Gerard in English so far.

    In 1948 I published the first life in English of the child-
martyr St. Maria Goretti. It is now in its ninth English
edition and has appeared in several languages, including
Zulu! The little Saint has shown herself very good to me
and got me to Rome for her canonization in 1950. While
in Italy I was given many privileges, one of the greatest
being that of meeting her venerable mother Assunta. I
found that the fact that I was the author of the first
English life opened many difficult locks and turned grumpy
and adamantine officials into charming and obliging friends.

Besides translating from the French the life of St. Jeanne de Lestonnac, canonized a few years back, I published three years ago, under the title of *A Fisher of Men*, the life of the Venerable Peter Donders, a Redemptorist contemporary and compeer of Father Damien on the leper mission field. His cause for canonization is far advanced.

To pass over smaller publications, last year I published a volume of conferences for religious of both sexes under the title of *Why Hast Thou Come?* It is already in its second printing. To bring matters up-to-date, *Grown Up*, a book for young women, was published in Dublin this year.

I thank the Lord Who has spared me so long and has strengthened me to reach the world of souls, if no longer from the pulpit, at least with the pen.

EDITOR'S NOTE: Father Carr's books include *Truly a Lover*, reflections on St. Therese of Lisieux (Herder, 1925), *Christ is All* (Newman, 1948), *To Heaven Through a Window* (McMullen, 1949), *A Fisher of Men* (Clonmore, 1952), *Why Hast Thou Come?* (Newman, 1957), *Blessed Maria Goretti* (Clonmore, 1948), and *Grown Up* (Clonmore, 1957).

SISTER M. CHARITAS, I.H.M.

WHEN I TOLD ONE OF OUR SISTERS I WAS WRITING SOME-thing autobiographical and didn't know what to say, she reminded me: "You were born and you will die: you're sure of those two things in your life."

I was born in Scranton, Pennsylvania, in 1888, into a musical household, the first of seven children of James F. and Mary McNulty Loftus. Two other certainties I knew of very early: I wanted to write and I wanted to be a nun. My grandmother Loftus was a writer for the *Irish World*, and though she died when I was very small, I heard my father speak of her delight in writing and of her reading, without spectacles, till her death in her more than eightieth year. I heard him say that she was a well educated woman, a surprising fact considering the scarcity of opportunities for Catholic women in Ireland during her lifetime.

She, however, lived much of her time in Preston, Eng-land, where my grandfather Loftus had a market for dairy

and farm products raised by the family in Ireland. My
father was born in Preston. On comparing his baptismal
record with the birth and baptismal dates of Francis
Thompson, the poet, I found that they were identical as
to time and town.

When my father was seven, his father being dead, my
grandmother Loftus with her younger children joined her
older boys who had previously come to this country. Her
oldest son, Matthew, on becoming mayor of Scranton and
interested in the development of the new city as well as
in sympathy with the lot of former friends and neighbors
in Ireland, invited them to come to his home and settle
in the city where their circumstances could be improved.

My mother's family and others accepted the invitation.
In the meanwhile, though his brothers were busy and satisfied with developing the new town, my father had preferred
to go west. He lived for a while with his older brother
near Shakopee, Minnesota, then roved further up and down
the country till he eventually returned to Scranton to stay.

After he came back he met Mary McNulty, a dark-eyed
brunette, whom he married in St. Peter's Cathedral. When
I was born it was there that I was baptized, confirmed,
and made my first Holy Communion. I attended school
at St. Cecilia's across the avenue, opposite the cathedral.
The school was a private academy for resident and day
pupils conducted by the Sisters, Servants of the Immaculate
Heart of Mary.

When I graduated from St. Cecilia's, I was advised by
the Sisters to take a course at the State Teachers' College
in Lock Haven, Pennsylvania; which I did. I had taken
music during all my school years so I continued to take it
at Normal where I received a music and a normal diploma
when I finished the course.

I was urged to make a career of music. I belonged to
a light-hearted family with music always in the air. My
father and his brothers had fine voices. My father played

the violin and cornet in Father Matthew's and other city
bands. My brothers inherited musical ability. One of them,
James W., became a priest of the Scranton diocese and as
a member of the diocesan priests' choir was selected by
Bishop O'Reilly for European voice training and future direction of the choir. He did not go, due to several circumstances. As he died in his forty-fourth year, his twentieth
in the priesthood, he would not have used the course even
if he had taken it.

I liked music and taught it, but it was not my chief
preference, even though I had abundant musical stimulation
of many kinds. For ten years at St. Cecilia's, my cousin,
Sister Matthew, was one of my teachers. Another gifted
cousin, Sister Paulus, was a music teacher in the Philadelphia community of our Congregation. Still another
cousin, Father Edmund Langan, rector of St. John's parish
in Pittston, and his brother John were also gifted with
exceptional musical ability. Surrounded by a family of
singers and musicians, I, poor lark with a small voice, would
peck typewriter keys.

I taught arithmetic at Robert Fulton grade school (old
Number 9) in Scranton and English at Technical high
school for a couple of years, during which time I felt a
strong urge to go to a liberal arts college and a stronger
urge to enter the convent. I knew, too, that I should teach
till I had enough money to satisfy both urges. The time
element became a problem; so I did clerical work in the
summertime in the Scranton branch office of *Collier's,* and
I typed letters and statements in the office of the International Correspondence Schools.

Then Mother Cyril, superior-general of the Sisters, Servants of the Immaculate Heart of Mary, settled my future
plans. I went to the College of New Rochelle where I received my A.B. after training to satisfy my heart's desire
in writing with English as a major. The English teachers

at New Rochelle were special and the saying was true:
"Everyone at New Rochelle writes."

I had another desire filled when I received the habit and
after two years in the novitiate was professed as a Sister,
Servant of the Immaculate Heart of Mary. The new person,
Sister M. Charitas, was trained by a very dear novice-
mistress, herself a music teacher, for the role of a teacher
of music.

After profession, I was assigned to classroom teaching,
first in high school subjects and finally in English at Marywood College. In all, I have lived on the Marywood campus
for forty-five years. Except for travel through many cities
in the United States and Canada for study and occasional
trips, I have dwelt on a one-mile road all my life, during
the first twenty years at one end of the road under the eye
of my mother and the next forty-five years at the other
end of the mile under the eyes of a religious mother-general.
Even without a vow of stability, I would thus become a
recluse, which I am naturally and by design.

I went to summer schools, to Catholic University, to Notre
Dame, to Columbia and to New York University. Finally
I acquired an M.A. and a Ph.D. at Fordham, meanwhile
doing all the writing necessary for academic, social and
moral obligations, as well as doing publicity work for the
Marywood schools, directing their publications, and writing
community histories. Of these last, four books have been
published: *Pastoral in Blue* (1946), the story of Mother
M. Casimir, superior-general and builder of Marywood Col-
lege; *Truth in the Morning* (1948), the history of Mother
Cyril's marvellous work for her community and her guidance of two other communities, the Sisters of SS. Cyril and
Methodius and the Sisters of St. Casimir; *Matins in a Leafy
Wood* (1950), the story of the beginnings of Marywood
College and its foundress, Mother M. Germaine; and *Con-
sider the Violets* (1953), the story of St. Cecilia's and of

Mother Mary, the first elected superior-general of our Scranton Congregation.

Short stories, poems and occasional articles which I wrote along the years were published in *The Magnificat, The Little Flower Magazine, The Rosary,* the Los Angeles *Tidings, The Little Missionary,* and in others. For many years such contributions were published frequently by Nic Gonner of Dubuque in his *Catholic Daily Tribune.*

And lastly, two devotional books. The association of Our Lady, the Mystical Rose, in her earthly appearances with the queen of flowers forms the unifying theme of *Lovely is the Rose* (1954). And *Hot Embers* (1948), aimed to honor especially Our Lady and her Little Flower, St. Therese of Lisieux, from St. Teresa of Avila, one of our community patrons. This book was inspired by and dedicated to a lifelong friend and spiritual mentor, Mother Francis of the Five Wounds, formerly prioress of Carmel, Philadelphia, but now of Mobile, Alabama.

I have a jubilee engagement to keep with her in person and in the near future, unless before that time the last certainty of my life in this world comes to pass.

SISTER MARIA DEL REY
DANFORTH, O.P.

WRITING? I GUESS I HAVE ALWAYS DONE IT. NOW AND THEN
I have taken flyers into other fields—photography, music,
teaching,—but I usually end up in writing as at my home
base.

My first try at journalism was at the age of nine. It all
started when my father bought a typewriter. One of those
ancient Olivers with a double shift. It had a cute device
whereby a pencil could be inserted between the banks of
keys and, by rolling the carriage, a pencil line was drawn
down the paper. This was fascinating! We children were
drawing column rules before we poked a single letter. Columns suggested a newspaper. So—right off—we started
a neighborhood newspaper. My part in the enterprise was
to visit all the homes around and get subscriptions, two
pins for a Lifetime Charter Subscription; one pin, for a
year. Since everyone around was either mother or near
relative of the editorial board, this was not too hard an

assignment. As reward, I was given a job on *The Trumpet*.

My rise was phenomenal. Within three weeks, I rose from Leg Man (literally) to Editor-in-Chief, without relinquishing any of the positions gained on the way up. The reason? The editors, reporters, copy boys, pressmen and columnists had all evaporated. They were enthralled with something new—marbles or jump-rope or playing house— and I was left holding all positions on the board and sole owner of all those pins I had collected for subscriptions. A troubled conscience bothered me. I felt I must work off at least the one-year subscriptions. My heart quailed at the thought of all those charter subscribers. Just what was their life-expectancy? Some of them might live for eighty years or more!

So you see, I started out in journalism under a heavy cloud of debt. I wonder if I shall ever be able to get into the black! For, even now I am working off a thousand debts collected since those old neighborhood *Trumpet* days. My vocation to Maryknoll, the forbearance of my superiors to whom I must be quite a trial, so many opportunities to see fascinating places and peoples,—all of these plus the greatest of them all, the invitation to spend my life with and for God, leave me forever and enthusiastically in debt.

In the *Trumpet* days, I did a lot of writing on things I knew nothing at all about. Once I ran a scorching editorial about divorce. It was not so well received. One of the lifetime subscribers was on the verge of divorce and she resented a child of ten hurling the Baltimore Catechism at her in smug self-righteousness. This taught me a valuable lesson in journalism: Don't try to force the reader around to your way of thinking. A lassoed steer is sure to buck. The wise editor, knowing his reader's limitations of mind and perhaps of heart as well, leads him gently around to the right position. In that way, he wins his point and still does not lose the subscriber.

To make a long story a bit shorter, I worked on our high
school paper at Seton Hill in Greensburg, Pennsylvania.
After a try at piano-playing in Carnegie Institute of Tech-
nology, I took to the typewriter again at the University of
Pittsburgh, majoring in journalism. Here, under Professor
Maulsby, we worked under a stiff but wise regulation. Each
semester, we students had to get 300 inches *printed.*

That last word is important. In journalism it is not
enough to turn in flawless copy if you do not have the
gumption to see an editor and get him to print it. He will
use it only if it says something of interest to his readers.
This saved us, thanks be to God, from writing reams about
nothing at all. Instead, we dug out stories that were worth
printing.

I went to cemeteries and museums and such dead places
and found some little fact that interested me. For instance, I found the grave of one Joshua Barney once an
Admiral in the Navy. It seemed odd to me that he should
be buried in Pittsburgh, far from the wild sea waves. Looking him up in the library, I unearthed quite a colorful
character. In the end, old Joshua was spread out in the
Sunday Supplement of *The Pittsburgh Press* with a full
half-inch byline for me—and this was pure unearned in-
crement—a number of big pictures of his grave and Joshua
in his Admiral's outfit. *The Press* sent out a photographer
on the story, which redounded to my glory in the class and
added quite a few succulent inches to the total.

However delectable as the inches might be, they were
merely a by-product. My aim was to prove to hard-boiled
editors that I could write. If they got some free samples,
they might be better disposed to hire me when I came
around looking for a job. Remember, those were Depression Days when jobs did not grow on bushes!

The reasoning worked. As soon as the sheepskin was
handed me on Commencement Day, I took my scrapbook

to the editor of *The Pittsburgh Press* and prevailed upon the Sunday supplement editor to introduce me. He did just that.

"This is Ethel Danforth, Bill," he said, and turned on his heel and left, probably not able to bear the sight of one tender cub crushed under the heel of a ruthless editor.

"Oh, yes?" said Bill to the Sunday editor's retreating back. "Well, what do you want?" he turned the full weight of his attention upon terrified me. Sink or swim, do or die, now or never, I plugged into my little salestalk. The outcome was that ten minutes later I rushed into a drugstore to the nearest telephone booth and called home. "I've got a job on *The Press!*" my mother heard over the telephone, just as did everyone within fifty yards of the booth.

In spite of the enthusiastic start, my career on *The Press* was not brilliant by any means. Those were depression doldrum days. I covered schools, hotels, and did feature stories. I interviewed visiting beauty queens, covered accidents and fires, sat through conventions and school board meetings, and once, to my intense joy, covered a State Fair, sampling all the prize-winning recipes and stroking all the beautiful horses. But the old urge came back again and again. God wanted me at Maryknoll and I should be there. In 1933 I entered.

Instead of writing at Maryknoll, I was put to something better. I read. I read aloud to the community almost every day. This, I think, is magnificent training for writing. The flow of different styles, the use of one word rather than another, the purposeful variety in sentence structures, become bone of one's bone. I am still one of the refectory readers in our community. I hope I never loose the job.

I taught in Hawaii for a year and a half. In the Philippines I stayed eleven years, three of them in a concentration camp,—the best years of my life in some ways. In those years I turned again to writing, knowing what a tremendous story was happening around me and loathe to

let it slide away without record. However, during one of
our recurrent terrors when our Superior and another Sister
were taken to the torture dungeons, I destroyed the manuscript lest it incriminate us all.

In 1947 I returned to the States for Maryknoll Sisters'
publicity work. A year later, back to the Orient I went
on a year's survey of mission work in Japan, China, Korea,
Guam, Hawaii, the Philippines and Western Carolines. This
resulted in *Pacific Hopscotch,* published by Scribner's in
1951.

It was just then that the Communists were expelling
American priests and nuns from China. I collected their
stories and wrote *Nun in Red China,* a first-person story
published under the name Sister Mary Victoria by McGraw-
Hill in 1953. A jaunt through Latin America covering
Peru, Bolivia, Chile, Panama, Nicaragua, Guatemala and
Mexico, resulted in *In and Out the Andes,* which Scribner's
brought out in 1955.

Of course these books were written on the margins of
time; my main work was still the ordinary channels of
publicity. In August, 1954, a young photographer, George
Barris, spent a week at Maryknoll taking pictures for a
story, tracing a young girl through the postulancy and
novitiate here.

It appeared in *Cosmopolitan* magazine for December of
that year, as "Bernie Becomes a Nun." However, Mr. Barris had been carried away with his subject; he took more
than a thousand excellent pictures. The best of these were
published in 1956 by Farrar, Straus & Cudahy in a book
likewise entitled *Bernie Becomes a Nun,* for which I wrote
the text. In this I tried to give the background common
to all women religious, so that a girl entering any order
would know what lay ahead of her.

My latest book to date, *Her Name is Mercy,* was published by Scribner's in 1957. It is the story of what seems
to me an epic of compassion, the setting up and operation

of a clinic to care for the million or more refugees in Pusan, Korea, during the recent war over there. We see the clinic through the eyes of army officials, relief workers, journalist, the nuns themselves and, of course, the refugees.

No doubt about it, writing is a little bit of Purgatory. The only thing that drives me to it—besides my Superiors —is the thought that it might lead souls to God. Also I hate to see a good story go by the board for want of someone to put it on paper. I make no pretense of writing deathless literature. My output is journalism, pure and simple, today's story told for today. What Tomorrow does with it, I really don't care. It is meant to serve its purpose Today.

HELEN CALDWELL DAY

(Mrs. Jesse Riley)

I WAS BORN ON DECEMBER 3, 1926, AT MARSHALL, TEXAS, where my father was a teacher at a small Negro college, Bishop College. I was one of three children, but we had an older half-sister, my father's daughter by a former marriage, and she also lived with us.

Despite the fact that we were always moving—or perhaps because of it—we were a very close family, for the most part preferring each other's company to that of others. However, we did have many friends, and most of these made ours their second home and the young people were soon calling mother "mother" and daddy "pop."

During these early years, we lived in Missouri, Iowa, Mississippi and Tennessee. Sometimes daddy was teaching school, sometimes he was going to school. My first book, *Color, Ebony* (Sheed, 1951), tells the story of this and all my life until I was twenty-three.

The hardest thing during these years and perhaps the

one that made the greatest lasting impression in my life was the divorce of my parents when I was twelve. Because of my own and my brother's hurt, I became firmly convinced from that time on, even though I was a Protestant and of no particular denomination, that marriage is indeed a sacrament, permanent and indissoluble. I think it was this conviction that helped to lead me later into the Catholic Church.

When I was eighteen I went to New York City to study nursing. While there at first I lost what little interest I had in religion. I believed that the only real good was personal integrity, and that whatever you believed was right was right for you; whatever you believed was wrong was wrong for you. However, as I came more and more up against the unchangeable realities—birth, death, suffering, courage and hope in the face of seeming hopelessness—I became more and more unconsciously dissatisfied with this belief. In theory it was perfect; in practice, impossible.

Finally, one day a miracle of grace happened, and out of the clear blue sky, for no reason either he or I can explain, one of the Catholic chaplains there at the hospital, Father Francis Meenan, asked me if I would like to be a Catholic, and I answered yes. He gave me instructions, and in due course of time I was baptized and received into the Church.

Meanwhile, despite my conviction of the sanctity and permanence of marriage, passion had led me into what I knew was an invalid union; but shortly after my conversion, I ended it; so that when the time came to take my baptismal vows, I could make them without reservation. However, later, from this union, I bore a son, Mcdonald Francis.

While I was carrying him, I left nursing school for a time and went to work as an undergraduate nurse. In my spare time I went everyday down to the Catholic Worker to help as a volunteer for this admirable group dedicated to the reconstruction of a Christian society based on the principles of love and peace and effected through personal sanctity and the daily practice of the corporal and spiritual works of mercy.

As my admiration for this group grew I felt more and more drawn to join them. Only concern for my son—I wondered if I had the right to impose voluntary poverty on him, although I might choose it for myself—kept me from joining in this work. These doubts continued for several years. Then Butch, as my son is called, became ill with polio and I with tuberculosis. By the time we both had recovered, my faith had grown enough to resolve my doubts and I decided to open a House of Hospitality in Memphis, similar to the New York House, differing only perhaps in the special needs of the Memphis community. The motive and the spirit, however, were to be the same.

In 1950, with the permission of the chancery, and the help of interested friends, I was able to open the Memphis House. Its special work was to care for the children of working mothers who could not afford to pay for their care, and to provide for women and their children who were in need of shelter. As it developed, actually most of this latter care became shelter for unwed or deserted expectant mothers and the children they already had. The House also served as a center for the study of Catholic Action, and frequently priests or laymen active in the apostolate of the laity came to give us talks. The work of the House was done by myself, the mothers of the children in the house and in the nursery, and by volunteer workers; although in the five years we were open we did have three full-time staff workers.

As in the New York House, the work was interracial both in those who worked and those who helped. The example of interracial living and working here in the heart of the deep south, did more, we believed, to help promote a greater understanding and tolerance than anything we might say. However, we did speak out our beliefs whenever the opportunity presented itself. This latter, especially got us into hot water from time to time, even with those otherwise friendly to the work of the House. My second book, *Not Without Tears* (Sheed, 1954), tells the story of this work.

While engaged in the work of the House, I was helped from time to time by a young colored man who was a fervent Catholic, deeply interested in helping others and in the other works of the Church. We had been friends for several years, but it was not until I saw his patience with the women and children of the House and his willingness to inconvenience himself for others that I really began to appreciate his fine qualities. In time we grew to love each other, and decided to try to serve God more perfectly together in marriage. So in September of 1955 we were married in the nearby Catholic Church by one of the priests who had long been a good friend to the House.

Together we kept Blessed Martin House open in Memphis until May, 1956, when circumstances made it necessary to close it. Now we are waiting for a baby of our own.

While I was in the sanatorium recovering from tuberculosis, I became acquainted with and later joined a group called The Catholic Union of the Sick in America. This group is one of Catholic Action for the sick by the sick. I have been so impressed by it that my latest book, *All the Way to Heaven* (Sheed, 1956), is the story of its founding and work.

Many times I have been asked how I came to write or why. As far back as I can remember knowing how to read, I have wanted to write. In Iowa City, Iowa, I first learned to use the Public Library and to choose books for myself with the librarian's help. I was six years old then and I used to fold tablet paper in book form and make up stories for my little brother. I said then that I wanted to be a writer when I grew up; but I probably would have

forgotten it, as most such childhood ambitions are forgotten, if my parents had not encouraged me in it and
shown faith in me and my efforts as I grew up.

Nevertheless, except for poems and stories for myself or
family or friends, which I had no desire to show to others,
I never tried to write for publication until I became ill.
While in the sanatorium I sold my first article and my
first story and began writing what was to become my first
book. Until then I had been too lazy to write and kept
putting it off to some distant tomorrow. So it was my
illness which made me grow up in this as in my faith and
in many other ways. I just hope now that I can hold on
to the things I gained then and learned then and become
a better person and a better Catholic and a better writer
because of them.

LOUIS DE WOHL

WHEN A MAN HAS REACHED A CERTAIN AMOUNT OF SUCCESS in his profession, people will come to him and ask questions. Now whenever someone asked me "Should I become a writer?" I invariably answered point-blank "No." Some were hurt, some angry, almost all of them were surprised. "Why not?" "Because you haven't got the stuff in you." "How do you know? You have never read anything I have done, have you?" "No. But I know all the same. I know because you asked me. If you had the stuff in you that makes a writer, you wouldn't ask me, you'd go and write and go on writing. You couldn't abstain from it."

And that goes, in my opinion, for all creative work; for would-be actors, architects, painters, sculptors, and musicians. Mind you, there are quite a number of people who cannot abstain from it, although they do not have the stuff in them, but that is beside the point.

As for me, I started writing at the age of seven or just

a little older, and what really set me off was that some of
the stories I read did not go the way I wanted. I simply
decided to change them, and change them I did. At the
age of eight I wrote a play, "Jesus of Nazareth," and the
great speech of the High Priest Caiphas in the market-
place of Jerusalem bore a strong resemblance to Mark An-
tony's speech in Shakespeare's *Julius Caesar*. Caiphas
praised Christ in the same hypocritical way that Mark An-
tony praised Brutus, to convince his audience of the contrary. Plagiarism or not, I was very much in earnest about
my drama. I decided to compose the music for it myself,
paint the posters and design the scenery, and of course I
myself would play one of the leading parts, Caiphas perhaps, or Mary Magdalene.

More than forty years passed before I came back to that
theme in my before-last novel, *The Spear*, the story of
Longinus who pierced the side of our Lord on the Cross.

When one meets a stranger, the first question one is
asked is usually: "Where are you at home?", and to most
people that is an easy one to answer. Not with me. A
dialogue almost invariably ensues. "I reside in New York."
"Ah, you're an American." "No, I am British." "Oh, I
see. Where were you born, in London?" "No, in Berlin,
Germany." "Ah, then you are a German by birth." "No,
a Hungarian. In continental Europe one inherits the nationality of the father, and my father was a Hungarian."
"Is that so? Then I presume your mother was German?"
"No." "I think I understand. She was English." "No,
she was Austrian." "A bit complicated, but now I do understand. Then your original language was Hungarian, of
course." "No, German. I don't speak Hungarian at all;
only English, French, German, a little Italian and Spanish
and a smattering of Latin, Greek and Arabic." At this
stage I must be glad if my interrogator does not think I
am trying to make fun of him; but what can I do? I have
given him only the bare facts.

I used to live in Germany, up to 1935. Then I could not take the Hitler regime any longer. I cannot stay in a country whose laws I can no longer respect. Justice, according to Hitler's official version was "what the Aryan man thought was right." Unfortunately, what the "Aryan man" thought right was a mixture of cruelty and drivel. Hitler had nothing against me at the time—I gave him good reasons for having something against me later—but I had enough of him and went to England. It was perhaps not quite as easy as it may sound. I had built up a career as a writer in Germany. Every line I wrote was printed. I had thirty-odd novels published, of which sixteen were made into pictures. Money came pouring in, and money is a good thing if you know what to do with it. And in England—to say nothing of the United States—I was totally unknown. What was worse, my English was only just good enough to get on in everyday life. It would take years before I could hope to write in English.

I soon realized that I was dealing not only with a different language but also with a different mentality. And then I had an idea. The mentality of a person is formed in early childhood. If I wanted to understand the mentality of the English, I would have to undergo a similar process myself. I bought myself children's books. Nursery rhymes, fairy tales, text-books of all kinds. I struggled through the books of the seven and eight year olds, then through those for children from nine to twelve, from thirteen to fifteen, and so on. I read history books, best-sellers, thrillers and adventure stories, newspapers and magazines, plays and poetry. A book a day was the minimum.

After five years I felt that I could start writing. And then the war broke out.

I volunteered. But the army, the navy and the R.A.F. all very politely declined. I was a foreigner. Even the A.R.P., the Civil defense people, would not have me. I was not allowed to dig a trench in Hyde Park. I was

angry. I was so angry that I decided that they would
have to take me. And as they would not have me as a
simple soldier, they would have me as an officer. For this
I needed an idea. I looked for it, found it, and went into
action.

A few months later I was a captain in the British army
with a Department of Psychological Warfare all my own.
My job started just about at the time when the Germans
began to bomb London, and I was stationed in London.
When the war ended, I had been through a little over a
thousand air raids.

When a man has to live very close to death year after
year, he is bound to undergo a certain change. It is not
just that he is afraid. He is that, of course, at least at the
beginning, unless he is devoid of all feelings. But fear is
not the main thing. First, the senses are sharpened.
After a few months I invariably woke up a few minutes
before the air raid sirens went off. When we have to live
in the jungle again, our sense of danger returns, that instinct of prehistoric times, the instinct of the animal. But
the intellect, too, undergoes a change. One no longer takes
things for granted. One realizes much more, much
stronger, that everything depends, not upon bombs, not
upon oneself, but upon God. If one has not prayed before, one prays now. And if one has, one prays better.

My parents had both been Catholics, and I was brought
up accordingly. I had never entirely lost my faith, but
I had become tepid—a constant danger particularly for
those who have had too much success at too early a stage
in life. Now I could not help asking myself: If I die
tonight—and I have a very good chance for that—what
do I have to show for this life of mine? I remembered the
parable of the talents. What had I done with the talents
God had given me? I had written "successful" books, but
to what was that success due? All my books were adventure
stories, thrillers. People read them in trains or when they

were too tired to read something really good. And they were written for just that purpose. They were not written in the service of God. Another seven years would pass before the late Cardinal of Milan, Ildefonso Schuster, would tell me: "Let your writings be good. For your writings you will one day be judged." But already then I knew that I had to undergo a radical change as a writer, and I knew that I had to make up for many years of time lost. I did not vow, like Franz Werfel, to write the life of some special saint if I would get out of the war alive. I just decided to serve God.

Thus in a way my career started at the end of the war. What it was that I wanted to write about became clear to me very soon. I had seen the terrifying effect of a false ideal. Millions of Germans fell for the dynamic charlatanism of Hitler, they tried to ape him, to become little Hitlers themselves. And there is no country where people do not look up to some one and try to imitate him or her. Most people want to be led, if only by some outstanding example in this field or that. Therefore much depended upon these examples. Now what would be the examples that God would wish us to follow? Christ, of course. But then, Christ was not only a Man, He was also God, the Second Person of the Blessed Trinity; and how could Mr. Smith hope to imitate Him?

Perhaps that was the main reason why the Church taught us to venerate the saints? They were all human, and many of them had to combat all kinds of faults to reach sanctity in the end. I began to read books about the saints. Soon I realized that most of them were written by devout people—mostly priests and nuns—for devout people. I could not imagine that anyone living at the outer fringe of the faith, to say nothing of a non-religious person, would read them. Yet it was exactly that type of person who needed a saint's example and guidance more than anyone else.

I began to ask questions and found that for a great many people a saint was "a person who was a religious fanatic," or "a medieval phenomenon," or simply "someone who prayed all the time" (which last was much nearer the mark, though not in the sense they meant). Saints were "plastercast figures," "goody-goodies," "disagreeable zealots." Of a hundred people I asked, not one replied "saints are what I ought to be" or "saints are examples to be followed."

But I had read enough now to sense, to feel, to know that apart from being just that, they were the most thrilling, the most interesting, the most courageous and even the most glamorous people of all. I decided to write historical novels whose heroes and heroines were saints.

Soon enough I discovered that the problems of the saints —and all around them—were the problems of our own time, and that they and only they were able to solve them. Who of us has not heard the rubbish about "Christianity having failed" or "Christianity no longer being modern"? That was exactly what Emperor Julian the Apostate thought and it was St. Athanasius who put him right. So I wrote my novel *Imperial Renegade*.

We all worry about the danger from the East. So did the Western world when Attila, King of the Huns, broke into Germany, France and Italy, until Pope Leo I stopped him and his huge army single-handed. So I wrote my novel *Throne of the World*. The most vital necessity of our time is the rediscovery of the Cross in our hearts. So I wrote *The Living Wood*, the story of St. Helena who rediscovered the True Cross. Then, in May of 1948, I went to Rome, had my first audience with that living saint, the Holy Father, and asked him whom he wanted me to write about next! He said "St. Thomas Aquinas." Two years later I gave him the finished book, *The Quiet Light*, and asked him for his next order. This time he said "Write about the history and the mission of the Church in the world."

And that will keep me busy as long as I live. So far
it has resulted in my novels on St. Augustine (*The Restless
Flame*), St. Ignatius Loyola (*The Golden Thread*), and St.
Longinus (*The Spear*). My most recent book, *The Last
Crusader,* is not the story of a saint, although St. Pius V
appears in it too at a decisive moment. But it certainly
is dealing with "the history and the mission of the Church
in the world," and it gives an example of the importance
of the lay apostolate so dear to the Holy Father. Besides
it shows a decisive phase in the struggle against the Islam,
—a struggle that is by no means at an end as the latest
developments go to show!

Now I am struggling with a novel whose hero is . . . St.
Paul. Need I say that it is not exactly easy work? And
need I say that I would not exchange it for anything else
in the world?

EDITOR'S NOTE: Mr. de Wohl is a Knight Commander of the Order of
the Holy Sepulchre and his wife (neé Ruth Magdalene Lorch, whom
he married in 1953) is a Lady Commander of the same Order. His
fifty books include *The Living Wood* (Lippincott, 1947), *Imperial
Renegade* (*id.,* 1950), *The Restless Flame* (*id.,* 1951), *Throne of
the World* (*id.,* 1949; published in England as *Attila*), *The Golden
Thread* (Lippincott, 1952), *The Second Conquest* (*id.,* 1954), *Set All
Afire* (*id.,* 1953), *The Spear* (*id.,* 1955), and *St. Joan, the Girl Soldier*
(Farrar, 1957) in the Vision Books series.

RIGHT REVEREND MONSIGNOR JOHN TRACY ELLIS

IN HIS RECENT VOLUME OF MEMOIRS, *Portraits from Memory,* Bertrand Russell has a brief chapter which he calls "How I Write." Granted that many readers may find a number of opinions in his book with which they will disagree, Russell has some sensible things to say on the subject of writing. He remarks, for example, that in his young years he would fret himself into a nervous state for fear that a given piece of writing might never come right but, he adds "Very gradually I have discovered ways of writing with a minimum of worry and anxiety." It is a familiar experience, of course, for new writers, although there are those to whom writing has apparently always been a rather effortless task. The late Theodore Maynard, it seemed to me, was one of those fortunate people. But most of us, alas, have not escaped the period of fret and frenzy that accompanied our first literary efforts. I certainly did not, and my recollections of the earliest manifestation of

this "fretting" process are related to the preparation of
themes for a college English class where the professor was
noted for his severe scrutiny and his close marking of
student papers. We knew that what we did would be critically read and corrected, and that in itself was a challenge,
to say nothing of trying to earn a high mark from one
who was notoriously stingy in that regard. It was in the
English class of this professor that I first learned the necessity of repeated rewriting of awkard passages, of the value
of a unified paragraph, of the search for more refined expression, and in a general way many of the hazards of
authorship which remain with a man to the end of his life.

After being awarded a Knights of Columbus scholarship
in June 1927, I enrolled for graduate studies at the Catholic
University of America and began my formal training in
history under the direction of Monsignor Peter Guilday.
During the next three years about the only writing I did
was for my master's thesis and my doctoral dissertation,
neither of which was ever the source of any special pride,
for although the research they embodied was, perhaps,
respectable enough, the style in which they were written
never rose above the pedestrian standards customary in
these academic exercises. After receiving my doctor's degree in 1930, I did very little writing during the next
decade, aside from one or two brief articles in *The Commonweal* and *The Catholic World,* since my time was devoted principally to the preparation of the courses I was
teaching and to my theological training for the priesthood.
It was only in 1941 that I decided to write another book.
The underlying motive behind *Cardinal Consalvi and
Anglo-Papal Relations, 1814-1824* (Catholic University
Press, 1942) was two-fold: a conviction that the English
aspects of the diplomacy of Pope Pius VII's great Secretary
of State deserved more attention than they had up to that
time received, and a desire to win an academic promotion.

A year before the volume on Consalvi appeared, however,

a change in my courses from teaching the history of modern Europe to that of the Catholic Chruch in the United
States altered radically my perspective about historical
writing in general. I now found myself suddenly catapulted
into a field that was teeming with subjects calling for treatment and, too, with an abundance of unpublished materials
such as many historians may only dream of. It was in
July, 1941, that the Rector of the Catholic University asked
me to take over the courses in the Graduate School of Arts
and Sciences of Monsignor Guilday, whose health had begun to break and who was to be moved to the School of
Sacred Theology where the burden would not be so heavy
for him to bear. It was not long before I sensed the opportunities for writing which this new field had opened
up. In the University I had fallen heir to Guilday's splendid tradition in productive scholarship, in the city the untold resources of the Division of Manuscripts of the Library
of Congress and the National Archives were only twenty
minutes removed by bus and trolley, and in the neighboring city of Baltimore the archives of the premier see of
the United States, the richest single collection of manuscript sources on American Catholicism, were only forty
minutes away by train. In other words, the situation was
ideal for one who felt the urge to bring to light some of
the hidden phases of the Church's history in this country.

Nor was I long in discovering an attractive subject. The
more I read about John Lancaster Spalding (1840-1916),
first Bishop of Peoria, the more did I come to admire him
and the more did I feel a desire to probe more deeply into
the life of one whose name had been a household word in
the diocese where I was born and raised. I started out,
therefore, with a vague idea of a biography of Spalding,
but I became so engrossed in the leading role he played
in the founding of the University that I ended up by publishing in 1946 a volume called *The Formative Years of
the Catholic University of America,* the heart of which

was in good measure Spalding's long, difficult, and inspiring struggle to found an institution for the higher education of the American clergy that would be worthy of the name.

  In history, as in so many other fields of writing, one investigation suggests another, and so it was with the volume on the University. My research in the archives at Baltimore put me in close touch with the man who had become the University's first chancellor, and the longer I browsed among the papers of James Cardinal Gibbons the more was the idea borne in upon me that here was *the* subject for a biography in American Catholic history. After four years of teaching postgraduate courses in that field I was fully aware—and not a little awed—by the vast scope of Gibbons' life and activities, and it was only after a considerable period of thought, and consultation with a number of advisers, that I embarked upon what proved to be the most ambitious piece of writing that I have ever done, or ever will do. I had, I suppose, passed through what Bertrand Russell calls "a period of subconscious incubation which cannot be hurried" before the Gibbons biography became a fixed idea in my mind. But once there, it could not be dislodged. What I hardly dared to express openly at first was suggested to me by two wise and discerning friends when Monsignor John K. Cartwright, Rector of St. Matthew's Cathedral in Washington, and Monsignor Robert Howard Lord, late professor of church history in St. John's Seminary, Boston, urged me to proceed without further delay. Encouraged by their judgment in the matter, I sought the permission of Gibbons' successor in the See of Baltimore, Archbishop Michael J. Curley, a permission that was granted immediately and without qualification through the kindly offices of his chancellor, Monsignor Joseph M. Nelligan.

  With this permission secured, there remained only the stamina and bravery to begin! Little did I know that on July 5, 1945, when I left Washington for Baltimore to

make my preliminary investigations in the thousands of
Gibbons Papers (filling more than 100 file boxes) the pro-
portions of the task I was tackling! For the next seven
years I lived, studied, dreamed, imagined and talked about
largely one subject—James Gibbons. The volume on the
University had brought promotion to the rank of full professor in the spring of 1947, so that motive no longer
entered into my calculations in undertaking the cardinal's
life. In fact, it became almost from the outset a labor of
love, but labor it was—to the extent of 1442 printed pages
in the two fat volumes which were issued by Bruce in
November, 1952.

After the life of Cardinal Gibbons, every other subject
seemed for a time to be almost trivial and anti-climactic
by comparison. But my experiences in the classroom and
in the direction of graduate students prompted two other
writing projects which might best be described as providing
'tools of the trade.' One was *A Select Bibliography of the
History of the Catholic Church in the United States*
(McMullen, 1947), the material for which I had begun
to gather in a serious way during the academic year 1941-
1942 when I had a sabbatical leave, a good portion of which
I spent at Harvard University auditing courses in American
social history and making the best of the opportunities
afforded for reading and taking notes in the magnificent
collections of the Widener Library and the fine collections
of St. John's Seminary, Boston. The other project, to
which I was goaded by one of my most resourceful and
able priest graduate students, appeared in November, 1956,
under the title *Documents of American Catholic History*
(Bruce). Neither of these books, to be sure, represents
authorship in the strict sense of the word, since the first
is only a bibliography with notes on the books listed and
the second is an edition of key documents in the history
of the Church in this country from 1493 to 1939.

While editing the volume of documents, in which I received valuable aid from the students in my seminar, I received an invitation to deliver four lectures on the Charles R. Walgreen Foundation at the University of Chicago with the understanding that the University of Chicago Press wished to have the manuscript of these lectures for publication in book form. How I came to write *American Catholicism* is, therefore, self-evident, and if the reception accorded the little volume continues to be as favorable as it has been since it first appeared in September, 1956, I shall have no cause for regret. At this writing, the first printing of 3,000 copies has been sold out and I have been informed that a second printing of 5,000 copies is now underway.

Along with my duties as professor of church history in the University, as secretary of the American Catholic Historical Association, and as managing editor of *The Catholic Historical Review,* time has been found now and then to write a number of articles for scholarly and popular journals. There is space here for mention of only one of these articles. For a long time I had been convinced that American Catholics had not attained the distinction in scholarship and the prominence in influential posts of national leadership that their numbers, resources, and educational efforts would seem to warrant. When I was asked, therefore, early in 1955 by the executive secretary of the Catholic Commission for Intellectual and Cultural Affairs to prepare a paper for their annual meeting on this very subject I decided to embody all the evidence I had been accumulating for some time on this puzzling problem. The paper was delivered at Maryville College in St. Louis on May 14, 1955, and I then worked it over and submitted it the following summer to the editor of *Thought.* It appeared under the title "American Catholics and the Intellectual Life" in the autumn, 1955, issue of Fordham University's quarterly. If I had little comprehension of what was awaiting me in the Gibbons biography when I undertook the task in the summer of 1945, I had less intimation of the hub-bub this article was to cause ten years later. In fact, the seven years of labor and the 1442 pages of the final product in the life of the cardinal received nowhere near the attention that was directed to the thirty-seven pages in *Thought*.

It is now well over a year since the article was published and the letters—to the number of about 250—have not yet ceased. It is apparent that what was said had been on the minds of a great many persons interested in getting at the root causes for the poor showing made by Catholics in this country in scholarship and national leadership. Needless to say, the reactions were not by any means uniformly favorable, but I cannot help believing that the very vehemence of the discussion in some circles will in the end redound to the benefit of all concerned. For as Father Henri de Lubac, S.J., says in his book, *The Splendor of the Church* (Sheed, 1956), the self-criticism that strives for realism in action is a good thing. If, as he maintains, it be carried out in humility, give proper recognition to the good achieved, and take its rise from an essentially apostolic discontent, "how very much better it all is ... than the naive self-complacency which admits of no reform and no healthy transformation."

In conclusion, I should like to express the wish that Father de Lubac's wonderful book be regarded as compulsory reading by every Catholic writer. It offers sterling advice and many sound correctives for the besetting sins that so frequently characterize those whose principal preoccupation is the intellectual life, a fact that is especially true of the chapter "Our Temptations Concerning the Church." Books like that of de Lubac and *The Intellectual Life* by Father A. D. Sertillanges, O.P. (Newman, 1952) help the Catholic writer to keep his work in proper focus. The pursuit of truth—in whatever form it takes through writing—can be an immensely thrilling and rewarding ex-

perience. Personally, I find the discovery of new truths in
the history of American Catholicism through the medium
of original research an experience of this kind, and for
that reason I feel the impulse to share these truths with
others by writing them down in a permanent form. And
there is no better way, it seems to me, for a person who
has the aptitude, taste and training for the intellectual life
to further the advancement of the Church than through
this means. He need not—and he should not—think of
what he writes as an apologetic, for as Cardinal Suhard
said in his famous pastoral of February, 1947, when he
counseled scholars to integrate the conclusions of their
several fields of specialization in order to try to form a
cosmic vision of the universe, "in this effort you must not
involve any consideration of interest be it even apologetical;
you must seek only what is." But the writer who sincerely
and conscientiously seeks "only what is" in theology, philosophy, history, literature, or science will be at the same
time doing an inestimable service to the Church in enabling
her to hold higher her venerable head amid the confused
and whirling intellectual currents of our time.

NORBERT ENGELS

I WAS BORN IN MUSKRAT CITY. THAT'S WHAT THE NATIVES called it, a settlement of French and Belgian truck farmers and general laborers, located on the northeast edge of the city of Green Bay, Wisconsin, bounded by the Fox and East River and the marshy shores of the bay. The natives also trapped muskrats by the hundreds, practically in their back yards, and stretched the hides on the graying clapboards of their simple frame houses to dry. Hence the nickname. My world started on September 4, 1903, on Day Street.

My father was a merchant tailor and my mother a gardener's daughter. As a result, I can do a neat job of pressing my pants (though I seldom bother), and my friends insist that I have a green thumb with a plant. Much more important is the fact that I received at my good parents' insistence not only a university education but a sound Catholic one.

My first spoken sentences were French, but old grandpa Pié died when I was four, and no one else seemed to want to talk French to little fellows, although the oldsters used it among themselves. It was a kind of Walloon Belgian-French dialect which my ear can still detect when I go back, although I have little understanding now of what they are saying. I have always regretted that I did not learn even this patois, and consider young ones very fortunate who pick up German, Polish, or any foreign language, along with their English, right in their own homes.

In those days we did not call out Catholic schools 'parochial'; they were 'Sister Schools,' and we were taught there, often sternly, sometimes in a very kindly way, but we were *taught*. I honestly believe I had a better education when I left the eighth grade than when I was graduated from the public high school, where things were easygoing and sociable but not very much devoted to the development of the mind or spirit. The nun who taught our eighth grade has just been elected Mother-General of the School Sisters of Notre Dame, Sister Mary Ambrosia, S.S.N.D.; and I want to acknowledge that she was one of the finest teachers any boy could have had.

And then in 1922 I went to Notre Dame, helping to pay for my education by playing with a hotel orchestra during the dinner hour. I remember entering as a very green freshman my first class at the university. The teacher had asked us to write briefly our experience with and attitude toward literature. Remembering high school, I scribbled hurriedly, "I think most writers are nuts," and left. *Mea culpa!* Of course, I was not thinking of myself as a writer-to-be and still do not in relation to that august term 'literature'; I was probably concerned with my empty stomach and figured my callow opinion to be a quick way of getting over to the cafeteria for a chocolate milk-shake and a package of coconut cookies.

But I had already started in a small way to write. There

were, successively, a war poem rhymed in the ninth grade;
an ode to an old-maid history teacher who had threatened
to flunk me, but then reconsidered; a music review of the
university orchestra concert which got me called up on the
carpet; acrostic love poems which the other lads in the
dormitory (Walsh Hall) requested, to send to their girl
friends; popular songs with words and orchestrations; and
many other miscellaneous bits. Nothing special about any
of them, but I suppose in a small way they could be regarded as early symptoms of the writer's disease, for indeed it seems to be a form of disease with me if only because I feel restless when I am not writing.

Yet, I am not a moody writer, one who must wait for
the right idea, the right disposition, and the right time
all to mesh neatly together. Neither am I the 'quota' type,
who relentlessly works it out from eight to twelve, or one to
four, faithfully every day, for better or worse. I always
have a bunch of ideas germinating in the back of my mind.
My teaching comes first, however, with its attendant student conferences, committee meetings, and piles of student
papers to read and annotate critically.

During the course of one academic year I read well over
a half-a-million words of student writing, and often rise
from my desk too benumbed to write even a single sentence
of my own, no longer sure of the purpose of writing, and
even unwilling to bet that the word is not spelled 'writting.'
I do not mean to suggest that my students are unusual
problems; they are good students, most of them, and are
here at Notre Dame to learn. Often I feel that I learn
as much from them, through their questions and comments,
as they do from me.

But every once in a while a break comes and my typewriter then chatters along easily and productively. So
the big thing with me is the problem of time and energy,
seldom mood or idea.

When I was a senior at Notre Dame I met Eleanore

Perry, of Hillsdale, Michigan, who was a junior at St. Mary's College, just across the highway. That was on February 22, 1926; a most agreeable day to recall. She was a writer, too, and has continued to be, through the years of being a good wife and mother. We were married on June 19, 1929, and have three fine children: John, who has an A.B. from Note Dame, and who served three years as an officer in the U. S. Navy, and who is now doing graduate work in Fine Arts at the University of Iowa; David, who is also a graduate of Notre Dame, in chemical engineering, and now a Navy flyer; and Julie, who is a student nurse and will soon receive her R.N.

Meanwhile, my wife and I have kept on writing. For several years she wrote the young people's column for *St. Joseph Magazine,* and has recently been included in a fine and important work, *Valiant Woman* (Grail, 1956), edited by Peg Boland. Now that our own children are grown up and gone away, she teaches at St. Mary's Academy, South Bend, in English literature and religion.

We never write an essay or poem without having the other read it over critically. Naturally, we do not always agree, but I feel that there has always been respect for each other's plan, ability, and integrity.

My book, *Man Around the House* (Prentice-Hall, 1949), is a collection of familiar essays about our family life, especially the things we have done together and built in our basement workshop. Doing these things helped to build our family together, besides giving us things for the house and garden we might not have been able to buy: twin beds turned out of solid maple posts, grandfather clocks made of black walnut bought at a used-lumber yard, tables from odds and ends of teakwood and mahogany gleaned from a friend's shipyard, pergolas, picket fences, boats, additional rooms, and even a north-woods cottage where we spend our summers.

My leaflet of poems is not so much as pages go, but it

does sincerely represent my own meditations on the meaning of the various parts of the Mass. It is called *Thou Art My Strength*, and was published by St. Meinrad Abbey Press in 1947.

Outside of these and numerous anthologies, most of my writing so far has been printed in magazines, but there are right now two more books in the making. My essays, stories and poems have appeared in most of the national Catholic magazines, as well as in *Science and Mechanics*, *Popular Science, Popular Mechanics, American Home, Woman's Day,* and the *Saturday Evening Post.*

I have often been asked about the diversity of my writing interests and publications, and can only answer that I am interested in everything, and feel I want to know everything there is about it. During World War II, I was teaching Shakespeare as usual, but also engineering drawing in the Navy Training Program at Notre Dame. One day I realized I was explaining a problem in sectioning by using an example from *Macbeth* to show that the external housing of an engine, like that of a person, may not always indicate what it is like inside; and next hour illustrating on the blackboard the meeting of two opposing forces in *Othello* by drawing the intersecting lines of two large cylinders of different dimensions.

May I also confess that I have a degree in music, but hurriedly add that this was little reason to 'hack-out' a magazine news story on atomic energy or to ghostwrite several articles on astronomy for *American Weekly?*

This insatiable curiosity is possibly one reason I have not concentrated more on writing so-called learned articles, although I have rewritten and edited any number of them for others. A second reason, which may be more valid, is that I prefer the creative and constructive kinds of composition; and a third, that the results of my literary and historical research have been intended for and devoted to my students rather than for publication.

I feel that a wide range of interests is valuable to one who teaches in a liberal arts college, such as I do, especially when it has its focus set on a central unity, a catholic curiosity revolving around a Catholic nucleus. The same wide range is invaluable for a Catholic writer.

Writing this brief autobiographical sketch, I became more and more aware of the fact that a man's opinions as well as his statistical figures are an essential part of his personality, and therefore of his life.

JOHN VILLIERS
FARROW

I FIRST THOUGHT OF BECOMING A WRITER WHEN I WAS ABOUT
ten years of age. The idea was suddenly born when I
received praise from my English master for a composition
that I had handed in. I still remember that this work
began with the words "Bang! Crash! The airplane
smashed into the deck!" The master, Mr. Moody by name,
thought that this was an unusual beginning and prophesied
to the entire class that I would become a writer. Thus the
thought was given, the seed planted. I can well remember
the glow of self-satisfaction that I experienced that day.
The resolutions that were made. The ambitions that were
formed.

By the time I was twelve, it was decided that I should
adopt a naval career. In the Australia (where I was born)
of that time, a boy took examinations for the Naval College
at about the age of twelve and a half—and I passed successfully. But these were the years when disarmament

was the mood and when one's instructors were being demobilized and, accordingly, disillusioned. Instead of continuing in the Navy, I joined the Merchant Service as cadet. The ship in which I served voyaged from Sydney to New Zealand, the Fijiian Islands, Honolulu and Canada. Sometimes an alternate run would take us to Tahiti and various other islands. During the tropical peace of the night watches I had ample opportunity to keep alive my ambitions of becoming an author and, in the off-duty hours of the long voyages, I had the time to read and study the great books.

My first work took the form of poetry and, when my name appeared in print, it proved an added and fierce spur. Short stories were my next effort. These too were sold and eventually I "swallowed the anchor," and took up writing as a full-time job. Almost immediately after leaving the sea, Hollywood engaged me, much to the disapproval of the late George Putnam, a publisher who had taken an interest in me and who possessed a deep conviction that script writing would spoil a promising novelist.

After writing a score of screenplays, I became convinced that a scenario writer had too little to do with the actual making of a film, so I left Hollywood and went to the Society Islands. In Tahiti, aboard a trading schooner, I commenced writing a novel which I enthusiastically thought would prove to be one of the best sellers of all time. I wrote the first part of the book while wandering around the Islands, the middle part on a long trip on a freighter to Europe, and I finished it while cruising on a fishing boat in the Mediterranean. The book was published simultaneously in France and the United States. While receiving fairly good reviews, it proved, from its sales, to be a failure.

I had written what I thought to be a popular book. Now I would write a book for myself, and one that probably would not sell more than a few hundred copies. I

had heard about a leper priest, called Damien, while I was
in the Islands. The idea of writing his life intrigued me—
his courage, his example, his inspiration. But, of course,
a book about a leper, and laid in the dismal confines of a
leper colony, could never be a success. Thus I thought—
but, nevertheless, I commenced writing the book. *Damien
the Leper* was completed in about ten weeks of actual
writing and the book, that I thought no one would read,
has seen thirty-three printings and has been published in
twelve languages. My publishers (Sheed & Ward) assure
me that it still has the same steady sale that it enjoyed
in the first year of publication.

After the emergence of *Damien the Leper,* I was once
again employed by a Hollywood Studio, but this time I
was given a chance to direct. This latter job did not leave
me much time to write, but I managed to get in a few
articles and to commence the arduous task of writing *Pageant of the Popes.* It was my belief that a readable one-
volume history of the Papacy was needed.

In 1939, World War II broke out, and I immediately
joined the Royal Canadian Navy. The war served to post-
pone my directorial career but not so my writing. I took
several crates of research books with me to sea. Once
again the long night watches gave me much opportunity
to think and plan the actual writing. I have told in my
introduction to *Pageant of the Popes* how, in relieving
a fellow officer on the bridge, I would be greeted with the
question: "Have you finished off another Pope yet?" *Pageant of the Popes* was first published in 1942 and won the
Catholic Literary Prize for that year. Since then I have
revised it and it has seen several printings and revisions.

In addition to directing, I am now producing films and
again I have little time to write, but in 1954 I managed
to finish and see published *The Story of Thomas More* and
a small book of poems.

Making films is a drudgery and requires much self-dis-

cipline, but I know of few greater or more triumphant
moments than when, putting down the pencil for the last
wonderful time, one realizes that one has finished another
book.

\

EDITOR'S NOTE: In 1936, Mr. Farrow married the actress Maureen
O'Sullivan, and they have seven children. Among his dozen decora-
tions is that of Knight Grand Cross of the Holy Sepulchre. And
among his books he did not mention is an English-Tahitian Dictionary.

REVEREND FRANCIS L. FILAS, S.J.

"LOVE ME, LOVE MY BOOKS" MIGHT BE THE MOTTO OF ANY author, but if I talk too much about my books, it is only that I wish you to love the man about whom all of them were written—St. Joseph. I honestly do not mean by that, that I think of myself as a worthy disciple of St. Joseph, because that is not true. In moments with myself I am almost aghast to think that my wagon has been hitched, as it were, to the star of St. Joseph. Without St. Joseph as my subject, I do not think I would have a single book on the market. The best I hope for is to be called a publicity man for St. Joseph, achieving the purpose of a publicity man to some worthwhile extent.

I was born in Cicero, Illinois, June 4, 1915; it was ten in the evening of a First Friday. My parents were the late Thomas M. Filas, a pioneer Cicero architect and builder whose ideas were two decades ahead of his time, and Emily Francis Seery, a mother who insists that her praises go unmentioned.

While in the fourth grade at parochial school, I was invited to be an acolyte. It is from this attraction to the altar as a boy that I trace my desires for the priesthood. For lack of funds I attended public high school. I had only the vaguest idea I wanted to be a priest. Between freshman and sophomore years I happened to read a newspaper advertisement for Loyola University, Chicago; and thinking in my ignorance that one had to attend Loyola to become a Jesuit, I sent a random speculative request as to what was really necessary. The late Father Joseph Reiner, S.J., told me to come down for an interview, and that was how I met my first Jesuit. At the suggestion of Father Clifford LeMay, S.J., who then took over my direction, I arranged to complete my high school in six semesters in order to have a year off to study Latin.

That year had two side jobs, both leaving strong impressions. I was hired as a garage bookkeeper who was to double as grease monkey. My talents in this field must have been unique. Within a month my employer told me that business was not good enough to warrant such noble tries (among them, mechanical efforts on a three-car "stable" kept by a west side gangster who later died of lead posioning, administered by sub-machine-gun.) The second job lasted for even less time—laboratory boy for two weeks amid the most immoral atmosphere I ever experienced. The miasma of raw paganism that permeated this commercial laboratory was too dangerous to risk much longer, and it was rather no job than that, even during depression times.

With the whole-hearted approval of my parents and elder brother and sister, I entered the Society of Jesus at Milford, Ohio, on August 12, 1932. My first vows as a Jesuit were in 1934, followed by two years of classical studies called the Juniorate. This period saw my first literary production, a translation of a French pamphlet on the Way of the Cross, which a kindly master of novices had earlier asked me to do as a means of relieving the strain of the novitiate.

In 1936 our class moved on to the three years of philosophy at the then recently acquired West Baden College in southern Indiana. This had been the West Baden Springs Hotel, a nationally known spa until depression and the inroads of competition from Florida hotels had closed it in 1931. Its owner, the late Mr. Edward Ballard, donated it to the Chicago Province of the Society of Jesus for use as a scholasticate.

Abortive visions were in my mind of attempting an article for some national magazine on "I Live in a Roundhouse"—a catchy title, and perfectly true, for the hotel had been built in circular form, with two concrete series of rooms surrounding an enormous central atrium that was topped by one of the largest domes in the world. Yet the great providential occurrence at West Baden, as far as my books on St. Joseph were concerned, was the discovery of a German history of the devotion to St. Joseph written by an almost unknown but very painstaking writer, Joseph Seitz. As a result of this accidental find, my first idea on seeing how much solid material Seitz had gathered was to translate his work, since I did not have the necessary background nor free time for original research. Above all, there seemed such a crying need for something about St. Joseph that was not dependent on the contradictory, doubtful, and merely sentimental statements that had been based on fragmentary history, pious legends, or private revelations.

My translation was an abysmal failure. It was too "German," at times not accurate, and every publisher I contacted told me he could never come close to breaking even. More than once I was inclined to throw the long manuscript into the wastebasket. The idea was shelved during my three years of teaching mathematics as a Jesuit regent at St. Ignatius High School, Cleveland (1939-41), and University of Detroit High School (1941-42).

Only in first year theology, back at West Baden now, did the old dream return. It was encouraged by Father Aloysius C. Kemper, S.J., a professor of theology, who very kindly offered to give a critical reading to what I wrote. Mr. William C. Bruce at this time also suggested that while the old translation could never be successfully marketed, his company would be agreeable to an original survey of the material it contained. From those beginnings came *The Man Nearest to Christ*, on the nature and history of the devotion to St. Joseph.

The title, highly fitting as it is, was the one I had vetoed most strongly cut of the twenty-two possibilities that were considered. I thought that it resembled too closely other "Man Who" books. I believe it originated with the wife of a Bruce editor. At any rate, the publishers fortunately overruled my veto, and the book appeared in the fall of 1944. The first printing sold out in two weeks. To everyone's amazement we finally went through four printings and a British and a Braille edition, with an Italian translation still projected.

It was this same school year of 1944-45 (my third of theology) that saw my ordination in June. Jesuits get a fourth year of theology, during which they somewhat grimly call themselves "toy priests"—still in studies, with little of the active apostolate permitted. But hard as this is for the eager young priest, the wisdom of gaining experience before publicly exercising Holy Orders is beyond all reasonable doubt.

During this closing year of theology (1945-46), I found extra time to write *The Family for Families,* a book equally divided in its emphasis on family life and the life of the master model, the Holy Family of Nazareth. Providence worked deviously again. In all the history of this book's

first publishers, only one manuscript has ever been lost—
and that was the original of *The Family for Families*. Fortunately I had carbon copies, but the delay entailed before
the loss was discovered and then by the long search meant
that the book appeared in off-season and missed the family-
life reading lists. None the less (to skip ahead a few years),
the disappointment over the mediocre showing in the hard-
bound edition acted as an incentive for me to be on the
lookout for some way of salvaging the idea. The chance
came in 1950, when Paluch Publications of Chicago began
their pioneering Lumen Editions, attempting to put Catholic pocket-size titles on the market. In this format, *The
Family for Families* has since gone through six printings.
I think in all fairness that when credit is given for opening
the pocket-size market to Catholic books, Paluch should not
be so completely overlooked in favor of later comers in the
field, even though the later "giants" accomplished the
break-through which the earlier and smaller companies did
not reach to the degree they desired.

My Jesuit course of training was still not finished in
1946; there remained the final so-called tertianship, the
"third year" of novitiate to be gone through as a priest.
My provincial superior postponed this for two years, in
view of the need for teachers after World War II. These
were very happy years at the University of Detroit where
I was primarily a teacher of religion. I say 'primarily'
because in the second year I helped open a downtown
branch of freshmen, to relieve the pressure on the uptown
campus. My jobs were (among others) Dean of Men,
Student Counsellor, Religion Professor, Sodality Moderator,
Assembly Preacher and Disciplinarian, Keeper of the Faculty Parking Lot, and Supervisor of the Gymnasium. You
can see why the students presented me with an album
bearing fourteen titles, so that I could make it clear at
any time in what capacity I was speaking to them. They
did not wish to incriminate themselves to Father F, Dean

of Men, while thinking they were telling Father F, Student Counsellor, confidential opinions about the teaching of Father F in college theology.

It was during this rushed period at Detroit that I was asked by the Detroit Council of Catholic Women to help organize the local Cana Conference movement for husbands and wives, which was a new idea then. I am proud to have been associated with Cana ever since, and still consider it one of the apostolates I prefer, as long as God wants me to exercise it.

Tertianship finally came in 1949-50, and then a chance to get a degree of Doctor of Sacred Theology under the new pontifical charter at West Baden College. I wrote my dissertation on the fatherhood of St. Joseph, aiming at the same time for the regular book market. This plan culminated in the 1952 publication of *Joseph and Jesus:* a theological study of their relationship. At the present writing this is the only single work in English, or any other language, that treats of the fatherhood of St. Joseph in such detail. Because of it and my allied work on Josephite theology, I was privileged to be a charter member in the founding of the Research and Documentation Center at Brother André's St. Joseph Oratory, Montreal.

My assignment to Loyola University, Chicago, came in the fall of 1950, as a professor of college theology. An unexpected new field opened up in lecturing on the Holy Shroud of Turin throughout the midwest. Ultimately, this lecture appeared annually on Good Friday telecasts both locally and nationally.

Throughout these years I had tried to keep up magazine articles and Queen's Work pamphlets as time permitted. One of the magazines on the list was a quarterly bulletin for priests called *Alter Christus*. When the little periodical had to be discontinued in 1950, it seemed a shame to bury with it the excellent material (especially on grateful devotion to the Sacred Heart of Jesus) which it had received

from so many Catholic writers. Accordingly, I edited many
of these articles aimed at the sanctification of priests under
the title of *His Heart in Our Work,* appearing in 1954.

Joseph Most Just: the logical questions about St. Joseph,
was published in the spring of 1957. To put it informally,
this might well be "the last of my wad" concerning St.
Joseph. But even though ideas for another book are being worked out on a new topic, I still wish I had more
material to use about Joseph. I wish I could write the
book of the ages about St. Joseph, not for any selfish satisfaction but to produce something remotely worthy of the
man whose nobility merited his choice as virginal husband
of Mary and virgin father of Jesus, closer to Jesus and
Mary than any other created being.

ANNE FREMANTLE

I WAS BORN ON ST. VITUS' DAY, JUNE 15, 1910, IN AN OLD
Saracen tower in the village of Tresserve, near Aix-les-
Bains, Savoie, France.   Mother had a tiny chapel under
the stairs—it used to be the dungeon—and I was baptized
there the following January, which was the earliest a
Church of England clergyman high enough to suit mamma
was around.   She was very devoted to Our Lady, and called
me Anne-Marie for Her and Her mother.   She had hoped
the village Curé, who was a great friend, would baptize me,
and chose a very Catholic name to please him, but he refused to do so unless mamma would promise to bring me
up a Catholic, which of course she would not.

When I was six months old, and christened, I was brought
to England, and Arthur Rackham, the painter, did a de-
lightful picture of the mermaids carrying me in my cradle
and pushing me to shore.   Until World War I broke out
I spoke only French and German, having a Danish nurse

and a French nurserymaid.   Mother always spoke to me
in French, father in German.

We went to France each summer, and my first memories
are of the sun and the bright flowers there, and of pushing
my sister down the garden slope (she was two years younger
than I) and being punished for it.   During the war we
were mostly in Sussex, where mother sheltered many
wounded soldiers in the house, and in the cottages many
Belgian refugees.   A Catholic priest came Sundays to say
Mass in the drawing room for them, and I remember trying
to stay as close as possible to the housekeeper, a Creole,
because she had just received Our Lord.   I had a tiny closet
of my own I made into a chapel; here was a crêche at
Christmas, and at other times, a crucifix.

When I was seven, the Archbishop of Canterbury prepared me for Confirmation and Communion in the Church
of England.   He wrote me later that I was the youngest
child he had ever confirmed.

I was writing a good deal by then—mostly poetry, and
unctiously pious:

> On Thursday night,
> As it was right,
> We went and got shriven,
> God has us forgiven,

is a sample.   Also screeds about Sir Roger Casement, the
Irish leader, who was hanged when I was six (I well remember being got out of bed at six A.M. to pray for him
the day of his execution) and the Chief of the Macdonalds
murdered in the Massacre of Glencoe by the Campbells.

On our birthdays we were allowed to come down to dinner, and always wore a wreath of flowers.   On my seventh,
I wore a wreath of red roses, which I placed on my favorite
book, *Lilith* by MacDonald—a book still one of my favorites,
that I edited for a new edition entitled *The Visionary
Novels of George MacDonald*, which the Noonday Press

published in 1954 with an Introduction by Wystan Auden,
another great admirer of MacDonald.

Religion was always my main interest, and I used to
come down to the drawing-room at six with my sister, to
spend an hour with mother, and insisted on reciting the
Nicene Creed, and often the Dies Irae too, to any friends
of hers that were rash enough to appear at that hour.
I loved learning by heart, and knew the Rubaiyat, Gray's
Elegy, and many of Heine's long Hartzreise by the time
I was nine. It was then that I became a Muslim, converted by a British author, Marmaduke Pickthall, who
rented a house on our place in Sussex. He had become a
Muslim and was a fluent Arabic scholar; he translated the
Qu'ran for me (I gave the manuscript to Princeton University in 1951) and his translation is the one published
in the Mentor series by the New American Library, and
is the one used at Princeton and at the great Muslim University of Al Alzhar in Cairo. Marmaduke took me to the
Mosque at Woking to make my profession of faith ("There
is no God but God, and Muhammad is His prophet") and
I faithfully kept the fast of Ramadhan (no food or drink
from sunrise to sunset for a month) and said the Islamic
liturgical prayers five times daily, to the fury of my governess.

When I was twelve my father died, after only a week's
illness, of pneumonia. In the following spring we came to
France for a year, where my sister and I learned French
and Latin with the Curé, who was horrified that I was a
Muslim. He taught me Latin from Cicero and St. Augustine, and at the end of a year I wished to become a Catholic.
Mother was cross, and said he had betrayed a sacred trust
by attempting my conversion, and we were sent off to
boarding-school in England. But only for a year. Then
back to France for six happy months, then another school,
where I passed School Certificate, and began my first novel.
It was about a girl called Cecile who lived in Savoie. It

was never finished because at seventeen, bored with doing
the London Season, I took the entrance exam to Oxford,
and won a scholarship to Lady Margaret Hall. While reading history there, I appeared for the first time in real print
(of course I'd written for school magazines, etc.) : a prize-
winning (five guineas) letter to the *Daily Mail* on whether
"you would prefer marriage or a career." Both, wrote I
firmly.

At seventeen, too, I met and became engaged to Christopher Fremantle, and we were married shortly after I
graduated in 1930, when I was twenty. The Archbishop
of Canterbury, who had married my parents, married us,
and baptized our first two boys. By this time, although
I knew that the Catholic Church was the only true Faith,
I had decided to remain in the Church of England with
my husband.

On our honeymoon I wrote a couple of pieces for the
Manchester *Guardian* and the London *Times,* and two
poems published in the *Times.* My one and only slim volume of *Poems* was published in 1931. In that year when
I entered *The New Statesman's* short story competition,
and tied first and second prize with myself (under an alias),
Sir John Squire asked me to work on *The London Mercury,*
of which he was then editor, and I did for a year. At the
same time I was writing a life of *George Eliot* for Duck-
worth's Great Lives series. It was published in 1931.

Then my husband had to have his appendix out, and
we went to stay with my in-laws while he convalesced.
In a great chest in their house I found lots of vellum-bound
diaries, written by his great-great-great grandmother from
the age of nine, in 1789, until her death in 1852. I worked
on them and three volumes were published under the title
The Wynne Diaries by the Oxford University Press in 1936,
1937 and 1939; since the war, the three volumes have
been compressed into one, and were issued in The World
Classics series.

In 1936, after his death, I was asked by Marmaduke Pickthall's widow to write his life. Hutchinson published it in 1936 entitled *Loyal Enemy*. It did very well, going into three editions, and is quoted often in books on modern Turkey (I had 'footnote fever,' my husband said, the first time I found myself quoted as an authority).

In 1935 I stood as Labour Party candidate in the General Election, my opponent being Sir Alfred Duff Cooper, then Minister of War. I 'ran' for St. George's Westminster, a hopeless seat, which I chose from the other hopeless ones offered me because it was Charles James Fox's old constituency (I was horrified when my Labour agent said "Charles James Fox, who's 'e?"). I got 5,000 votes, Duff Cooper 20,000; but I had not forfeited my deposit, so all was well!

In 1936 I went to the USSR for the London *Times* to cover the Moscow Theatre Festival (I had already covered the Greek Theatre Festival in Sicily in 1931, and edited a *Guidebook to Sicily* for Methuen as a result). I was writing a good deal for the *New Statesman* and other magazines, also selling short stories to the *Daily Herald, Blue Peter, Sphere,* etc., and poetry to the *Spectator* and Sunday *Times,* and I was a steady reviewer for the *Times Literary Supplement* from 1930 until I left England in 1940.

When war broke out, I got a job driving an ambulance for the London County Council as I had taken the Red Cross exam, and after but a few months I went to work for the Joint Broadcasting section of the BBC, broadcasting in German and in French (I had had several plays broadcast: on Sidney and Stella, on Racine, and on Woodrow Wilson).

In the late summer of 1940, I brought my two boys to America and left them with friends, returning to England in 1941. It was also in 1941 that my first book to be published in the United States appeared: *Come to Dust*, a novel about France. In 1942 I was given a job in Wash-

ington, in the Indian section of the British Embassy. I
got it through a kind of courtsying to my ancestors: of
course I have an Oxford M.A., but my grandfather, Sir
Mountstuart Grant-Duff, was Governor of Madras, and then
Under-Secretary for India, and his father, James Grant-
Duff, was the author of the classic *History of the Mahrattas*
as well as an officer fighting the French in the eighteenth
century wars there. I had corresponded with both Mahatma Gandhi and with the Ali brothers as a little girl,
and was extremely sympathetic to Indian Nationalism.
Now I was called upon as a British official to work against
that nationalism and to vilify it. I both loved and hated
my job: loved it because I loved the Indian atmosphere
and personnel with whom I worked (my boss was an Indian, Sir Girja Bajpai), and hated it because I was, as
Research Assistant, obliged to justify the imprisonment of
Gandhi and Nehru and thousands of other Indians by the
British by attempting to prove that they were pro-Japanese,
which, of course, was completely untrue.

On July 11, 1943, I was received into the Catholic Church
in St. Matthew's Church, Washington, D. C., by Monsignor de Menasce. The Monsignor and my godmother,
Mrs. John Wiley, were also both converts.

In 1945, when my Washington job ended with the war's
end, I came to New York, where my husband joined me in
1946. Our youngest son was born in Washington in 1944,
the result of compassionate leave I took in England in 1944
when my mother died. I had named my three sons after
the Victorines—monks of the Abbey of St. Victor near
Paris, who lived in the twelfth century and were not related but all wrote: Adam and Richard of St. Victor were
hymn writers and theologians; Hugh of St. Victor was a
mystic.

In 1947, I went to North Africa to gather material for
a life of Charles de Foucauld; this was published by Holt
in 1949 under the title *Desert Calling*. In 1948, my historical

novel, *James and Joan,* a Literary Guild recommendation, was also published by Holt, and *Desert Calling* was published in England by Hollis & Carter as Catholic Book Club Choice and Book Society Recommendation. In 1947, I was appointed to the Department of Communication Arts at Fordham University, a post I still hold, and in 1949 I worked as an editor at the United Nations during the General Assembly, a job I have held six times since and again this year, 1956-57. I had begun to write for *The Commonweal* in 1944 and in 1950 I was made an associate editor. I have done reviewing for the New York *Times* and the New York *Herald Tribune,* and have also written for *Vogue, Town and Country, Harper's Bazaar,* the *Catholic World, Psychoanalytical Quarterly,* etc.

Since 1950, I have written, edited, translated or contributed to the following books: *The Face of the Saints, Fifty Years of the American Novel, The Commonweal Reader, The Lives of the Saints, The Greatest Bible Stories, Mothers, Christian Conversation, Christmas Is Here, The Grand Inquisitor, Europe: a Journey With Pictures, A Maurois Reader, A Treasury of Early Christianity, The Age of Belief,* and *The Papal Encyclicals.*

My husband, children and I live at 252 East 78th st., New York City, where we have been since 1946, and at 156 Mercer st., Princeton, N. J., since 1951.

REV. ROBERT IGNATIUS GANNON, S.J.

AS A BRIEF OUTLINE OF A "WRITER'S" PAST, THIS MUST BE the story of a misspent life. I have studied and taught and travelled and preached and lectured and engaged in endless wrangles on education, public relations and finance, but the literary output of the last sixty-four years has been practically nil: a textbook, a book of after-dinner speeches, a fat brochure, some magazine articles and now in 1957 a biography. There is no sense of guilt however. Everything can be blamed on my vow of obedience. I have been a Jesuit taking orders for forty-four years and not being regarded by my superiors as an intellectual, have never been ordered to write a book. Without such motivation, it always seemed to me that there should be an excellent reason for giving in to any such weakness and only a few times have I felt comfortably justified about rushing into print.

The first time was in my teaching days at Fordham Uni-

versity. I had Freshman English and Dramatics. I wanted
a Play Shop and there were no helpful texts that would
prepare for an appreciation of all dramatic literature, get
boys interested in writing plays and at the same time teach
them the art of the short story. So in 1923 I wrote *The
Technique of the One-Act Play*. It was published by the
Fordham University Press. It is being used now chiefly
in television circles.

Thereupon mine ancient wisdom and austere control returned and except for occasional dissipation in a magazine,
I let the public alone until the good Paulist Fathers asked
me to do a hundred pages or so on *God in Education* for
a series that they were getting out at this time. That must
have been about 1942. Nothing further happened until a
Fordham boy starting a publishing venture, came to me
with the idea of making a book of after-dinner speeches.
I was appalled. Such curiosities of American life are hard
enough to listen to, impossible to read. But he persisted
and *After Black Coffee* appeared in 1945. It was published
by Declan X. McMullen.

That should have been the end, but to my astonishment,
His Eminence Francis Cardinal Spellman decided in 1953
that I should write the authoritative story of his life. The
vow of obedience made up for the usual qualifications, ac-
cess was granted to all the necessary letters, diaries and
reports, and a five-hundred-page book resulted. It was published by Scribner's in 1957. I thought it was going to be
pretty dull, one cornerstone after another, but I found
that the Cardinal Archbishop of New York had done several
things that made the true and unvarnished account read
like fiction.

So that *is* the end. I am at work now on my epitaph.

EDITOR'S NOTE: Father Gannon was born at St. George, Staten Island,
in 1893, joined the Jesuits in 1913, and was ordained in 1926. He
was an instructor at Fordham from 1919 to 1923 and president of

the University from 1936 to 1949. Besides his S.T.D., earned at Gregorian University, Rome, he holds an A.B. from Georgetown and an M.A. from Cambridge, and has had honorary doctorates conferred upon him by nineteen institutions. Since 1952 he has been pastor of St. Ignatius Loyola Parish in New York City, as well as rector of The Loyola School and Regis High School.

SELF PORTRAIT

ERIC GILL
(1882 - 1940)

IN A CERTAIN SENSE, LIFE BEGINS WITH BAPTISM. FOR WITH baptism we begin life with a kind of God-given perfection. But from then on to the grave, we are subject to countless conflicting possibilities and powers for good and for evil which we have to co-ordinate if our lives are to become integrated, if we are to achieve and maintain our integrity. It is this sense of lifelong consistency of mind and heart for truth and goodness that characterized the career of Eric Gill.

His life, in his words and in his deeds, while of course not always perfect, were intact and complete. And in our modern way of living a departmentalized life, a life divided into separate compartments—our home life one thing, our work life another, our leisure life still another, and our religion something apart from all of them—we whose lives are disjointed and full of compromises and contradictions, can and should learn more than just admiration for the integrity of Eric Gill.

Christened Arthur Eric Gill, he was born in Brighton, England, in 1882. He was the second of the thirteen children of a minister of a religious sect founded by the Countess of Huntingdon. The sect was so small and its doctrines so vague that one writer referred to it as having three persons and no God. But like so many witticisms, this one was not true. Eric's parents were so sincerely religious minded that he never lost his grasp on the eternal verities, even though in a later period, for reasons which will be explained, his grip was weakened. And even then, he never fouled his family nest by recrimination.

As could be expected under the circumstances, his family was poor. Poor but upright and cultured and loyal and happy. And that was the starting point of Eric's lifelong crusade against men or even nations dedicating themselves to the amassing of material wealth. Yes, nations too; for he was never deceived by the bringing of the blessings of civilization to benighted countries which just happened to have rich natural resources, where the white man's burden consisted chiefly in shipping them home.

Eric's formal education consisted of six years at a private school in Brighton and two years at an art school in Chichester. He was weak in speculative subjects; strong in those he thought worth doing for their own sake, chiefly mathematics and drawing. While at art school, he joined his parents in becoming a member of the Church of England. And so he was an Anglican when he soon afterwards became apprenticed to a London firm of architects which engaged largely in ecclesiastical building. He was there but a short time when he lost his faith in what was called religion and lost faith in what was called art. On the one hand, the unnatural and tyrannical division of labor which reduced the builder to a mere copying of things designed on paper to the smallest detail by ponderous. pompous artists who held religion in tolerant contempt while making a living off it, and, on the other, the self-centered, soft-cushioned Anglican clergymen and their indifference to the intellectual, moral, and physical well being of the people —these among other things drove the young man into a vague and hungry agnosticism. He had thought that God meant a Supreme Being to be proudly loved and served and he had thought that architecture meant building. But, while he lost his illusions, he did not lose his head. He left his fictitious world and began to build a real world for himself. He wanted to be a workman, with a workman's rights and duties, to design what was to be made and to make what he had designed. An artist, he held, is not a special kind of man, but every man is a special kind of artist. What work could he do that was wanted? He soon found it: letter cutting in stone. He studied lettering under the great Edward Johnston and after a year got his first small commission, and from that day on was never out of a job. And he just walked out of the architect's office.

It is an evidence of the fact that his supposed agnosticism was just youthful bewilderment at the abuses of religion which he had witnessed that it was at about this time that Gill formulated the idea of his philosophy of work which began with the idea of God. In sorites or extended syllogistic form, it ran something like this: God is first of all to us the Creator, first, for it is to that power in Him that we owe our very existence as well as that of all the rest of the world in which we live. But God said that He created man in His own image and likeness. Therefore God intended man to be primarily a creator. But a creator is one who makes at least an appreciable part of a thing and who controls the means of its making. Therefore assembly-line mass-production in particular and our modern mechanized industrialism in general are contrary to man's nature as God created him. We should need no elaboration—much less proof—of Gill's reasoning. Have you ever met an assembly-line worker, seeing one of his company's finished products, and commenting on the quality of the job *he* did? And we see the results: workers with one eye on the clock and the other on the paycheck, and their hearts in beer-gardens to help them forget the kind of work that gives them no satisfaction of accomplishment, work that makes them servants rather than masters of machines, work that leaves them old at forty. Flowing naturally from this philosophy of work, of man as a creator, as a maker, was Gill's doctrine on the matter of the ownership of private property. Contrary to prevalent opinion, he held that it was not primarily a moral right, one flowing from man's free will. Gill denied that it was as a moral being that man had a right to private ownership. That right, he held, came primarily from man's material necessities and man's intellectual nature, deriving not from his need to *use* things but from his need to *make* things.

It is, then, to man as workman, as an intelligent being who must manipulate things in order to make them serviceable, that private ownership is both necessary and a natural right, and only when there is control of the means of production can there be proper and efficient production. Unless a man—be he a farmer, a miner, a craftsman, an artist, a laborer—unless he own, either individually or jointly with others, the field or mine or other necessary property or materials, he cannot properly control his work. This necessity of manipulation it is, according to Gill, which gives the right of private property in the means of production. Maritain has put this truth in philosophical terminology: "The exercise of art or work, whether it be that of craftsman or manual laborer, is the formal reason of individual appropriation."

It is obvious that, as things are here and now, the only grounds upon which productive goods can be validly made, have to a great extent been destroyed. The factory worker, for example, can make no claim to private ownership and the big machine industries and the utilities are not private industries—they are, as they publicly boast, public services; and hence they are fair prey to socialists and communists, for what are public services should be publicly owned for the profit of all. Bonds, bonuses, money in the bank, even profits sharing are not ownership, they are not control of the means of production, they do not restore the intellectual operation of the workman by which he imprints on matter the mark of rational being. This is the philosophy of the Distributists to which Belloc, Penty, Pepler, McNabb, the Chestertons, and scores of other leading thinkers, Catholic and non-Catholic, subscribed. The only possible reform of our world, Gill believed, must begin with the distribution of ownership.

In 1904, Gill married Mary Ethel Moore, a clergyman's daughter, and set up housekeeping in a block of workmen's dwellings in the London suburb of Battersea. Soon after the birth of their second daughter, they moved to Ditchling in their native county of Sussex. There was no back-to-the-land sentiment behind this, though Gill always loved the earth, and especially "the earth that man has loved for his daily bread and the pathos of his plight." What was behind the move was the conviction that crowded city quarters were no place to raise children. For to Gill, marriage meant babies—if it were not for babies, he once asked, would there be any more marriages?" He also believed that the coming of children aided in their parents' development of character: the father, for example, was no longer simply concerned with what conditions were best for his work or even for his personal comfort,—he became concerned with what conditions were best for a growing family.

In 1909, Gill interrupted his successful inscription-cutting business to carve a female figure in stone. His first sculpture. Most sculptors, at least at that time, modeled their statuary, building it up in clay, and then have this model reproduced in stone by a professional carver with various machines and gadgets. Gill carved his subject himself directly out of the stone. Moreover, he thought in terms of stone (not of clay) and of carving (not of modeling). In his *Autobiography* he records the event in these words: "So all without knowing it, I was making a little revolution. I was reuniting what never should have been separated: the artist as a man of imagination and the artist as a workman. I was really like the child who said, First I think and then I draw my think—in contrast with the art-student who must say, First I look and then I draw my look. At first the art critics didn't believe it. How could they? They thought I was putting up a stunt —being archaic on purpose. Whereas the real and complete truth was that I was completely ignorant of all their art stuff and was childishly doing my utmost to copy accurately in stone what I saw in my head."

Despite this misunderstanding, the art world soon opened its doors to receive him. But before it could close them behind him, he escaped. He found the atmosphere stuffy with aesthetes, dillitantes, poseurs, and agnostics.

He returned to his home and family and work, and he began to examine his own relations to God. The religions he had known were ineffectual, insufficient, and warring among themselves. So he set about making up a religion for himself, or rather, a metaphysic, a preamble to religion. And then he began to discover, slowly and gradually, that his new invention was an old one. Invention, in its old meaning, of course,—to discover, to come up with, to find. For man can approach faith through reason but not fully apprehend it. Belief in God means that you believe Him, that you accept His revelation. Of this experience Gill said: "I found a thing in my mind and I opened my eyes and found it in front of me. You don't become a Catholic by joining the Church; you join the Church because you are a Catholic." It is interesting to recall the similarity of Gill's expression to Chesterton's when he entered the Church some nine years later.

The importance that Gill attached to his reception into the Church is indicated by the fact that he concludes his *Autobiography* with the record of that event. The remaining third of the book he designated as a Postscript.

For the next four years, 1913 to 1917, he was engaged principally in carving the Stations of the Cross for Westminster Cathedral, the work which put him in the front rank of contemporary English sculptors.

Then in 1918, he was conscripted into the British army. His stint was brief—only four months, and entirely on the home front. But it helped him to formulate his opinions regarding Christians engaged in organized violence at the behest of the civil power. He was not a pacifist, as he has sometimes been called. He believed a just war possible, and hence one in which a Christian man could be obliged even in Christian charity to engage in. But he found it increasingly difficult to understand how one could be fighting for justice when the powers that attack each other are economic and financial powers, unrelated to the moral law, and unredeemed by Christianity. Modern war, he maintained, is mainly about money. And he carved his belief in stone by choosing as his subject for the facade of the war memorial at Leeds the scene of Christ driving the money-changers out of the Temple.

With the recently deceased Hilary Pepler, Gill founded the still-existing community of Catholic workmen at Ditchling. Although the community adopted the Rule of the Third Order of St. Dominic, it was not in the strict sense a religious community: its members remained laymen and they took no vows. They lived in their own private dwellings and, after Mass and Communion each morning, they went to their separate labors. The basic principle of their life was poverty, voluntary poverty; not penury or want for the necessities of decent human living, but a spirit of detachment from material possessions. Money as a means, not an end. Absurd? Do you know anyone dedicated to amassing material possessions who has peace? Do you know of any nation so dedicated which has peace? For at least in this all the nations are united: all our modern politics are based on a denial of the Gospel. Capitalism is based on the notion that those who have money have the duty to get more, and that who have none must be enslaved, or exploited or employed—until machines make their very existence unnecessary. Fascism aims at creating empires as rich and great as the others. Communism wants to make the rich poor in order that the poor may become rich. But the Gospel of God wants the rich to be poor and the poor holy. That is the peace that Christ promised. That is the peace that Gill sought—to be detached and free, and so to possess his soul in peace. That was the ultimate secret of the integrity at which he aimed.

Following a brief illness, he died in a London hospital on a November night in 1940, during the second World War. In fact, there was taking place overhead at the time an air raid.

EDITOR'S NOTE: This chapter is based on a number of sources, principally "A study in integrity: the life and teaching of Eric Gill," by Father Conrad Pepler, O.P., in the May, 1947, issue of Blackfriars. Evan R. Gill edited a thorough *Bibliography of Eric Gill* (Cassell, 1953). *It All Goes Together* (Devin-Adair, 1944) comprises his selected essays and numerous reproductions of his art. See also his Autobiography (id., 1941), *Beauty Looks After Herself* (Sheed, 1935), *Money and Morals* (Faber, 1934), *Art* (Devin-Adair, 1950), and his *Letters* (id., 1948).

HILDA GRAEF

AT THE TENDER AGE OF SIX I MADE TWO DECISIONS THAT affected my whole future career: I resolved to test my literary capacities by composing a poem of my own, having just learned to write, and I told my father I wanted to learn Greek. This strange idea had entered my head when he had taught me for fun the first three or four letters of the Greek alphabet. He was a teacher at a Berlin girls' school, though his ambition, like that of his small daughter, had always been to be a writer; but the plays he had composed had never found their way on to the stage or into print.

I was seven when the first world war broke out; my father died three years later and, in 1918, when the German revolution brought havoc to the country much of my small world, too, was destroyed. I had been brought up a Protestant in name, though both my parents were unbelievers. Nevertheless, I had been really pious as a child. But now a cousin of mine, who was much older than I and was considered the genius of the family, told me that all the New Testament stories I had learned were no more true than fairy tales. It was a great shock to me that there should be no Father in heaven and no Lord Jesus to pray to; but if Werner said so it surely must be true. So my childish faith collapsed within a few moments. It left no conscious gap, for the next years were far too exciting for me to feel any lack: there was the aftermath of the revolution, political orators on soap boxes, general strikes when I had to do my homework by candle light, and the like. Later in the early twenties, came the inflation, the nightmarish time when a loaf of bread would cost a million and even a milliard marks. At this time I first took up private coaching to help mother, who was teaching at a school; for our small capital had dissolved into thin air.

When I was seventeen I had a strange experience. By way of broadening my horizon, I went into a Catholic church one evening, where they were having May devotions. Then something extraordinary happened. I, who had hardly ever gone into a Protestant church because I found the services intolerably boring, was completely carried off my feet. I could not imagine why. So strong was the inexplicable attraction I felt that I went again two days later, and after that to Mass on Sunday. That finished me. I felt sure that if I went once more into a Catholic church I should want to become a Catholic—without even believing in God. This was absurd, and I decided then and there never again to enter one.

A year later I finished school and began to study German, English and Scripture at Berlin University, having developed an unaccountable interest in religion despite my complete unbelief. My student years were filled with work, dancing, theatre going, and also with my first journalistic efforts. My mother wanted me to take a degree enabling me to teach so as to have a secure background, whereas I

wanted to be a fashion journalist and very near got on to
the staff of *Vogue*. That plan, however, miscarried, and
I resigned myself to my mother's wish and, after taking
my state's examination at Berlin, went in for a two years
educational training from which I emerged as a full-
fledged teacher. For eighteen months I taught at a Berlin
church school, mostly English and Scripture. Then came
Hitler—and I had even more than one Jewish grandmother!

During my university years I had done a fair amount of
writing for some provincial and also some Berlin papers,
mostly on fashions and small sketches in the manner of
the popular Erich Kaestner. This too would now have to
stop. I therefore decided to take a course in cooking, as
I was quite good at that and it would give me an opening
anywhere. After a short spell as lady housekeeper, I emigrated. I first went to Holland, where I stayed for a few
months, and in May of 1936 I landed in England. I had
quite a difficult time during my first years there. I started
off doing domestic work and then got a job as German
'Fraeulein' at an incredible little private school near Eton,
whose principal was addicted to the brandy bottle. During
my first winter there I had every conceivable variety of
a cold; but I would nevertheless sit undeterred on my bed
(my chair in the icy room I shared with the gym mistress
was too dilapidated to sit on), wrapped in my dressing
gown, and wrote articles for Swiss newspapers. My great
worry was: would I ever be able to write English sufficiently
well for publication?

After four terms at this somewhat purgatorial school, I
was offered a bursary if I would study Church of England
theology and take the Archbishop of Canterbury's Diploma.
I accepted with alacrity, and soon found myself writing
theological essays at top speed at King's College, London,
which invariably received high marks from my profes-

sors. It seemed that I might, after all, be able to write articles in English.

Though I had in the meantime been confirmed in the Church of England, I was still not much of a Christian during the first year of my theological studies. Then, in my second year, when I was introduced to the doctrinal teaching of the Church in the first five centuries, the incredible happened: for the first time in my life I saw that the Christian religion is not, as my German Lutheran teachers had presented it, something totally unreasonable which one had just to 'experience'; I realized that it was a perfectly logical whole, hanging together in all its parts, and by no means 'absurd.' I duly took my examination, in January of 1940, a few months after the outbreak of World War II. Though I received a First class degree, conferred on me in Lambeth Chapel by the Archbishop of Canterbury in person, I could not find a post, owing to my German nationality, but just managed to keep alive in a London attic frequently shaken by bombs, on a small allowance from a charitable organization. So I had plenty of time to read, and immersed myself in St. Thomas Aquinas and St. John of the Cross, with an admixture of G. K. Chesterton and Monsignor Benson's novels by way of lighter relief. Besides, I started making a regular morning and evening meditation according to the Ignatian method. It is hardly surprising that, with such a spiritual diet, I should soon have turned my eyes to the Catholic Church. In fact, on one cold morning in January of 1941, I made my way to the famous Jesuit church in Farm Street and asked to see a priest, to the accompaniment of the noise of roaring planes and anti-aircraft guns. Within two months I was received into the Church.

As I had built my career on an Anglican theological diploma, all prospects for a job seem to have collapsed. While I was still an Anglican I had written a series of articles on "Prayer in the Bible" for a religious teachers' periodical. I now began to interest myself in mystical theology and published articles on German mystics in the Oxford Dominican monthly *Blackfriars*, besides writing on German questions in the London *Tablet* and other journals. In autumn of the same year (1941), I was appointed senior assistant to the editor of the *Lexicon of Patristic Greek* that was being compiled in Oxford.

I had never thought of writing books but contented myself with articles, when, as the war was nearing its end, in July of 1945, I received a letter from an Irish publisher (Mercier Press, Dublin) asking whether I had a manuscript that I would care to submit to him; he had seen my spiritual articles in *Blackfriars* and was interested in publishing something I had written. I was dumbfounded—I—write a book? It seemed an impossible proposition. But gradually the idea grew on me, and after consultation with the editor of *Blackfriars* I enlarged some of the material I had published in that periodical, added some other studies, and finally sent in the manuscript of my first book, *The Way of the Mystics*. It was still on the press when the publisher asked me to do a second book for him, on Therese Neumann, whose name was just then much in the news. Little did I know what I was letting myself in for when I gladly accepted this offer. I had no doubt that Therese was a genuine mystic and, as my remuneration for the *Lexicon* work was scarcely sufficient to keep body and soul together, I was hoping to quickly write a 'potboiler.'

I had never studied Therese Neumann's case before; but as I was now reading the various previous publications, doubts arose in my mind that all was not so clearly supernatural as it seemed, and, though I should have liked to write a popular hagiographical account, I felt I could not do so without first investigating the case. I wrote in this sense to the publishers, fully expecting them to draw back; but to my surprise they replied that I should examine the case as fully as I could and then present it as it seemed to me.

In order to gain some firsthand impressions, I decided to go to Konnersreuth myself—not an easy undertaking, for the year was 1948 and the American occupation authorities refused me a visa until I produced a formal permission from Therese's own diocesan, Monsignor Buchberger, to see her. The journey—from Switzerland where I had spent a holiday—was also difficult; the electricity broke down and the train stood for three hours between two stations in the middle of the night; besides, it was invaded by American soldiers who had, understandably enough, drunk far too much of the excellent Bavarian beer and had to remind each other from time to time that "there was a lady in the compartment." Nevertheless, I eventually arrived at Konnersreuth and had a short conversation with Therese; I did not, however, see her in one of her ecstasies, since the Friday I was there was the feast of Our Lady of Mount Carmel. When I expressed my regret to her director, Father Naber, that I had not been there on the previous Friday, he informed me that the phenomena had not appeared on that day either. In fact, as I was assured on very good authority, they had lately become very infrequent.

Back in Oxford I completed my book, having come to the conclusion that a supernatural explanation of the strange case was no more probable than a natural one. I thought I had given the evidence for my view with sufficient fairness, and two prominent Jesuits, Archbishop T. D. Roberts and Father C. C. Martindale, gave the book very favorable reviews in English papers, so that there it was hardly attacked at all. Hence the violent controversy the book aroused in the United States came as a surprise to me. It brought me, by the way, very little 'fan mail,' though I remember a letter from one of Therese's American admirers expressing the conviction that I must be either the

willing or the unwilling instrument of the devil. When
the book appeared in a German translation in Switzerland
the controversy flared up even more violently; immediately
before publication the publishers received, among other
threatening mail, a post-card calling the work "the vile
book of the vile witch of Albion," though it appeared with
two Imprimaturs.

It was a relief after all these attacks, to which I replied
in an article published in the *Commonweal*, to immerse
myself in the works of the Greek Church Father, Gregory
of Nyssa, whose sermons on *The Lord's Prayer and the
Beatitudes* (Newman, 1954) I translated, with introduction and notes, for the Ancient Christian Writers series.
While I was still engaged on that, I received a letter from
a German Dominican nun friend who asked me whether
I knew Edith Stein. I replied that she did not interest me;
I thought her too much of a blue stocking. About three
months later I received a letter from an American Capuchin
in Italy who also asked me if I knew her. I replied in the
same strain. By way of answer he sent me the first biography of her, written by her Prioress. I approached with
the greatest misgivings—only to be so completely bowled
over by it as to want to write a life of her myself, more
suited to English-speaking readers and stressing also her
intellectual and spiritual development. To collect more
first-hand information on her, I made a lightening tour
through Belgium, Holland and Germany, during which I
stayed at her own convent at Cologne for two nights, having
to climb over the bomb-damaged roofs of the surrounding
houses to get to my bedroom *The Scholar and the Cross*
(Newman) was published in the spring of 1955.

At the same time my work on the *Greek Patristic Lexicon*
came to an end. After more than thirteen years of it,
this seemed a suitable moment for some stocktaking. My
mother, who had joined me in England in 1939, had suggested several times that I should write my autobiography.

I now settled down to it, and the outcome of my delvings
into my past was published by Newman in the spring of
1957.

At the moment, I am busy carrying out a long cherished
plan to write a larger and, I hope, more mature book on
the mystic life than my first one had been, which is probably to be called *The Light and the Rainbow*. While collecting material for its first chapter on Jesuit spirituality,
I had the privilege of being admitted—the first woman
ever!—with the permission of the provincial and many
smiles and rattling of backdoor keys, to the enclosure of
the Jesuit house at Enghien (Belgium) to choose my books
from their magnificent spiritual library. For the spiritual
life has remained my chief concern. It was the purpose
of *God in Our Daily Life* (Newman, 1952) to adapt it to
the normal routine of contemporary men and women, and
I have tried to present it in an even simpler form in a series
of twelve articles that began to appear in June of 1956 in
the Dominican publication *The Torch*.

LUCILE HASLEY

OFFHAND, IT SOUNDED LIKE AN ENCHANTING PROPOSAL. IT wasn't every day, I told myself, that a writer was given a free hand in writing up his own charms and virtues— especially in a reference book of this sort—and so why, pray, not make the most of it? With only your conscience as your guide, and taking the sweet privilege of quoting only from the good reviews, would not it be possible to build yourself up as a literary figure, beloved by all, who . . .

And then, as with most enchanting proposals, came the sobering thought that this was not for the likes of me. That is, had I not *already* set down in cold print, in essay after essay, and in fulsome detail, an only too candid and thorough picture of myself? Was it not a little late in the day, then, to try to present a more glorified Lucile Hasley?

Or, for that matter, why bother to write up even an old Hasley?

Surely, the simplest way to introduce myself—if not the

most delicate—was just to point out, quite reasonably:
"Look. Why don't you just read my *books?* Heaven knows
they contain no plot, and heaven knows they will never capture a Pulitzer prize, but they certainly expose *me.* In fact,
it's practically like reading a private diary."

Few writers can make this claim. And few writers,
let us face it, would even want to. The personal essayist
(that's me) is a breed apart: the writer who is willing to
stick out his neck, for better or worse, in order to reach
through—in a most personal way—to his audience. Reader
identification, I think you call it: based on the tried and
true dogma of Original Sin that links us all together.

For instance, one has only to flip to page 22 of *Reproach-
fully Yours* to get a rough idea of my besetting sin—a slight
tendency toward exaggeration—that is offset only by my
beautiful (if Utopian) faith in my readers' ability, and
willingness, to take it in full stride. I quote:

"The real sore spot for me, however, is that an accepted
manuscript calls for 'biographical data' about the author.
I gaze with chartreuse envy at that lucky author who can
start out: 'Born on a river barge on the Ganges, I grew up
alone, untamed, unlettered.' Or 'I wrote the outline for
this story on the back of a soap wrapper while in a concentration camp. After three years as prisoner (during
which time they never discovered my name was really
Countess Amerila von Steuppenguard), I finally escaped to
Lapland . . .' "

This is what is commonly known as dangerous writing
(indeed, it frightens even my husband sometimes), because
some literal-minded if careless reader—somewhere in the
world—is sure to say thoughtfully: "Lapland? Countess
Amerila von Steuppenguard? But I always thought
Mrs. Hasley was just a South Bend housewife."

As indeed she is. That careless reader has only to move
on to the next lyrical paragraph:

"Who, I wonder, is going to be entranced with my bio-

graphical data? I start out, in forthright, deadly fashion:
'I have spent my entire life in South Bend, Indiana. At the
age of six I broke my leg while roller skating. In high
school, I made the second string volley ball team and...'
No, no, I can't go on. It's so dull that I'm sorely tempted
to toss in a couple of divorces and illigitimate children and
just show those editors what an interesting contributor
they've snared."

But enough nonsense. Actually, I'm quite content with
my lot (Notre Dame faculty wife, mother of three, convert) but you can see for your self that I—at least in the
beginning—had no choice *but* to write about the everyday things that happened right in my own back yard.
Not for me could there be any high-flung essays on the
grandeur of the Alps, life behind the Iron Curtain, the joys
of solitude, or my last interview with Winston Churchill.
Not for me, either, could there be any ladylike essays on
raising African violets or the joys of liturgical cooking or
cleaning Venetian blinds... for I am not passionately addicted to any of these pursuits.

No, I had no choice but to write about that sterling
character, *Myself,* and all the people around me... especially the clerical friends who were polishing my little
soul to a fare-thee-well... and, naturally, a certain amount
of Catholic atmosphere was bound to creep in. (*Creep*
in? What am I saying! The essays were fairly leaping
with Catholicism. The only creeping was done by me: the
inquisitive convert, creeping around... and sniffing... and
exploring her new Home.)

Anyhow, as I was saying, my essays were so very personal
that I prudently wrote the following inscription for *Re-
proachfully Yours:* "Dedicated to my children—Susan,
Janet, and Danny—with the high hope that they won't sue
me for libel when they grow up." Then, to handle my
mother, I lovingly dedicated my next book, *The Mouse
Hunter,* to her. (It seemed only decent, considering that

the lead-off essay entitled "Charlotte Mary Josephine" had not left a stone unturned in presenting her to the world.) Then, quickly running out of any more books to dedicate, I could only hope for the best as regards the other possible law suits—such as from my non-Catholic relatives (who appeared in "Swing Low, Sweet Chariot") and my long-suffering husband. I figured, though, that my non-Catholic relatives wouldn't be caught dead reading the Catholic press, and as for my friend Louis . . . well, heavens, didn't I hand over all my royalty checks to him? Believe me, it wasn't every professor of English who had a wife toiling over a hot typewriter from dawn to dusk . . .

(Oh, all *right*, Louis . . . I'll change that last sentence, only I don't see why you have to proofread *everything* I write. You talk about poetic license but you never let me . . . look, why don't you just take care of the punctuation?)

What my upstanding Born Catholic husband wants me to admit, you see, is that I'm a very lazy writer . . . and with practically no ambition worth mentioning . . . and that I *waste time* writing hundreds and hundreds of personal letters that, in themselves would be saleable essays . . . maybe even novels. What's worse, it's the ugly truth. But can I help it if the mailman dumps bushels of fan mail (and vice versa) from all over the world on my doorstep? Don't I *prefer* a live audience, that responds with either yelps of pain or yelps of delight, rather than a faceless numerical blob, as indicated on a sales report? Yes. Too, there is a very special delight in the letters from fallen-aways . . . interested Protestants . . . grateful but bewildered converts . . . and the keep-it-up-girl clergy: all saying "Thanks."

Thanks for what? Well, one version comes from Ed Fischer, the TV columnist, who once did a "Toast of the Month" magazine feature on me. I quote, with pleasure unconfined:

"The scribblings on the note propped up against the sugar

bowl on the kitchen table read: 'Dear Mother, I'm being baptized a Catholic tomorrow. Hope you don't mind. Love, Lucile.' In fourteen words Lucile Hasley told her family of her conversion. Then in thousands of words she told the world how it feels to be a convert. And every word about her life in the Catholic Church has the simplicity, directness, and explosiveness of those first fourteen. Her sentences, although carrying heavy bundles, dance along on tip-toe. She has the ability to make theology as exciting as a detective story. She knows how to fit big truths into little words."

This is high praise... "big truths into little words"... and I try to remember it whenever I'm tempted to show off with a three-syllable word I've picked up from playing Scrabble. But there I go! Actually, I'm a prolific reader and *love* to play around with words. Too, I will spend hours lovingly revising a manuscript and whittling it down to the bone so as to live up to my famous remark, that I fear will follow me to the grave: "If I have any literary standard at all, it is this. I consider it a mortal sin to bore people."

I try, too, to carry this slogan into the lecturing field. Hence, I positively refuse to be saddled with edifying topics ("The Dignity of Woman"... "Bringing Christ into the Home") and wing merrily around the country with exactly one speech in my repertoire. Of course I conscientiously change the title ever so often, to mislead people, but my favorite choice, and the one that appears most often on programs, is The Joyful Christian. (There are moments, though, when The Petrified Christian would be more apt, for I suffer, most frightfully, from chronic stage fright. For instance, how do I know... for sure... that the Bishop, sitting at my right, will not interrupt me with hoarse cries of "Heresy!")

Anyhow, me and my speech (and I surely hold the national championship for getting the most mileage out of

my limited talents) have traveled from Spokane to Boston
to Dallas to Mobile to ... well, you name it.

Now if you will kindly translate my lecturing career onto
the printed page, that is, see the close parallel between the
writing and the talking, you'll discover the same theme:
namely, a thin talent that has been spread far and wide,
and greeted with a response that is awkward to explain.
(Indeed, the *worthwhile* writers and speakers of this world
have every good reason to hate me passionately. It's getting
away with murder, that's what ... especially my fantastic
book sales. Bitterest of all is the fact that I never wanted,
or intended, to become a writer. It just *happened*. I just
started to write—out of sheer stark boredom—when I was
put to bed for four months with a heart ailment. Moreover,
I never even collected a decent quota of rejection slips.
Moreover, I was approached by the publishers, not vice
versa, and had to be literally coaxed into letting them collect my essays in book form.)

Let it be said,. though, that Sheed & Ward appear to be
just as puzzled as I am about the popular response. For
instance, they once put on a contest (requiring no box tops)
and invited their customers to write in and explain, if possible, the secret of my success. Frankly, I think things
have come to a pretty pass when even your own publishers
can't figure out why anyone would buy your books ... but
let it pass. Let me just quote from the winning entry by
Mrs. Mary Reed Newland of Massachusetts who, incidentally, got fifty dollars worth of free merchandise for
her efforts:

"The secret is that Lucile Hasley is to the Catholic reading public, both the initiate and the still-to-be-initiated,
what used to be known as duck soup for poppa. She is
the All-American Roman Catholic Wedge. She is the gal
you can hand to anyone—any size, shape, color, class, and
intellect—and get them softened up and ready for the kill.
She's the lethal lollypop that the doctor hands little kids

with one hand while he goes at them with a hypodermic in the other. For instance, she got the first faint smile I'd seen in over a year out of a woman afflicted with one of the most nearly fatal cases of scruples in the history of the Church. Lucile the Wonder Worker, she was known as in our parish after that. I'm putting in a bid for a small case of first-class relics if her next plane trip should prove disastrous."

I suspect that this last eerie note sums up my status quite neatly. That is, you can see for yourself that *some* readers would like my bones for holy relics. Others . . . just my bones.

SISTER MARY XAVIER, I.W.B.S.

(Mercedes Claire Holworthy)

I WAS BORN IN DENVER, COLORADO, ON FEBRUARY 28, 1890, of Reverend Alfred J. Holworthy and Annie Betz. My father, a graduate of Oxford University, came to America seeking work and wealth. Of the first he found plenty, of the latter, very little. After his marriage, he went to Denver to study for the Anglican ministry, and it was during his second year there that the first of his two children was born. I was baptized a week after my birth, my father insisting that I should be named for Our Lady of Mercy. Though he was a "low-church" Episcopalian, he had a singular love for the Mother of Christ. He was very happy when I was given the name of Mary at my investiture.

My father's first assignment after his ordination was to the little town of Wallace, Idaho, where he was pastor of a small church with several outlying missions. I was then four years old.

As far back as I can remember, I always accompanied

my father on his journeys over the mountains of Idaho to Murrey and other missions; and when I was five years old he permitted me to sit on his lap and hold the reins of his horse as he taught me to drive. At six years I was able to guide the horse over the mountains with very little help. The horse was not gentle, and my father need merely show him the whip to encourage him to move faster. One day I showed him the whip, but accidentally touched him with it. That both of us were not killed as the horse dashed over those mountains in a mad run-away race, is because God had something else for us to do. Though thrown out of the buggy, neither of us was hurt, and after a fifteen minute chase we caught up with "Billie," merely because he could go no further—an on-coming wagon and its occupants brought the run-away to a halt.

Even while at home, I much preferred to play dolls and study my lessons in my father's office than to help mother with the dishes and sweeping. I always tried to do everything I saw my father do, so that before I was seven years old I had learned how to set type and help him get out his little four-page church paper. He taught me to read, write and spell each morning, and then on Saturdays there would be no playing until I had learned my Sunday-school lesson.

After four years in Idaho, my father was transferred to Corpus Christi, Texas, and given charge of the Church of the Good Shepherd. Up to this time, he had been my teacher, but now I must go to school. I was very happy about that because my new friends were going to school, and that sounded "bigger." What was my disappointment when I found myself registered at the Convent. I argued, begged, cried—all to no purpose. My father was firm in his determination that a common school education was not good enough for his daughter, so when I gave too much trouble (I often played "hookey" and went to the public school with my chum), he sent me to the Episcopalian school

in San Antonio. The break came when I returned home
one morning saying that I would not go to the Convent
school any more, that they were trying to make a Catholic
of me. The reading lesson that morning happened to be
a story of the Blessed Virgin Mary. I refused to read it.

A few nights away from home conquered me. I wrote
to my father that I would go to school anywhere, do anything, and be the very best girl in the world if he would
only bring me home. He did not relent. After a year and
a half of persistent crying and begging, of manifest discontent and rebellion at school, the principal finally wrote
and asked my father to take me home before they should
have to send me. They were all tired of me.

I arrived home at nine P.M., and had to sit for a two-
hour lecture. The next morning I was back in the Convent
school—this time as a weekly boarder—Monday to Friday.
After a few weeks of tears and rebellion, the Sisters finally
won me over to a state of contentment, and finally of happiness with them. Soon I did not want to go home on
Friday afternoons.

One evening during the month of May, I attended the
regular devotions in honor of Our Lady with the other
boarders—just through curiosity. Like St. Paul, I was
"thrown to my knees" during the singing of the Benediction
service, tears flowed from my eyes, grace was poured into
my soul, and from that moment, though not yet twelve
years of age, I was determined to be a Catholic. I consulted my father. His answer, "Are you crazy? Don't mention that subject to me again." I said no more, but after
a year of hard study in the Catechism, which I concealed
inside my geography, I was secretly baptized on December 6,
1903, by Father Claude Jaillet, the subject of one of my
books.

We moved to St. Louis shortly after that, so in order to
practice my Faith I had to tell my parents. One of the
Sisters told my father and I told mother. Both were

broken-hearted. What my father said to Sister I do not know, but I shall never forget my mother's words: "There is no use crying over spilled milk, but if you are going to be a Catholic, for God's sake be a good one; a good Catholic is a saint, but a bad Catholic is the devil himself."

Neither of my parents would give me permission to make my First Holy Communion or be Confirmed until I would be eighteen. I consulted my confessor, the saintly Redemptorist at St. Alphonsus (Rock) Church, Father Enright. He gave me instructions privately, and I had the happiness of receiving my First Communion on the first Friday in May, 1904. Since I had not eaten before leaving home, and was on my way to school, Father Enright insisted on my going to the Monastery for breakfast. As I entered the door he said, "You are the first lady to be permitted to eat in our Monastery." I was confirmed by Archbishop Glennon a few days later. When my parents found out that I had disobeyed them they gave up on the question of religion.

In February, 1907, I returned to Corpus Christi, ostensibly on a month's vacation. My intentions were to remain, and I applied for admission into the novitiate. My parents were shocked, and my mother said I was carrying things too far. They forced me to wait until I was eighteen, and since the Superior would not receive me before that time without their consent, I had to submit this time. On February 28, 1908, I took the step with my father's blessing, but not with mother's. I received the habit of the Sisters of the Incarnate Word and Blessed Sacrament on January 6, 1909, and made my final vows on December 29, 1910.

My first years in the Convent were devoted to teaching music and the elementary grades. I received my B.A. degree at Incarnate Word College, San Antonio, Texas, in 1929, and after my courses in Library Science, and some education courses from the Catholic University, I entered St. Mary's University, San Antonio, from which I received my M.A. in History in 1939. For some years I was head

of the history and commercial departments in our high
school in Corpus Christi, but since 1936 I have been librarian while still holding my position in the commercial
school.

Since 1941 Our Blessed Mother has given me opportunity
to make reparation for my irreverence toward her in my
early days when I refused to read the story about her—I
am Moderator of the parish and high school Sodalities.

My first book was written as my thesis, *The History of
the Diocese of Corpus Christi* (1939). During my research
for this story I became so fascinated with the life and
work of the early missionaries in southwest Texas that I
resolved to continue. My second book, *Diamonds for the
King* (1945), is the story of the Sisters of the Incarnate
Word and Blessed Sacrament in Texas, 1852-1945. Bishop
Claude Dubuis' missionary labors fired my enthusiasm, and
the more material I found, the more desirous I became to
write his life. As I was about to launch on that endeavor,
I learned that Dr. Leo V. Jacks had written it, and that
it was soon to be published. I then turned to one of his
priests, the pioneer missionary, Father Claude Jaillet. It
appeared in 1948 under the title *Father Jaillet, Saddle-Bag
Priest of the Nueces.*

I am not really a writer. Research work has become a
hobby. At the request of the By-liners of Corpus Christi
I am collecting material on the pioneer families of this
City which may be printed some day. The year 1953 was
the centenary of the foundation of the first parish in Corpus
Christi, and I gathered material for a souvenir brochure
for that occasion. It was entitled *A Century of Sacrifice:*
the history of the cathedral parish, Corpus Christi, Texas,
1853-1953. Our Bishop Mariano S. Garriga graciously contributed its foreword.

I am a corresponding member of the Texas Knights of
Columbus Historical Commission and have enjoyed work-
ing in their archives with the worthy custodian, Bishop
Laurence FitzSimon of Amarillo.

RILEY HUGHES

NOT LONG AGO I WAS INVITED TO CONTRIBUTE A CHAPTER TO Frank Sheed's book of non-convert stories, *Born Catholics*. I was attracted by the idea of an antidote to the spate of convert stories we have had—that of my wife, Josephine Nicholls Hughes, to be found in Gilbert Oddo's *These Came Home,* interests me most—but I felt that my own story merited inclusion only if I wrote of myself as a type: the Irish-American of New England origin. Thus I wrote my piece in the third person. It occurs to me now that the problem for the writer, particularly when he inhabits the academic world, is to be sure to live in the first person, whether or not he writes in the third.

I have decided, this time, to try to see myself as "I," and not as "one." I was born in New Haven, Connecticut, in 1914, and I had my early training there, part of it literally in the shadow of Yale, which I was later to attend for a time as a graduate student. It was in New Haven too that

I had my professional start as a writer. A year after graduating from high school and a year before going to college, I began writing book reviews for the *Journal-Courier,* a morning newspaper. The summer just before college I was what I believe is called a "relief" reporter for the evening paper. I was not yet a writer, but I was on my way to becoming one. College, I hoped, would help.

Attending Providence College was one of the important influences in my life. I entered college having read enormously yet not systematically; I had already written a few hundred book reviews. But for all I had read and written, I was distressingly ignorant. I had neglected much of my formal education to read the classics of English literature; of science and philosophy I had no idea whatever. College perforce opened my eyes—happily there was no elective system—to fields I had casually ignored. With the Dominican Fathers I had found guidance, inspiration, and a living ideal of truth and learning. *Veritas* is the college motto, as it has been of the Order of Preachers for seven centuries, and truth I learned to know and love.

From my sophomore year I found myself writing for the Sunday book page of a distinguished newspaper, the Providence *Journal.* In my freshman year I had made up a book of humurous sketches which I had published, and many more I had not. By my junior year I had the good sense to consign the manuscript—much worn after rejection by nine publishers—to the flames. I left college the author of an unpublished and happily destroyed book, with the odd literary honor of having written a book column for a race track magazine. I went on to graduate work, first at Yale and then at Brown. Every summer I pounded the sand of the Connecticut shoreline as a "shore correspondent" for the New Haven *Register,* bringing news of weiner roasts and other stirring events to a waiting world.

My first full-time position—these were the late Depression years—was a writing and editing job. In 1940 I was appointed a state editor in the Connecticut WPA Writers' Project. Two years later I was head of the Project, slightly before it was dissolved, as Dr. New Deal lay dying. My chief writing task on the Project was to do a book on officer training in the United States Coast Guard. Devin-Adair brought the book out in 1944 under the title *Our Coast Guard Academy: A History and Guide.*

By that time I was back at Providence College, as public relations director and instructor in English. I had had a year in the English department at Brown; now I was engaged in teaching again. Fifteen years later I am teaching still, now as associate professor of English in the School of Foreign Service at Georgetown University.

When I take stock now, I have an enormous quantity of journalistic reviewing to look back on—I have been writing book reviews constantly for a quarter of a century—and three books. My first writing for the Catholic press was in the pages of *America,* at the kind invitation of Father Harold Gardiner, S. J. I have written reviews often for *The Commonweal, Best Sellers, Books on Trial* (where for some years now I have had a quarterly column on reprints and new editions), *Renascence, Thought,* and other Catholic magazines. I was the second critic to succeed the famous Brother Leo in *Columbia.* My reviews have also appeared in *The Saturday Review.* Since 1951 I have been fiction critic of *The Catholic World,* to which I contribute a monthly column.

In all my years of book reviewing, I tried my hand at various literary forms, and I have published something in every form. For a long time the stern demands of professional competence I held up for others acted as a brake on my own literary ambitions. My novel, the first of what I hope may be not a few, was written more or less as an accident. *The Hills Were Liars* existed first as a short story—a short story no one would publish. Then an editor from Bruce invited me to dinner one November day; I took

along, as conversation pieces, a short story I had published
in *Four Quarters* (our only Catholic "little magazine" and
a most distinguished publication edited from La Salle College) and a short story in manuscript. I came away from
a pleasant dinner finding myself pledged to spin the un-
publishable short story into a novel.

This, after some three years of constant writing, I did.
I wrote the book in long hand, in pencil mostly, in a huge
business ledger. For much of the time I was baby-sitting
with our children. Every day I would write what I could
—sometimes only a few lines, never more than a few pages
—stopping to tie a baby's shoe, or to referee a children's
free-for-all. You see, I am what is known in the trade as
a "bleeder." That is, I write with excruciating slowness.
I don't write books—I write *words*—one long word after
another. Fortunately I do not have the problem of revision
most writers have. And I have nothing to throw away,
not more than a paragraph or two for an entire book. One
reviewer of *The Hills Were Liars* commented on what he
was pleased to consider the polished perfection of my sentences. He concluded that they were the result of long
and careful revision. In a sense he was right, but the revision was in my mind, not on paper. Style has always been
less of a problem for me than finding something to say.

In *The Hills Were Liars* I found something to say, I
think, a way to give voice to the thoughts and the anxieties
of some years. This book is the story of our world as I
imagine it to be one hundred years from now, after the
atomic wars are over. Men live cut off from other men
in small islands of humanity. Men live; the Church lives.
I wrote *The Hills Were Liars* to work out imaginatively
what Christ's promise to the Church might mean in a world
almost destroyed. The theme is from Scripture, in the
words of Jeremias: "In every deed the hills were liars,
and the multitude of the mountains; truly in the Lord our
God is the salvation of Israel."

The novel came out, published by Bruce, in 1955, and in the following year P. J. Kenedy published my anthology of short stories from the American Catholic press entitled *All Manner of Men*. I had long hoped to publish a novel, but for even a longer time it was my ambition to edit a volume of short stories. I think that my collection is an important one for the new talent it introduces and for the attention it calls to the work of quality being published in our Catholic magazines. The sponsorship of this book by the Catholic Press Association is a hopeful sign, I think; it shows unmistakably the vigorous interest of the Catholic press in fiction of literary merit, professional in its competence, modern in spirit, and wrought out of our great tradition of Christian art.

At the moment (January, 1957), and before I can get down to a novel now only a skimpy group of notes, I am engaged in three book projects. First to be completed will be an edition of Monsignor Robert Benson's novel *By What Authority?;* this for a series of reprints of Benson which P. J. Kenedy is putting out. I am working on a freshman English text for Harper, and I have copious notes for a biography of Bishop Bruté, first bishop of Vincennes, Indiana, which I am to do for the Catholic Treasury series of juveniles being published by Bruce.

I am doing all this in the midst of normal family chaos. When I was writing the introduction to my short story anthology workmen were immediately below me banging together a new main beam in our house. The children can tie their own shoes now, but I must break off my writing to hear Winifred read me a story, or to ask Austin his catechism questions. Dennis and Hildred are not in school yet, but they bring drawings or "book jackets" which demand instant attention. Much as the children interrupt my writing schedule, I interrupt it far more often myself. Writing, even in the midst of one's family, is a lonely job; one is cut off by a self-constructed wall of concentration. I break out of the wall now and again, and get away from my usual round, by going on lecture tours. I was thrown into lecturing quite by chance. Some years ago I went, as one of three men in an audience of six hundred women, to hear the late Theodore Maynard speak on Chesterton. At the last minute, illness prevented the speaker's appearance, and with fifteen minutes' preparation—a rough outline on the back of an envelope—I walked out on the platform to give the talk instead. After that experience, no audience has had the power to terrify me, and I have spoken to literary and other groups in twenty-four States, and at some sixty colleges and universities.

For a quarter of a century of writing I have, it seems to me, but little to show; I have begun to feel only recently that I have achieved technical competence, and have at last found things to say. Next to my personal and religious heritage, my life has been influenced most by my college, my wife, and my children. From all of these I have learned, as more than a notional thing, that reverence for life which is the stuff of all good writing. As Francis Bacon says, "The joys of parents are secret, and so are their griefs and fears; they cannot utter the one, nor they will not utter the other." In *The Hills Were Liars* I tried to utter the "griefs and fears" of all parents in this fateful atomic age of ours. I can only hope that it will be granted me to live purposefully in the first person and to continue, gathering effectiveness and skill, to write in the third.

KATHRYN C. HULME

I'M A CALIFORNIAN, BORN AND RAISED IN SAN FRANCISCO, a "vintage San Fransiscan" as I sometimes call myself proudly, since my father was also born in that city to which my grandparents came in the 1850's via covered wagon and clipper ship. Educated in the public schools and later in the University of California, I concentrated as heavily as the curriculum allowed on literature courses, and I cannot remember a time when the idea of becoming a writer was not the number one desire in my heart. The taste for books came from my mother, a confirmed bookworm who was perennially in debt to the publishing houses which in those days sold "sets" of Mark Twain, Stevenson, and Victor Hugo on the installment plan, their salesmen going from door to door with their handsome offerings. Thanks to her never being able to say 'No' to a book-peddler, I fed on the classics from my earliest reading days.

From that California childhood there emerged many years

later what I called my first real writing—an autobiographical story, thinly disguised as fiction, entitled *We Lived as Children*, published by Alfred Knopf in 1938. A book of African travel sketches and a novel set in Tunisia preceded the autobiographical story, but I never boasted much about these first two fruits bursting with purple passages. Willa Cather was my literary idol at that time. Her clean beautiful prose made me look at my own with dismay. Maybe I wasn't meant to be a writer after all. Then one day, as I sat in a little café on the Left Bank of Paris, where I was living and earning my living, I began to write the first of the stories that belonged to me: *We Lived as Children*. It was a story of early San Francisco, a divorce and a broken family and a gallant little mother who tried to protect her children from the sense of shame that the word 'divorce' implied in the early 1900's. I wanted the book to be a tremendous indictment of divorce, but perhaps I treated the mother-love theme too tenderly to achieve my aim. The book, nevertheless, was a success, reviewed warmly as a charming period piece of a California childhood and praised for the quality of its prose. At last I could believe that I was beginning to learn how to write.

There was another beginning, in that fictionized autobiography, which I can see clearly today, although at the time I was completely unaware of it. There was the certain beginning of my interest in the Catholic Church which forbade divorce, an interest which many years later was to lead me to the doors of the Jesuit rectory in Phoenix, Arizona, to ask for instruction in the Faith.

World War II intervened and the desolate post-war years in Germany afterwards when I gave heart and hands to the Displaced Persons, working as a United Nations relief officer in Bavaria from 1945 until 1951, when at last I was free to come home and try to write again. And I came home burdened with the story of what I had seen and experienced in the refugee camps and so produced the book,

The Wild Place, which to my astonishment won the Atlantic Non-Fiction Award for 1953. It was published by
Little, Brown & Company, Boston. It was while writing
that report on the human debris of World War II that I
became a convert and was received into the Church at St.
Francis Xavier's in Phoenix. Incidentally, I had chosen
Phoenix as the place to try for a writing come-back for
two reasons: one, I knew not a soul in the entire State
and would not therefore be tempted away from my typewriter by friends; and two, after six winters in the Gotter-
dammerung fogs of Germany, I felt I needed at least a year
of hot sunshine to burn the mould out of my bones!

Phoenix did just that for me, and something more besides. At the risk of having this autobiographical note
sound contrived, I've got to confess that my latest book,
The Nun's Story, also published by Little, Brown, first took
shape in that city as a story possibility, when I was talking
one afternoon with my little Jesuit Father in St. Francis
Xavier rectory. I had not yet completed *The Wild Place*
and had no inkling even that it would sell. I confided
to the Father that I thought all writers were slightly mad
to imagine they could earn a living by writing in these
days, especially writers like myself who wanted to do serious themes and not escapist stuff. America was fed up to
the gills with stories of refugees, I said. Anyone with a
grain of sense knew that there was no market for them,
yet there was I slaving away day after day on my sorrow-
ful story, fully aware of its dubious saleability but unable
to stop the compulsive flow of words . . .

"Because you *are* a writer, Miss Hulme," the Father
said. His Irish blue eyes twinkled as he looked at me wring-
ing my hands. Then he said thoughtfully: "You'll go on
writing because that is your gift. And I'll even venture the
prophecy that one day you'll use your pen in an apostolic
work."

His calm statement startled me into vigorous denials. I

should never have the temerity to try such a work: I am
a convert barely three weeks old in the Faith. Even if
such a desire arose in me, I'd have the good sense to sup-
press it, I said. What could I possibly have to say about
anything religious, I who had spent half my life outside
of any church?

Four years later, almost to the day, *The Nun's Story* was
published by Little, Brown. In the long travail of writing
it I never once thought of it as "an apostolic work," nor do
I now. I thought of it as a salute to the dedicated life
which I have always revered wherever and whenever I
have encountered it—in my own mother dedicated to
motherhood, first; later in some of my teachers and finally
in the relief workers I met overseas, most notably of all
in the Belgian nurse on one of our UNRRA teams who is
the living counterpart of my "Sister Luke," who told me
her story in bits and parts through the long winter nights
in Germany. And that heroic story of a dedicated life was
lying within me like a powerful yeast when I walked away
from the Jesuit rectory so certain that never would *my*
pen be used for the writing of anything with a religious
theme!

I've learned my lesson. I'll never again sound off on
what I can or cannot, will or will not, write. The unexpected warm reception of *The Nun's Story* guarantees that
I may go on writing and that I shall do, God willing, and
that is the happiest statement that an author can make—
a fitting way to end this little résumé of my writer's life.

LEO VINCENT JACKS

I WAS BORN IN GRAND ISLAND, NEBRASKA, IN 1896. AS A child, I read a great deal. At first in English, then in other languages. In grade school I had a teacher, a German Ursuline nun, who was interested in language experiments with children. She obtained permission from the parents concerned and organized a group of youngsters to study German. I began in the fifth grade. When I graduated from grade school I had had four years of German and two of Latin. In Prep school, at St. Mary's, Kansas, I added Greek to the list. Subsequently I studied other tongues.

In Prep school I had as a teacher a man deeply interested in good writing, Father Charles J. Scott, S.J. He got the boys to form a small group called the Academic Literary Society. Members were required to produce a daily composition. It taught us a great deal about prompt writing. He corrected and annotated these papers for us. I owe him much.

In college (St. Mary's, Kansas), I was fortunate again in a teacher, Father Francis X. Reilly, S.J. He took a deep interest in writing. I had the luck to work with him for three years. He had a critical mind, and could call a spade a spade. Working with him would do much to sharpen anyone's wits.

In 1917 I graduated from college, and served two years in the army. I was in an infantry regiment, later light field artillery. Subsequently I was a machine gunner. I was in the Thirty-Second Division, Michigan and Wisconsin national guardsmen, and that division, as you know, saw a lot of fighting and suffered heavy losses in killed, wounded, and gassed. I had many experiences which doubtless did a great deal toward shaping my viewpoints.

In competitive examination I won a Knights of Columbus fellowship to the Catholic University of America. In 1922 I read Greek for a Ph.D., writing my thesis on *St. Basil and Greek Literature.*

I got into publication in an indirect way. I had written a lengthy memoir about World War I, an amplification of a journal I kept. A friend of mine at Catholic University, the Reverend Dr. Marshall Campbell, saw it and gave it to George S. Brooks, one time editor of *McClure's* and later a screen writer. He passed it on to Maxwell Perkins, at that time managing editor at Scribner's. Mr. Perkins published it under the title *Service Record of an Artilleryman* (1928), and subsequently accepted two other books from me, *Xenophon, Soldier of Fortune* (1930), and *La Salle* (1931). Maxwell Perkins was a great editor and a wonderful friend. I think my ideas about writing were still in a formative shape, but he gave me much advice and help, as indeed he did for many other young writers.

Since I have taught at Creighton University, Omaha, I have had less time to write.

I have no particular creed about writing. You write what interests you, you write it as well as you can. J. K.

Huysmans said about the same thing, but not many people read him today. I like a good western, or a good mystery. There are not many of either. I have written five books (not including my thesis) and about fifty short stories and articles. I am interested in writing western fiction more than any other type. But it is largely a question of finding a good story. Any good story is valuable on its own account. It makes little difference if the story is tragic or comic, supposing it has the quality of holding the reader's attention. A writer has to discover some knack for discovering a story that is attractive and also one that he can write. Some writers are sympathetic to certain types of fiction, but cold to others. One ought to discipline himself to work at any kind of writing task. Anyone who wishes to be a professional writer had better learn to discard prejudice and write what comes before him.

The early history of our country contains a wealth of material. Nearly every State has its historical society. If one would probe into the records, he would find something good, and once in a while phenomenal. Not a complete story, of course, only an idea. The history of the Spanish southwest and the missionaries there is a case in point. In this field I wrote *Claude Dubuis, Bishop of Galveston* (Herder, 1946). My other book was *Mother Marianne of Molokai* (Macmillan, 1935).

I believe in realism. Of course realism and vulgarity are not the same thing. I believe in writing what a story calls for, no more, no less. A writer has to write his story as he sees it. I do not believe in censorship. Certainly some bad books are published, but that has always been true. A censor is a worse danger than a bad book.

In 1949 and 1950, I was manager of the writers' workshop at Catholic University, Washington, D. C. In the years between 1946 and 1953, and again since 1956, I was and am chairman of the Omaha Writers' Club, managing the annual writers' conference in Omaha. I had the pleas-

ure of seeing several very good professional writers develop
here under my first program, and now I hope to repeat
the same accomplishment. Writing is a difficult profession.
The only people who make a success of it are people with
some ability and a great deal of determination. We need
more of them.

CHARLOTTE M. KELLY

WHEN I WAS TEN I WROTE A POEM THAT BEGAN:

> Blarney Castle is now very old,
> About it a story is told
> Of a wonderful stone in the wall:
> If you kiss it you're likely to fall.

After this remarkable effusion the Muse mercifully abandoned me, and for the next twenty years my pen was inactive. Not so myself. I finished my education at the Bar Convent, York, the oldest school for Catholic girls in England, I spent a year in Lille, teaching English and studying French, with a passing glance at the history, literature and art of France. There was a winter in Switzerland, some leisured months on the Riviera, a delectable spring on the Italian Lakes, and a rapid tour of Belgium. Here was material for the aspiring writer, but it just never occurred to me to use it, except in voluminous letters to my friends.

Only when I settled down in Dublin, my native city, did chance—or more properly, Providence—start me on a career that, despite its trials and tribulations, has given me untold joy.

It all began when someone was asked to review a novel by Maurice Walsh for an Irish periodical. That someone passed the job to me—if I would do it. I would, if I could. I doubt if many books have ever received such attention from a reviewer. I read and reread, I wrote and rewrote. Restricted to a few hundred words, I found space for a colourful quotation and a moral reflection. Then I copied the final draft in my best handwriting and sent it off. I can still recall the excitement with which I saw my masterpiece in cold print. It seemed incredible that I—I had written it. That review was followed by others, but still it never struck me to "write," until an enterprising editor of the same periodical gave me my first commission. It was one that today would fill me with dismay, but then I tackled it cheerfully. Would I do three 3,000 word articles on the brothers Vrau, industrialists in the north of France and pioneers of Catholic Action? The source from which I was to get my information was a closely printed 400 page biography published early this century in French. I had never heard of the Vraus, but the town in which they lived was, by the dispensation of Providence, the one where I had learned my French. I knew the background, I knew the language. All I had to do was to write the articles. Well, I wrote them—I don't know how long I took, months probably—and they were published unaltered. I was a writer.

About this time, I began to work in the Central Catholic Library, Dublin, and, fired with enthusiasm, took a course in library training in University College. I was duly conferred with my Diploma, but I never got a job as a librarian, though I did and still do voluntary work in the Central Catholic Library. This is the place to pay tribute

to the invaluable help that I and many other writers have
received from the Library. But for it, I should never
have been able to continue writing.

In 1931, I used the first money I had earned with my
pen to visit my old school in York and was invited to record my "impressions" in the school magazine. This is
where Providence really took a hand. One of the "old girls"
to whom the magazine was sent was married to a member
of an English Catholic publishing firm. He read what I
had written and sent me a friendly and unofficial—how unofficial I was to learn later—invitation to write a book for
girls, using the school as background. "But I can't write
a *whole* book!" I protested. I had never even written a
short story. A well-known writer had told me: "You can
either write fiction or you can't." This was my chance to
find out if I could, or not.

I began. My characters came to life, spoke, moved,
thought, apparently of their own volition. That was an
unforgettable day. My pen (I could not type at this period)
travelled fast, presenting a photographic and embarrassingly
eulogistic picture of my school days, and with the sketchiest
of plots. As an expression of affection and gratitude it was
a pleasing production; as a story it was an arrant failure.
The publishers returned it with polite regrets. It seemed
the end of everything. In fact, it was only the beginning.
That manuscript, unpublished to this day, not only sup-
plied me with the material for countless short stories, it
proved that I could create characters, but that I knew nothing about plot-making. This defect was remedied by my
taking a correspondence course in short story writing,
which taught me the technique, if little else. Following
that rejection, however, came the suggestion that I try another tale, with a Swiss background. I wrote the story.
It was refused, fortunately. For it was to be the first of a
number of serials that the editor of *Ave Maria* has accepted
since then. I had never heard of the magazine until some-

one said to me about this time: "Why don't you write
something for the *Ave Maria?*" Without much hope, I sent
it a little tale about a gentle French demoiselle I had met
abroad. It was accepted and I was asked for more. Thus
began a long and happy association that continues to this
day. Stories, articles, juvenile and adult serials, found a
welcome in its pages, and two of my books, a juvenile,
Those Terrible Trents (1948), and a novel, *Laughter of
Niobe* (1949), were published by the Ave Maria Press.

Now my years of travel began to yield a harvest as I
wrote for other American periodicals, and for Catholic and
secular publications in England and Ireland. I have always loved writing for children. My first story for the
Catholic Children's Realm, an old-established English magazine, appeared in the mid-thirties, and I am writing for it
still, as well as for the fat shiny Annuals that appear in
London at Christmas time.

My endeavors to find publishers for my books were a
series of triumphs and disappointments. My story about
Switzerland, *The Mystery Man,* was eventually (1948)
brought out in book form in London by Newnes, years
after it had been refused. An English publisher accepted
one book and put me under contract for two more. Five
years later I bought back the unpublished manuscripts.
There was a slump in the juvenile market . . . if I could
wait. I had waited long enough. The books were subsequently serialized in the United States.

I did not confine myself to fiction, however. An article
intended for a minor Catholic magazine was passed on to
the editor of a learned quarterly, whose contributors had
strings of letters after their names. It was accepted, and
others suggested. The payment was negligible, but it was
the honour and glory to be there at all. It was then that
I learned the mingled pleasures and pains of research; the
wearisome plodding through old letters, old documents, the
dusty files of newspapers, for some essential information,

the exultation of finding in a yellowed newssheet a three
inch paragraph that supplies the clue to a baffling problem.

But a newly appointed editor, looking in vain for letters
after my name, began to wonder what I was doing in such
company. Diplomatically he accepted my next article,
but delayed publication so long that I demanded it back—
something that I'm sure none of his other contributors have
ever done. We parted without ill-feeling, but with mutual
relief. (Perhaps he had heard about the shiny Annuals!)

Should Catholics write only about Catholics, and on subjects of Catholic interest? That is a question one often
hears. To my mind, the answer is this: if you want to
make money don't write such books or articles; if you want
to write them, don't expect to make money—at least in the
British Isles. It's as simple as that, so take your choice.
Some writers have no choice, if they depend on the pen
for a living, and the living of others. But for those who
write for jam, rather than for bread and butter, the choice
is there, unless you happen to be a Graham Greene or a
Frances Parkinson Keyes.

Personally, I am in the "writing for jam" category. I
write fiction for both Catholic and secular publications, but
my articles have usually a Catholic interest and are published in Catholic magazines. I am a little chary of Catholic
novels, because I feel that no form of writing has so many
pitfalls. It is comparatively easy to write a poor Catholic
novel; it is immensely difficult to write a really good one.
My ambition is to write books for Catholic children; not
'pious' tales, but good honest stories such as the non-Catholic
publishers will produce, *with* the important addition of the
background of religion that a Catholic child takes as a
matter of course. I am never quite satisfied when I write
any other kind of tale for children. Such a book as I described, *A Year for Sally Ann*, was published for me by
Walker of London in 1957.

What advice would I give to young writers? First, to

thank the Almighty for an inestimable gift; and secondly, to write and write and write, until your fingers ache, your eyes burn, and the words cease to have any meaning, and the pile of rejection slips mounts steadily, while the acceptances can be counted on the fingers of one hand. If this prospect appalls you, throw your typewriter into the river and take a job as a dishwasher, a band leader, anything you like. But if, disappointed, disillusioned, weary to the point of exhaustion, you still pound away, then you have within you that something that neither school, nor course, nor "easy-aid" can give you: the God-given gift of creative power.

FRANCES PARKINSON
KEYES

WHEN ASKED—AS I VERY FREQUENTLY AM—WHERE I COME
from or where my home is, I often find it difficult to answer this seemingly simple question without completely
confusing my interrogator. The facts of the matter are
that my mother, Louise Fuller Johnson, was a New Yorker
transplanted to Newbury, Vermont, a little village which
had been settled by her paternal ancestors, and my father,
John Henry Wheeler, was a Bostonian transplanted to the
South, where he became head of the Greek department of
the University of Virginia. There they lived in James
Monroe's house and there I was born, thus making me a
Virginian. After my father died, however, my mother remarried, another Bostonian, and I spent my winters in
Boston and my summers in Newbury, with the exception
of two years in Europe. When I married, I moved to my
husband's home in New Hampshire and that still remains
my legal residence. When my husband was elected to the

Senate, we went to Washington and, from there, it seemed just a step across the Potomac to Alexandria in my native Virginia. Later, after his death, when it became evident that I would have to spend the greater part of my winters in Louisiana, because of my work there, I established a writing center in historic Beauregard House in New Orleans.

According to present standards, I am afraid my formal education would be considered somewhat sketchy. My father's mother, for whom I was named, taught me to read from the Bible and supplemented what formal schooling I did have with lessons in Latin, French and mathematics, which have proved invaluable to me. During the winters in Boston, after my father's death, I did attend private schools—at one of which, incidentally, three of my granddaughters are now pupils. These winters were broken by trips to many parts of the United States and two years, about a decade apart, which were spent in Europe, where I studied in Geneva and Berlin, besides travelling a great deal on the Continent and in England. When we were not in Boston or travelling, we were at "The Oxbow" in Newbury, living in the house built by my great-grandfather and which has been in our family ever since. (In the summer of 1956, we celebrated the sesquicentennial of its building.) When we were not in Vermont, I was instructed by a German governess, who was a graduate of the Sorbonne; and her teaching, plus my sojourns abroad, laid the foundation for any linguistic ability I may possess.

When I was eighteen, I married Henry Wilder Keyes, whose home, "Pine Grove Farm," was near Haverhill, New Hampshire, just across the river from Newbury and only five miles from "The Oxbow." Until my husband became Governor of New Hampshire in 1917, our family—by this time we had three sons, two of them born before I was twenty-one—lived at the Farm both summer and winter, except for occasional visits in Boston, where my mother-in-

law opened a house and where I continued to keep in touch
with members of my father's family, my former schoolmates and other friends. (When my novel, *Joy Street,*
was published in 1950, many of these were among the
guests at the "birthday dinner" for that book.)

I have always felt that my writing career really began
at the age of seven when a young friend and I collaborated
on a "pageant" which, unfortunately—at least from our
point of view—had only a "one-night stand" in my mother's drawing room! However, it is my firm belief that
there can be no true vocation without a long novitiate and
those unbroken years at the Farm formed a valuable period of apprenticeship for me. Despite the fact that I was
the companion, as well as a nurse and teacher to my children, there were very few days when I did not manage to
write a little, for my determination to be an author dated
back to the production of that "pageant," and was not intensified by the need of adding to the family budget.

My first novel, *Old Gray Homestead,* was published just
after my husband entered the Senate. As I became more
and more familiar with the different phases of life in Washington, it seemed to me that there must be many isolated
women throughout the country who would be interested in
reading about it and that, perhaps, I could write about what
I was seeing and doing in a way which would please and
interest them. The editor of *Good Housekeeping* agreed
with me and thus *Letters from a Senator's Wife* came into
being. The response to these *Letters* was so immediate
and so generous that, in spite of the publication of a second
novel and a series of short stories, I suddenly found myself
switched from fiction to current events, both national and
international. Consequently, I began to spend more and
more time in ranging the world. Eventually, however,
after years of working on it in odd moments on trains and
ocean liners, a novel of Washington life, *Queen Anne's*

Lace, was finally on paper and was published in 1930. After that, there was less and less political writing and more and more fiction and, in 1936, *Honor Bright* became a national best-seller in the United States. (I had become a best-seller in England sometime previous to this, with the publication of *Senator Marlowe's Daughter.*)

For a long time, Normandy had been one of my favorite provinces in France and I have often referred to it as my "second home." I had become interested in the Little Flower first, when I attended her beatification in Rome and later, when I read her autobiography. A friend suggested that I report this feeling to my publisher and, when I did so, he immediately asked me to write a book about her. I retorted that I was much better fitted to write about sinners than about saints, but he urged me to make the attempt. The result was a summer spent with the Benedictines of Lisieux, in the course of which I wrote *Written in Heaven,* which was published by Messner in 1937, and reissued in revised form in 1950 under the title of *Therese: Saint of the Little Way.*

The warm reception accorded *Written in Heaven* so encouraged both my publisher and me that, in 1938 and 1939, I went to France again, with a companion volume as my objective and although, in the course of the latter trip, I was caught in the second World War, I managed to secure the material for *The Sublime Shepherdess,* the life of St. Bernadette of Lourdes, and for *Along a Little Way,* a more personal record, before returning home. (When the former book was reissued in a revised version in 1953, under the title of *Bernadette of Lourdes:* Shepherdess, Sister and Saint, and received a Christopher Award, I was deeply touched, as well as greatly honored.)

With Therese and Bernadette so warmly welcomed, it seemed natural that I continue working on religious subjects and I turned to Our Lady of Guadalupe; consequently,

1940 found me on the way to Mexico to write the story of Juan Diego and his devotion to the Queen of Heaven. It was published by Messner in 1941 under the title of *The Grace of Guadalupe,* and was the Catholic Book Club selection for March of that year.

The next few years seemed to indicate a return to fiction again until one of my personal Christmas cards, which I always write myself, entitled "Our Lord Had a Grandmother, Too," brought numerous requests for a book on "Good St. Anne." Research on this took me to shrines in the Holy Land, in Greece, in France, in England, in Spain, in Canada, and in various parts of our own United States; to museums in most of these countries, as well as in Italy, Belgium and Holland; and the search still goes on for material to be included in each new edition of *St. Anne: Grandmother of Our Saviour,* which already has gone into three.

I now have three more books of religious character on my present agenda, one with Spain as its setting; one telling the story of our own North American Saint, Mother Cabrini; and one about our South American Saint, Rose of Lima. My newest novel, with a Louisiana setting, *Blue Camillia,* was published in the Spring of 1957; and, in addition to the three religious books mentioned above, I am also under contract to write several more novels.

I have had to curtail my speaking engagements to a very large degree because of the uncertainty of my health and the pressure of other work; and though I do not write as many articles as I did in former years, I always try to find time to wedge in those whose subject is of particular interest or appeal to me. All in all, I have written twenty novels and five books of religious character; I have also written four books of non-fiction, which include travel, politics, and personal and professional experiences as their themes, besides a cookbook, a juvenile and a volume of verse.

EDITOR'S NOTE: Mrs. Keyes, a convert, was received into the Church in 1939; her *Along a Little Way* (Kenedy, 1940) gives an account of the steps that led to her conversion. She interrupted her research work in Avila, Spain, to write this autobiographical chapter for *The Book of Catholic Authors.*

REV. ANDREW J. KRZESINSKI

ON NOVEMBER 20, 1884, I WAS BORN IN THE CASTLE TOWN of Niepolomice, near Cracow, where my parents owned a thirty-acre farm. It was near a great forest of pine and spruce where in the past the Kings of Poland had come to hunt the deer and the elk.

From childhood I was deeply impressed with nature and the universe around me, and I remember reasoning, while still very young, that if nature and the universe are so beautiful, how much more so must God be Who created them and maintains them in their perfect order.

Following my elementary education at Niepolomice, I took the eight-year course (high school and college) of the Gymnasium of St. Hyacinth in Cracow. From the beginning I found my school work very easy, especially my favorite subject, mathematics. In 1906, after passing the "matura" examinations with honors, the way to the university was open to me. But I had long since felt the call to the priesthood and so instead I entered the Grand Seminary in Cracow. After ordination in 1910, I was at first employed in parochial work; later I taught philosophy and religion in the college department of the Ursuline Gymnasium in Cracow. At the same time, I was continuing my own studies, and in 1919 received the degree of Doctor of Theology and in 1923 that of Doctor of Philosophy, both at the Jagiellonian University in Cracow. Next came postgraduate work at the Universities of Paris (the Sorbonne), London, Rome, Berlin, and Leipzig.

My first book, *Reality, Knowledge and Truth in the History of Philosophy,* was published in Polish in 1924 and won me the appointment as dozent of Christian philosophy at the Jagiellonian. The following January, I was invited by Warsaw University to the chair of Christian philosophy, which had been restored for me by the Polish government. Less than four years later, however, I resigned, for ideological reasons, and returned to the Jagiellonian.

In 1927, while still at Warsaw, I wrote *In Defense of the Transcendent World.* With but minor revisions, it was translated from the Polish and published in Paris in 1931 under the title *Une Nouvelle philosophie de l'Immanence.* A critique of the positivist and modernist teachings of a Warsaw professor formed the basis of my book, *Positivism, Modernism and the Polish Clergy* (in Polish, 1928).

My philosophical studies, begun in 1931, on Western culture as exposed to the attacks of atheistic Communism and Nazism, both of which sought to destroy its Christian ideals and built their own world domination on its ruins, I treated in a well-received work, *Modern Culture and Its Tragedy* (in Polish, 1934). I was convinced that Western culture, due to its Christian character, would not only eventually triumph, but would become a point of contact with other world civilizations and thus a much-needed harmonizing force in the world. To contribute all I could to this ideal, I entered upon an intensive study of the cul-

tures, ethical systems and religions of the Far East. With
the encouragement of my University rector and our Archbishop, I left the Jagiellonian on February 2, 1936, for the
Orient to make these studies at first-hand.

My travels took me around the world and lasted a year.
First I went to London where the India Office arranged
with the British-Indian Government to facilitate my research by making contacts for me in Indian intellectual
circles. Then, in crossing the United States, I delivered a
lecture at Duquesne University, Pittsburgh, on "The Critical Situation of Western Culture" which Monsignor G.
Barry O'Toole, head of the Philosophy department, urged
me to put into book form. From the United States I went
to Japan, China, Manchuria, Indo-China, Thailand (Siam),
the Malay States, Burma, India, Sikhim, Tibet, and Ceylon.
In all of these countries I had frequent opportunities and
ample facilities to study their social, religious and cultural
ways of life. In all of them, too, the universities invited
me to lecture on Western civilization; in India alone I
spoke before some twenty such groups composed of professors, students, and other intellectuals. While in India
I met the poet, Rabindranath Tagore, who invited me to
lecture at Santiniketan College which he had founded and
endowed to educate youth in the pure Hindu tradition. In
his residence at Allahabad, I also met Pandit Nehru, then
President of the All India Congress and later Prime Minister of his newly independent nation. He had recently returned from Russia and was strongly influenced by Communism, the true ideology and practice of which I tried to
expose to him. It was at his invitation that I attended the
All India Congress meeting at Tilak Nagar in South India.
While there I met Mahatma Gandhi who, despite the pressure of Congress affairs, took the time to discuss problems
of religious truth and the social and cultural life of India.
At his suggestion, these discussions were continued at his
home near Wardha some days later.

My host in Calcutta, Archbishop Ferdinand Périer, warned me that for years the bishops of India and China had in vain sought permission from Lhassa for priests to enter Tibet. "It is impossible," he said. But the English-Indian government finally succeeded in securing the necessary permission for me. What I learned there was well worth all my efforts. The people of Tibet live according to Buddhist principles in every detail. Tibet is unique in the world in that probably one third of its population lives in monasteries, and that representatives of no other religion are allowed in the country.

At the end of April, 1937, I took leave of the Far East, leaving there not only many friends, but also my heart.

They form the largest part of the world's population but, despite their ancient cultures and many and splendid works of art, the majority live under the most difficult social and economic conditions; and, while deeply religious, have only sparks of religious truth. How important it would be for the glory of God and the good of humanity if these nations were in possession of full religious truth, of the highest Christian ideals! I was filled with the desire to contribute to their cultural and spiritual unity with the Christian nations. One Christian civilization among all nations, with a variety of national characteristics, all enjoying full independence and freedom, and living according to the principles of the one true religion. With this vision in my mind and heart I left the Far East.

En route home, I visited Palestine and Egypt and again London. Laden with the riches of my researches, I arrived back at the Jagiellonian in September, 1937.

Some of the fruits of my travels appeared in *Researches on Far Eastern Culture* (in Polish, 1938), *The Problem of the Catholic Missions in the Far East* (id., 1939), and in two other books.

To do the work I wanted on Far Eastern and Western cultures, I needed a better understanding of culture in

America, particularly in the United States. In June of 1939, I had everything ready for a visit to the United States but, unfortunately, I delayed starting until September. By then World War II had broken out, in fact, Cracow was already surrounded by the German army. Amid bombing and machine gunning, I eventually made my way to Lithuania (already overridden with Soviet spies), then through Latvia and Esthonia to Sweden whence I sailed to the United States, arriving in New York on October 14, 1939.

Since then I have lectured on the Far East at Pennsylvania and Columbia Universities and have been visiting professor of philosophy at Laval University, Quebec, Montreal University, and Fordham.

Due to my hasty and hazardous flight from Poland, much of my Far East research materials were left there, and as a result I have so far been unable to write my work contrasting Eastern and Western cultures. However, since coming here I did have published *Is Modern Culture Doomed?* (Devin-Adair, 2nd ed., 1944), a French edition of which appeared in Montreal the following year. Fides of Montreal also published *Christianity's Problem in the Far East* in 1945, with a French version following in 1946.

During World War II, I thought that an expose of Nazism in the light of Western culture was called for and so I had published in Boston in 1945 *National Cultures, Nazism and the Church, The Religion of Nazi Germany,* and *Nazi Germany's Foreign Policy.*

The injustices to Poland of the Yalta agreement evoked *Poland's Right to Justice* (Devin-Adair, 1946). That same year my defense of Poland's western frontiers appeared under the title *Poland, Germany: a Lasting Peace?* (Devin-Adair).

To comfort and strengthen the suffering Polish people I wrote for them, in Polish of course, these four books: *In Defense of Poland, Amid the Bombs and Fires, The*

Individual Action in Saving Poland, and *The Congress of the American Poles.*

I have long been interested in the problem of mental health. Due to the pressures of life here, it is a particularly acute problem in the United States, and so I was happy to be able to act as an observer with the Psychology Department and Psychiatric Institute of Columbia University through the years 1950 to 1953. I hope soon to complete my work on the results of this experience.

Up to the present I have written some thirty books and about eight hundred articles. My knowledge of twenty languages has proven very helpful to me.

On January 30, 1950, I became an American citizen.

I would be grateful to God if He grants me the time and energy to realize my complete program.

ANNA KUHN

LIKE MANY OTHER WRITERS, I HAVE ALWAYS BEEN AN OM-
nivorous reader, that is a kind of preparation for potential
authors. However, one must have a strong urge to say
something himself and my particular urge came from an
article which I read in *Fortune Magazine* some two dec-
cades ago. I can not even recall the title, but the theme
was the Shrine of Lourdes about which I knew nothing
whatsoever. After reading the exciting story of the tiny
hamlet at the foot of the Pyrennes in southern France
where the Blessed Virgin appeared to Bernadette Soubirous
and where miraculous cures occurred each year, I studied
everything I could find in books, magazines or pamphlets.
In fact, the theme took such a hold on my imagination
that the following summer I sailed for Europe with Lourdes
as my destination!

An unforgettable sojourn in this hallowed spot as part
of an English pilgrimage resulted in a book for children

entitled *A Queen's Command* (Bruce, 1940) which nar-
rates the story of the humble shepherdess, who, in 1934,
was enrolled in the canon of the saints and is known since
as St. Bernadette. Other juvenile books followed, but none
ever brought the tremendous inner satisfaction that came
with the publication of *A Queen's Command!*

Currently my creative work has taken a new turn, and
I am engaged in writing magazine articles and book reviews in the hope of making the vast field of Catholic
literature better known and appreciated. However, the
juvenile books written some time ago continue to follow
me with deliberate and constant pace as clubs or schools
ask for the author of *The Quest of Don Bosco* (Bruce,
1942), *Royal Banners Fly* (*id.*, 1946), and other works to
speak on juvenile writing.

Fan mail from children in the course of a year, especially
during Catholic Book Week, is always gratifying. Recently
I received a heart-warming letter from a parochial school
lad in the West telling me that he enjoyed *The Quest of
Don Bosco,* and that he hoped some day to be a priest like
Father John Bosco.

In my series of children's books I wrote a short biographical sketch of Rose Hawthorne, the daughter of the
famous Concord (Massachusetts) writer of the nineteenth
century. Rose eventually established the first free cancer
clinic in the United States and became Mother Alphonsa of
the Dominican Sisters of St. Rose of Lima. This particular story, included in *Watching At My Gates* (Bruce,
1948), has had many interesting ramifications. Frequently I am asked to write the story for some national
magazine. Recently a Catholic visitor to New England
learned for the first time of this famous daughter of the
Puritan Nathaniel Hawthorne, called me on the telephone
and requested me to write the story for a magazine with
which he was associated. Calls also come for me to speak
about Rose and her magnificent work for the cancerous

poor. Thus a tiny acorn into a great oak grows; and once a subject has taken hold of an author's imagination, it is astounding to realize in how many different ways it can be presented to audiences.

Research work on Catholic subject matter is always easy as there are such vast resources from which to draw. Also as one writes of the heroes and heroines of Christendom for youngsters, there is a glow of satisfaction and inner happiness because one is cognizant of the fact that he is going to produce a book with order and beauty inherent in the theme, and that it will in some way be appealing and challenging to teen-agers who may eventually read it. The human interest element in the lives of the saints is often more dramatic than that which is found in ordinary lives, and this feature of my writing I have stressed in my books for children.

My early background and training in public schools (Somerville High, Somerville, Massachusetts) as well as my college education (Tufts University, Medford, Massachusetts) did not prepare me for my career as a writer for Catholic readers. Although I did receive an excellent general education, I cannot say that any course or any instructor ever stimulated me to such an interest in the world about me that my dormant potential for writing was drawn out. It was only when eventually I was admitted to the Graduate School of Boston College that the Jesuit Fathers in their quiet and scholarly way made me aware of the truth and beauty of Christendom and gradually taught me the discipline necessary for writing. It was about this time that I received a degree of Master of Education in English from Boston College that I read the article mentioned at the beginning of this brief biographical sketch; and somehow these two incidents are responsible for the auspicious and satisfying career of writing which I have pursued in my leisure time.

REVEREND LAWRENCE
G. LOVASIK, S.V.D.

ON JUNE 22, 1913, I WAS BORN OF SLOVAK PARENTS IN Tarentum, Pennsylvania, a steel-town about twenty miles northeast of Pittsburgh. I am the eldest of eight children. At the age of twelve I was accepted as a student at the Sacred Heart Mission Seminary, Girard, Pennsylvania, conducted by the Fathers of the Society of the Divine Word. The object of the Society is to train boys for the holy priesthood and through them to propagate our Faith in foreign lands. At present more than 2,250 of its priests and 1,750 of its Brothers are working in the United States, Europe, and in the foreign missions.

After an intensive training of thirteen years, I was ordained to the priesthood at St. Mary's Mission Seminary, Techny, Illinois, August 14, 1938, and was sent to the Gregorian Papal University in Rome for further studies. Later, after spending three years as a teacher and prefect of seminarians, I was assigned to do missionary work in

the coal and steel regions of the United States. At this time
I published a standard prayerbook and New Testament and
other brochures in the Slovak language for the benefit of
the people to whom I preached. My present work consists
in giving missions and retreats to lay people and religious,
—a work I love and at which I have spent the past fifteen
years. My headquarters are at the Divine Word Seminary,
Girard.

A question I am frequently asked is: "Father, how have
you gotten interested in writing?" There were several influences that urged me to write, which I shall touch upon
here. Being a missionary, I had occasion to observe the
life of people at close range and to deal with their problems in the confessional and in private interviews. I became acquainted with their spiritual needs, with their
personal and family difficulties, and with their individual
plans and longings. As a priest I was to take Christ's
place among them and imitate His compassionate Heart.
He once said of priests: "You are the light of the world
... Go, therefore and make disciples of all nations, bap-
tizing them in the name of the Father, and of the Son, and
of the Holy Spirit, teaching them to observe all that I have
commanded you; and behold, I am with you all days, even
to the consummation of the world." In answer to this
command of the Savior, I wanted to reach the hearts of
people, but my voice could be heard only by those to whom
I was able to preach. There were thousands of others who
needed the help I could give. I realized that one of the
most powerful means God has given us for spreading Christian principles and combatting non-Christian influences is
the press. Though I was not specially gifted with a talent
for writing, I was determined to work at it till I was able
to present our Catholic people with the teaching of Jesus
Christ in print. If God has chosen me to preach His
truth and love among men, I wanted to do it in the most
effective way I knew how, and that was by writing. My

publications would reach souls to whom I was unable to
preach, and I could thereby continue teaching the truths
of the Catholic Church and its wonderful means of salvation long after my mortal remains had been laid in the
grave.

Life is short, and we must all give an account of it on
the day of judgment. I am in earnest about using the time
allotted to me by God on this earth to the best advantage
in carrying out the ideal of my life—to make God more
known and loved through my writings. A personal love
for Jesus Christ, Our Lady, and immortal souls, as well as
for Holy Mother Church, has been my inspiration to dedicate as much of my time as possible during and between
missions and retreats to writing.

Since I have published about ten books and more than
fifty booklets and pamphlets since 1943, I have often been
asked how this was possible in my busy schedule of missionary assignments. The only answer I can give is that at
least ninety percent of any writer's accomplishments are
due to plain and ordinary hard work. In the case of a
priest, it is the grace of God that brings blessing upon this
work so that it may be profitable for the salvation of souls.
In order that my work might be most effective, I have always tried to write with simplicity and sincerity, and to
present my material in a practical manner. This is the
reason why almost all my publications deal with spiritual
subjects. This is my way of doing priestly work for the
salvation of souls.

One of my special aims in writing is to teach people to
pray much. Prayer is one of the channels of grace. It is
the cure for most of our daily problems. Hence, almost
half of my writings are in prayer form. Such books as
Mary My Hope and *Treasury of Prayer* and *Praying the
Gospels* (Marian Action Publications, 211 W. 7th av.,
Tarentum, Pa.) have been distributed far and wide. I have
given special emphasis to Eucharistic devotion—the Mass,

Holy Communion, Real Presence—which is the very heart-
beat of our Catholic religion. This is the reason for booklets like *Mass Prayers, Communion Prayers, Eucharistic
Visits, Communion Crusade, Novena of Holy Communions,*
and *Stepping Stones to Sanctity,* one of my most popular
books.

In many of my writings I have tried to give help and
consolation to those who are sick and afflicted. *So Gentle
His Hand* and four pamphlets on various diseases (cancer,
tuberculosis, heart condition, nervous and mental conditions), with a patron for each, have been widely distributed. The apostolate to the sick is one of my favorite projects.

One of my hobbies is teaching by the use of visual aids.
This accounts for publications in rich color, like *The Catholic Picture Bible* and *The Mass for Children;* illustrations
in story-form like *Catechism in Stories* (Marian Action
Publications), and sketch talks in *What Catholics Believe.*

My earliest and perhaps most encouraging experience
in the field of writing was the publication of the letters of
my brother Leo who was killed in the service of his country. He was in the Air Corps, and though he was the
only Catholic in his crew, succeeded in naming his Libera-
tor bomber "Valiant Virgin," in honor of Our Lady. I
wanted our boys in the service, and also our Catholic people, to know how much this youth loved his Faith and his
heavenly mother, and so I wrote *Knight of Our Lady,
Queen of the Skies.* This booklet was reprinted three times
in 1943, and a hundred thousand copies were distributed
during World War II. In 1956 I published two books: one,
a tribute to Our Lady, *God's Mother and Yours,* and the
other a tribute to my brother Leo, *High Flight* (Marian
Action Publications).

One of the greatest experiences of my life was the
founding of the Sisters of the Divine Spirit in August,
1955. This modern American religious Congregation of

home and foreign missionaries is an answer to the appeal of Pope Pius XII for the adaption of the religious life to the needs and problems of our time. His principle and wish is: Modernization without mitigation. Accordingly the Rule of the Sisters is based upon our American traditions with a double ideal: sanctification of the individual and sanctification of the Christian family. The Sisters wear a modern garb, much the same as that worn by women in the military service. They teach in schools, conduct catechetical classes, visit homes for census and instruction, aid in social work; in short, they do any type of apostolic work that the Church may call upon them to do. It is the first "modern" community of its kind in our country and its growth has been very rapid—fifty members and approval from Rome in one year! The Sisters of the Divine Spirit also spread the printed word to Catholics and non-Catholics alike. Through these generous women, consecrated to the Divine Spirit, the Spirit of Truth, I hope to further extend the influence of the Catholic Press in our country and beyond its shores.

It is only by the grace of God that souls are saved. This grace can be obtained by prayer and sacrifice. Realizing the fact that I am an unworthy and very imperfect instrument in God's hands, I have always appealed for co-missionaries who will pray for me and offer their work and suffering at least one day each week that God may bless my work. If I have any success as a writer, it is certainly due almost entirely to this apostolate of prayer and sacrifice and, above all, to the grace of God!

PATRICIA LYNCH
(Mrs. Richard M. Fox)

I BELIEVE THE MOST INTERESTING THING ABOUT A STORY-writer is the stories, but if readers would like to know more about me, I will tell them. I was born in Cork City in 1898, and have written stories ever since I could write. I began by telling them and, when I was a child, I was selected by popular acclamation to tell stories to the class in convent school during sewing lesson. As I did not like sewing, we were all satisfied. I was so small the nuns made me sit up on a high desk facing the class.

The stories were bits of folklore and legend I had heard in Cork, tales told me by my mother and by Mr. Hennessy, a famous "shanachie" who visited our house on Faer Hill. I read a good deal too, but I soon found that to keep my class going I had to make up stories of my own. This was not difficult for there were the quays, the river, the old houses, and the bells of Shandon church pealing out from where it stood amid a huddle of rising streets. Cork is

really an island with bridges and water all around, and it
is just the right place for stories.

I didn't stay very long in Cork, for I left the city while
still a child and spent several years in various schools, convent and secular, in Ireland, England and at Bruges.   My
father had interests in Egypt for, at one time, he edited a
journal there.   But he died when I was too young to know
him.   After his death, my mother and brother led a wandering existence, first in search of a fortune he was supposed to have and secondly for business reasons.

The changing scenes of my schools and the varying people I met were of great help in making me a story-teller.
They enlarged my experience and understanding.   But I
often felt very lonely and driven in on myself when I was
left at a new, strange school.   I would dream about Ireland
and think of its people, its hills and valleys.   These dreams
would centre on Cork and I would try to recapture all the
stories I had ever heard in Ireland.   Perhaps that is one
reason why all my books are rooted in Irish life and character.

A curious thing is that my Irish stories have appealed
to a wide circle of readers outside Ireland.   In France
there are now five of my books published in translation.
They have also been issued in the United States, in Germany, Switzerland, Holland, Sweden, even—strangest of
all—in Malaya.   In spite of different national customs and
traditions, readers find a common ground of appeal in books
which have the sun, the wind and the rain in them, as well
as the joys and longings of ordinary humanity.   And that
is what I hope may be found in my books.

What do I write about?   One of the earliest of my books
is called *The Turf-cutter's Donkey* and tells of the white-
washed cabins on the Irish bog, of Long Ears, the patient
little grey donkey, of the turf-cutter and his wife but,
most of all, about the adventures of Eileen and Seumas, the
two children who meet with the tinkers and leprechauns

but who keep their simplicity and kindness even if they do—like Long Ears—kick over the traces once in a while.

Critics have said that they find in my writing a blend of ordinary life and of fantasy. I appreciate the compliment, for usually it is meant that way. But I have always considered that ordinary life—all life—is a fantasy, though it is certainly reality as well. What can be more fantastic than those bonds of friendship and affection that spring up out of nowhere and bind people together? What is more fantastic than our world of sea and sky, of red sunsets and golden moons. Yet if among the waving white bog cotton (canavaun), I spy just one little leprechaun, people who accepted all the other wonders as "ordinary," think that this is most fantastic. It is time we saw life as a whole and realized its magic. What I have tried to do in my books is to reveal the magic of ordinary life.

Perhaps because I began by telling stories, my books have been found specially suitable for reading aloud and for radio. My *Brogeen* stories—Brogeen is a leprechaun who keeps running away from his home in the fairy fort because he likes humans—have proved very popular with children over the B.B.C. and other stations. The Brogeen books have been dramatized in serial installments. In France they have given Brogeen the name of Korik, which is, I understand, a little gnomish creature who belongs to the Breton country. Brogeen, in Ireland, is the little shoemaker with the golden hammer. The name has the same derivation as that of the shoes we call "brogues."

In *Knights of God* I have written about the saints of Ireland. This book was a choice of the Catholic Children's Book Club in New York. I see there saints as brave, adventurous people who were warriors on the side of spiritual truth. They have the same qualities of humour, common sense and kindliness that we can find everywhere in humanity but, because they were more richly endowed and had greater resolution, they became saints. I have also written of the old Irish legends in my *Tales of Irish Enchantment,* for I believe that these legends enshrine what is worth preserving in the early history and memory of the race.

Most of my books—I have now written twenty-five—are stories, with an Irish background, stories of fairs and firesides—with the turf glowing on the hearth—of journeys and of home. Sometimes my people travel on ships and sometimes they set out across the bog with a little grey donkey and a load of turf. But everywhere they go they find adventure, whether they turn to the heroic past or the unknown future.

There are no desperate fights with gangsters in my books, with bands of children defeating hordes of crooks and criminals in pitched battles, over roofs and through alleyways. I do not care for the unreal "tough" books because I do not know of any groups of children who fight with gangs of robbers. That is altogether too fantastic! And I do believe that reality—including imaginative reality—is essential to a good book. I am not keen on "mamby-pamby" books either. My characters have their temptations and meet their villains, because there are plenty of temptations and villians to be met with in life and we must all—children and grown-ups—be on our guard against them. Yet, like most story-tellers, I do not want to preach. I want the story to tell its own lesson just as the lives of the saints do.

I have written of my early life in some detail in *A Story-teller's Childhood.* Of the many incidents recorded, I will pick out one, the day I met Sister Francis in the garden at a convent school where I went to stay during the holidays before the other girls came back. As the gate clanged shut she looked up and leaned on her spade, watching me, and when I came nearer, her eyes smiled. I stopped at the edge of the earth she had been digging.

"I am Sister Francis," she told me.

"I am Patricia Nora Lynch!"

Her face was brown but very thin, her golden brown eyes were dancing. They changed every moment, they laughed, they grew serious, sad, kind.

"I dig too much. I walk too much!" she said in a breathless whisper.

"Are you sick?" I asked fearfully.

"I have been near the doors of death," she told me. "They opened a little way, then closed. I remained on this side."

"Were you frightened?"

Sister Francis looked at me. Her strange eyes were keen.

"When you came to the high wall with the barred door, and the bell clanged, you were frightened. Unknown eyes looked through the grille. You heard bolts pulled back and you stood there, alone and suffering. The door opened and you came in to find a garden and a friend!"

Such chance encounters helped me to understand the direction in which I was going. So, too, did my meeting with Miss Carmichael who stayed at the Baerasel's pension in Bruges. I had been left there by my mother when I fell ill during our journey to Egypt. Miss Carmichael wrote travel articles and would pound them out on her typewriter. I brought her hot, creamy coffee in the mornings and we talked. I told her about my family and their quest for riches.

"Perhaps writing will be your gold mine," she said. "You've had a few little nuggets already. You should learn shorthand and typewriting. With them and a good knowledge of English, a girl can go through the world."

"You mean I'll be a writer—like you?" I asked.

"It's a good life!" said Miss Carmichael.

Later I had a letter from Egypt. My mother wrote saying that a cotton factory had been built on my father's land. There was money, though not very much, because a great deal had to be paid in taxes. But there was enough for me to go to college and become a teacher or a civil servant.

"Which will you be?" asked Miss Carmichael. "A teacher or a civil servant?"

"I'll learn shorthand and typing and go through the world!" I declared. And I drank my glass of wine.

EDITOR'S NOTE: Books by Patricia Lynch, who now lives in Dublin, include *Strangers at the Fair* (Browne, 1945), *A Story-teller's Childhood* (Browne, 1946), *Lisheen at the Valley Farm* (Grayfield Press, 1949), *The Seventh Pig* (Dent, 1950), *The Dark Sailor of Youghal* (Dent, 1951), *The Boy at the Swinging Lantern* (Bentley, 1952), *Grania of Castle O'Hara* (Page, 1952), *Brogeen and the Green Shoes* (Burke, 1953), *Delia Daly of Galloping Green* (Dent, 1953), *Tales of Irish Enchantment* (Clonmore, 1953), *Orla of Burren* (Dent, 1954), and *Knights of God* (Regnery, 1955).

SEUMAS MacMANUS

I FIRST OPENED MY EYES IN DONEGAL, IRELAND'S NORTHWEST corner stone. It is the wildest, most remote, most rugged and mountainous, the most barren and the most beautiful, as well as the most Irish territory in Ireland.

I am of the mountain people. As a buachaill of a boy I herded on the hills, spaded on the farm, dallied to the mountain school where I got the daub of schooling that is mine. At night I moved from cottage to cottage, squatted in the groups that always surrounded the big, blazing turf-fires, hearkening to the women telling their fairy stories and the old men reciting ancient folk tales, singing the old songs, or chanting some thousand-year-old poem.

Ere I crept out of childhood I was myself a shanachie— carried in mind and could tell a sheaf of the old tales, as I had learned them by a hundred firesides. I told the tales to the lads who companied me to the herding, the lads who with me scudded three miles over the hills to Mass on

Sunday, to the lads who loitered with me to the little
school. Many of my tales I gathered in that little school
—for oftentimes when the master looked pleasedly on five
or six small students with heads together, puzzling (as he
thought) over a mathematical problem or posed on some
other noxious subject, we, the boys from five to six mountain glens, were, each in turn, telling the best story he had
heard the night before. Or we were communing over the
latest fairy escapade—for the Donegal hills are, perhaps
more than any other part of Ireland, favored of the Gentle
Folk.

During my boyhood, I devoured every book that was to
be found within a six-mile radius, altogether as many as
thirteen or fourteen or fifteen.

At the age of sixteen I began verse-making—made songs
while I herded or plied the spade on my father's hillside—
chiefly, songs that dealt with Ireland's struggle for freedom, and with the heroes who had fought and died for love
of Shiels Ni Gara. Within a year I was publishing prose
and verse in the *Tir-Conaill Vindicator,* the little weekly
paper of our county, published in Belashanny. I filled the
columns of this paper every week—songs, sketches, stories,
news-reports—written in school copybooks, on my knee, at
the fireside after my day's work was finished. At the
end of three years' contributing I got my first pay from
good John MacAidan—a check for ten shillings, almost two
and a half dollars. And I was indeed a proud man as well
as a rich one. Then he printed for me my first book of
poems, with the Irish title *Shuilers,* meaning Vagrants.
Twelve hundred copies of it were bought at a shilling each
—making me a millionaire.

But to wealth I had now become no stranger, for I had
been appointed master of our mountain school, teaching
sixty to seventy boys in a room that was nearly thirty feet
long by fifteen feet wide—for a great salary of three
pounds, or fourteen dollars, a month, as well as a school

penny which every scholar brought me each Monday morning.

Now also *The Shamrock,* a penny weekly story paper in Dublin, ordered from me a series of nine stories at two and a half dollars each—which I did in nine days in school copybooks, on my knee, at my father's kitchen fireside at night.

Hearing that American story papers would pay more than two and a half dollars a story, I wrote a bagful of them and, closing my school, with the bursting bag sailed for America in the steerage of a big liner. Arrived in New York I asked the names of magazines that would pay well for stories, and was told that *Harper's* and *The Century* were the wealthiest. I brought to *Harper's* seven of the copybooks, and kind old Mr. Alden, the editor, deeply interested in the mountain boy dressed in homespun, read the stories himself, and kept six of them. And to my dumfounding, gave me one hundred dollars and upward for each of them.

I went to *The Century* with ten stories, and they bought eight. With other stories, then, I tried the other seven or eight magazines that America knew at that time—and every one of them bought stories.

I arrived in America in September, and sailed back to Donegal the following May, with a fortune—wherewith I bought a fairy hill of which I had always been enamored.

I returned to America the next Fall, with a new bag of stories, and carried home in the following Spring three times as big a fortune as that of twelve months before. My Donegal neighbors, knowing that anyone who wished could shovel up bags full of such stories among our hills, could hardly credit the gullibility of the American people!

American publishers began putting out my books, not only folk-tale books, like *Donegal Fairy Stories* (Doubleday, 1900), *In Chimney-Corners* (*id.*, 1899), *The Donegal Wonder-Book* (Stokes, 1926), and *The Well o' the World's*

End (Macmillan, 1939), but also novels like *A Lad of the O'Friels* (Irish Pub. Co., 1903), and original stories of Irish life, as well as Irish history, *The Story of the Irish Race* (Devin-Adair, 4th ed., 1944).

And I, who had never seen a college before I came to America, found a fruitful field lecturing and telling folk-tales to the big American universities, as well as to the big Clubs. This I have been doing for many, many winters. But for my summers I always go back to my own Donegal hills and my own Donegal people and my own Donegal fairies.

Under the ocean, off the coast of Donegal, lies a fairy paradise, Tir na'n Og, the Land of Perpetual Youth, which, on beautiful summer eves, is often seen by our fishermen, rising over the waters, afar off. It is a special province of heaven set apart by the good Lord for His favorites, the Irish, whose bliss He desires and safeguards from the intrusion of Americans and other common peoples of earth—and there I hope to go when I die.

That is, *if* I die.

IRENE MARINOFF

IN VIEW OF LATER DEVELOPMENTS, IT SEEMS PROVIDENTIAL
that, although not of British stock, I should have been born
in England, a privilege the value of which I was to realize
only in later years. My father, of Russian origin and
Bulgarian nationality, had met my mother at Geneva,
where he was studying medicine, my mother having left
her home University of Berlin to pursue her French studies
in Switzerland. Owing to the different marriage laws
obtaining in both countries, they decided to marry in England. So it happened that I was born in Hove, on September 20, 1901. By way of compromise between the Orthodox
Church of my father and the Judaism of my mother, I was
baptized in the Church of England and received my first,
very deep impressions of Christianity in a Low Church
milieu. Though German is my mother tongue, I began
English in a kindergarten at the mature age of three, and
went to various schools, mainly in London, till I was ten.

As my father died young, my mother decided to return to Germany to her parents. Here a German education was superimposed on my English foundations. As my mother had been one of the first, though not the very first, students at the University of Berlin, she wanted me to have the same classical education she had received. So I was sent to one of the best schools of the German capital, and learned Latin and Greek with great delight.

In choosing a career, I was torn between my two heritages. Was I to be a doctor or a teacher? Fortunately, the question was decided by our financial position which did not allow me to go in for so expensive a training as the medical. As I had a good command of English, I decided to study English, mathematics, physics and philosophy at the University of Berlin, where we lived. Only I could not take my doctorate there, owing to my queer combination of subjects; so I went to Marburg for that. After six years I was proud possessor of the Prussian Diploma for Secondary School Teachers, taken in Berlin, and a Dr. phil. (Ph.D.) of the University of Marburg, with a thesis on the British post-war novel. From 1929 to 1933, I taught at various schools in Berlin and the neighborhood, continuing my English studies in my spare time with a view to becoming a university lecturer in that subject.

Meanwhile, one of my early childhood wishes was by way of finding fulfillment. I remember quite distinctly, at a time when I could scarcely write myself, being thrilled at the sight of an adult's notebook filled with hieroglyphics from cover to cover. How I wished I could do the same—write my own stuff, I mean. I had written my first poem in 1926, and now made my début, though not yet a Catholic, in a Catholic teachers' periodical with an essay on some of the abuses of the educational system then prevailing in Prussia. Other essays on educational subjects followed, and as I was at the same time elaborating my thesis, I was kept fairly busy. In 1932, Tauchnitz published my first book: *Neue Wertungen im Englischen Roman*, on the English novel of the twentieth century.

My future seemed assured. But then I had not reckoned with party politics. Alas, or rather, thank God, my mother was a Jewess, and I lost all my prospects of making my way in Germany. Then I bethought myself of the land of my birth and early years, which I had revisited only once, in 1927, previous to an important examination, to "brush up my English." After making some very valuable contacts in Switzerland, I went to London and started at the bottom of the ladder again. It took exactly eight years for me to recover what had been mine in Germany, a university degree (a B.A. from the University of London with first class honours in German and subsidiary Ethics), a good position at a secondary school, and publication of another book.

Yet how much more had been granted to me than I had lost! For one thing, I now possessed a second country with whose language and culture I was thoroughly familiar—a year's studentship at Westfield College, University of London, had given me an insight into English student life, while a series of lectures and war work of various descriptions brought me into contact with members of different social classes. But, above all, in November of 1939, I had found the Faith.

This was the culmination of a search which dated from 1930. Before that year, in spite of my childhood impressions in England, religion had been more or less dormant in my life. The Berlin of my school and university years provided no suitable atmosphere for the pursuit of God, especially for one whose relations were Jewish and whose friends for the greater part were agnostics. Yet even then the need for a Supreme Authority in life and morals made itself felt. Together with others of my generation, I questioned the validity of the then prevalent philosophical relativism, and even went as far as to doubt the reality of

my own authority as a teacher. However, it was only in
1930 that the pursuit began in earnest. I began to study
Catholic as well as Protestant theologians, and the experience of exile only served to intensify my desire for Absolute
Truth. This led me from the Evangelical branch of the
Church of England, with occasional visits to Nonconform-
ist services, via the Buchman group to High Anglicanism
which, as with so many others, proved a stepping stone to
the Catholic Church. However, it took the whole weight
of Jewish persecution—how we laboured to rescue as many
Jews as we could from Germany, my own mother among
them!—and the agony of the early months of the war till
I was prepared to take the final step.

My real life began on March 7, 1940, and with it a re-
orientation of all my powers. I was then doing part-time
work at an excellent school in Sussex, the Burgess P.N.E.U.
School, and had sufficient leisure to study and live in the
light of the Faith. The first practical result of the mental
and spiritual strengthening was a renewed occupation with
a book on National Socialism, which I had begun at Westfield College and had never finished because it would not
"come right." Now I experienced the truth of the saying
that without the Faith we can do nothing, and as a corol-
lary, that with it we can do everything. What had seemed
so difficult before, to explain the nature and rise of National Socialism to myself and others, became easy. Considered as a heresy, National Socialism lost both its evil
power and its fascination. I was fortunate in finding a
publisher, Burns, Oates & Washbourne. In 1941, *The
Heresy of National Socialism* appeared, with a foreword
by His Grace, the Archbishop of Liverpool.

It was well received, and its author turned to subjects of
more immediate interest to a recent convert—subjects connected with the new life that was growing within her.
Spiritual subjects became my main concern, and articles
of mine were published by *Blackfriars, Carmel,* the *Fran-*

ciscan Annals, the *Tablet,* and the *Catholic Herald.* Meanwhile, encouraged by my spiritual director, I wrote an account of my spiritual Odyssey entitled *Two Passports and No Home,* which however, together with two plays— a nativity play, *The King's Quest,* and a full-fledged five-act play, *The Five Talents*—have not yet been published. *The Five Talents* was written when already a higher call had sounded, and the apostolate of prayer had revealed itself as even more effective than that of the pen.

In September of 1949, I entered a Benedictine Convent in Belgium. We are preparing a new foundation of Benedictines of the Byzantine rite who by prayer, study, and the recitation of the Divine Office in Slavonic, labour for the union of the Eastern and Western Churches. We work under the guidance of the Benedictine monks of Chevetogne, Belgium, who, for the past thirty years, have devoted themselves to this apostolate and are known throughout the Catholic world as the editors of the periodical *Eirenikon.*

Whether I shall be allowed to write again, I do not know. I leave the decision to my superiors. What I do know is that this work for the reunion of the churches is what God wants of me now. And that is all I need to know.

EDITOR'S NOTE: In 1955, Miss Marinoff was back in England as a member of a conference on Christian ethics held at Downside during Low Week. The papers contributed to this conference, hers among them, were edited by John M. Todd, and published by Burns, Oates & Washbourne in 1956 under the title *The Springs of Morality.*

ANNABELLE McCON-
NELL MELVILLE

EVEN AFTER FINDING A THIRD BOOK IN PRINT, I AM STILL a little surprised to be considered an author; and, having been reared a good Protestant, it is especially edifying to be considered a Catholic author. With an opening sentence like that, I am almost bound to tell in subsequent ones how I became a Catholic, and then how I became an author, if such I am.

I became a Catholic, at the age of twenty-six, owing to four factors. First, through fortunate accident it happened that the finest intellects I encountered among my contemporaries were possessed by actively practicing Catholics. Second, I was given almost a year of instruction in the Church's teaching by Father Arthur Cunningham, the pastor of the church in St. Johnsville, New York, where I did my first five years of high school teaching. Third, I read the *Imitation of Christ*. And, finally, I did my master's thesis on the subject of G. K. Chesterton's philosophy.

The first factor roused my interest; the last three, pursued simultaneously, brought me to the baptismal font in May, 1936.

As for writing, the story is almost as brief. One institution and one man were largely responsible. The institution was the Catholic University of America in Washington, D. C.; the man was Monsignor John Tracy Ellis, professor of church history in that institution. My first book, *Elizabeth Bayley Seton,* began as a term paper in one of Monsignor Ellis's courses and emerged as a doctoral dissertation in 1949. Whatever excellence that work possessed was chiefly due to the direction of Monsignor Ellis, whose standards of scholarship have notably influenced the work of anyone who worked under him or will work under his direction in the future.

Elizabeth Bayley Seton brought several benefits to her biographer. Not only did I begin to have entree to the fascinating stores of church history materials in the United States, but I was also able to see something of the European connections with our history. In 1951, as a result of studying the life of a woman whose cause has been proposed for beatification, I was introduced to the Sacred Congregation of Rites in Rome and given a glimpse of the process of documenting such causes. My own work was given Roman approval prior to publication. In Livorno I had the pleasure of meeting descendants of the Filicchi family about whom I had written, and saw materials still in their possession which relate to Washington's administration. At home, in Emmitsburg, Maryland, I had the supreme satisfaction of discovering a document relating to Mother Seton that had never before been used in clarifying her career. On the material side, the *Seton* brought me a publisher, Charles Scribner's Sons, and a wise editor, Mr. J. E. G. Hopkins.

My second book stemmed rather naturally from the first. *John Carroll of Baltimore* was a contemporary of Mother

Seton's, and I was already at home in the field of American church history archives. Again the direction of John Tracy Ellis, the editing of J. E. G. Hopkins, and the kind publishing of Scribner's gave my work what excellence it possessed. This time I had the added encouragement of the interest of Archbishop Patrick A. O'Boyle of Washington, the commendation of the Thomas More Book Club which selected it for their readers in July, 1955, and the recognition of the American Catholic Historical Association which awarded it the John Gilmary Shea prize in December, 1955.

As a result of this interest in American church history, I began to be asked to lecture to Catholic groups such as men's clubs, seminaries, Newman clubs, the Catholic Library Association, etc. One such engagement in 1956 led me to spend a night in a Boston Fire Station! I was scheduled to speak at a Communion Breakfast in my home town of Albany, New York, and I started out just as the famous blizzard of March 16 began. We left the Boston bus station at about five in the afternoon. At one the next morning we had progressed as far as the Museum of Fine Arts of Huntington Avenue, just blocks away, had to be rescued from the bus, and wound up on cots furnished by the Red Cross at Fire Station 67. I now accept speaking engagements with the proviso, "weather permitting."

In 1956 the *Library Journal* described me as "a new creative writer of 1956," and that raises the question of how I happened to write a "who-dunnit." Certainly not because I was abandoning my first love, church history. In the days when I traveled rather regularly between Albany and Washington or Baltimore I was an inveterate reader of mystery novels. In the course of writing the *Carroll*, there was one period of almost a year when the manuscript was in the hands of advisory readers. In order to escape my own impatience while waiting for the return of the *Carroll*, I decided to keep my typing hand in practice by doing something else. "I've *read* enough mysteries," I told myself. "Why not try to *write* one?" Many years ago I had read somewhere that amateur writers do well to stick to the scenes they know, so I chose the little town where I had lived for nine years prior to 1945, described events that had actually taken place, but re-arranged them to make a mystery plot. Several people read it upon completion but none with intent to publish. The Carroll manuscript came back, I went to work on the revision, and it was not until publication was under way that I got out the mystery again to see what, if anything, could be done with it. I still liked it the way it was first written, so I took another chance, sent it to the Bruce Publishing Company with apologies that it was not history, and they decided to risk it. The editing of Mr. Bernard Wirth cut it down a bit, but it remains substantially what it was the first time I typed it out in Emmitsburg. The Catholic Literary Foundation used it for an August selection in 1956, and my students in the State Teachers College in Bridgewater read it, I suspect, in preferencee to my more substantial work.

I have no idea whether fiction will lure me again or not. At present, I am back with my first love, busily working on a biography of Boston's first bishop, John Cheverus. This time research took me to France where I have just finished nine weeks of most happy delving. Hopes are high that 1958 will see the completed book. But only time, scholarly readers, editors, and publishers will decide the issue. Meanwhile I have a very full schedule at the Bridgewater Teachers College of Massachusetts, and teaching is my true profession.

On the side I dabble in amateur theatre, when I can be type-cast in middle-aged roles. I putter over African violets, experiment with cooking, whip up a new dress when I am desperate for something to wear, continue to be a devotee of the Boston Symphony, write book reviews for

Books on Trial or the *Catholic Historical Review,* and try to
keep track of my five godchildren who live in the District
of Columbia, Maryland, New York, and New Hampshire.

As far as details of education and teaching experience
go, I think that *The American Catholic Who's Who* has
most of these.

The only comical thing that has happened to me as a
result of taking up writing occurred in June of 1956 when
Stonehill College of Easton, Massachusetts, conferred an
honorary Doctor of Laws on this budding author. I mis-
interpreted the dramatic pause of the reader of my citation,
galloped across the platform midway through his speech,
and will undoubtedly go down in the college history as
the only woman who just couldn't wait for her degree. I
certainly disrupted the dignity of the occasion.

I'm afraid none of this is very exciting. I'm a pretty
run-of-the-mill small town school teacher and that suits me
fine. I like small towns, and I have always enjoyed teaching. If I can find archives for historical research nearby,
I also enjoy doing some note-taking during my free time.
With the excellent archives of Boston so near my present
teaching position, I am likely to finish another biography.
After that, who can say?

DAPHNE D. C. POCHIN MOULD

I DO NOT REALLY REMEMBER WHEN I DID NOT WANT TO
write. I remember composing stories and poems before
I learned to write, and dictating them to members of the
family who wrote them down for me. None of these early
efforts, which so far as I remember were often about
fantastic animals, have, fortunately for me, survived!

My background is English, but I have been so long out
of the country, out of contact with its thought and way of
life, that going back there in recent years, I found I passed
readily enough for a born Irishwoman! Actually, I was
born in the very heart of the "Englishry," in the south
country, in Salisbury with its ancient Cathedral, whose
spire is the landmark seen from all the rolling downs
round about. Stonehenge was not far off, and when I
was very small, I tried out my climbing instincts on its
stones,—to be immediately hauled off by an irate official!

I was born in 1920—oddly enough in view of later events

on November 15th—the feast day of the great Dominican, St. Albert, teacher of St. Thomas Aquinas, and patron of scientists. With the urge to write, I also had an urge to study science, especially the natural sciences. I used to go out in the country and identify the plants and trees, watch the birds, go quietly through the English woods so that the red squirrels came playing past me, unnoticed. I looked at the rocks too and found fossils in the English chalk pits which pit my "calf country" with white scars.

Science for me meant the discovery of truth, reality, the nature of being, finding out what things were, what life was about.

My family were Anglican—the Church of England in its "High Church" department. I was brought up to be an Anglican too, but I doubt that I ever really believed. I had a phase of belief around the time I was confirmed and given a course of instruction in church doctrine, but my scientific studies made me question the foundations of such teaching. Could the existence of God be proved? If it could not, then all religious belief was false, a myth, something to attack in the name of truth. Accordingly, I deliberately abandoned my Church of England allegiance, and determined to devote myself to an agnostic attack upon religion in the name of truth. Leaving England for Scotland in 1939 was the time of my final break with the Church of England, and my coming into a country of the Presbyterian Faith probably hastened this step.

Scotland has always fascinated me, even before I knew the clear, bright skies over her winter snowfields, or felt the rasp of rock under nailed boots. That country had had my loyalty in my childhood, never England; the glamour of Prince Charles, of Scottish history in general, of the pipes and the tartan, the mountain streams, the heather, the silent blue waters of the lakes, the magic of her islands, held me enchanted from the very time that I heard first of their existence. So to Scotland I came in the first months of the Second World War, to Edinburgh, where I began my University B.Sc. degree with the wail of sirens and the crackle of machine gun fire as the first air raids took place on the Forth Bridge.

Four years in wartime Edinburgh saw me with my degree with first class honours in geology—the science of rocks. I got a research fellowship too, and permission to start work on it from the Ministry of Labour—for work was still under war controls then—and went up into the Highlands to do research on the granite of Foyers, beside Loch Ness. Study of this hitherto unmapped bit of country—some one hundred square miles of it—gained me the Ph.D. from Edinburgh in 1946. It also crystallised my ideas about my writing—to begin with something Scottish, something Highland, and to live in the Highlands.

So I came to live in Fort Augustus—also on Loch Ness (but I never saw the Loch Ness Monster), and beside the Benedictine Abbey of Fort Augustus. I intended to begin my writing about Scottish history, topography, and the like, and attack religion when it came into my story, eventually working up to an all-out attack.

My first book was the *Roads from the Isles,* published by Oliver & Boyd of Edinburgh. It was the story of some of the old cross-country tracks of the West Highlands, along which in the old days the black cattle of the Hebridean islands and of the Scottish mountains, used to be driven in great herds to the markets in the South, where numbers were bought by drovers from England. Naturally, the next move for me was to the islands themselves, and I wrote a book about the Outer Hebrides (*West over Sea*). But some of those Outer Islands are wholly Catholic, and here I came up against Catholic life and thought for the first time. In this country too I came up against the old churches and monastic ruins originally founded by the Celtic Saints, by men like St. Columba of Ireland. My first two books told the history of some of these churches

and their founders, but from a neutral point of view. Now
I intended to write about the Inner Isles—including Iona of
St. Columba—and to "show-up" the Saints and the Church
for what I thought they really were.

But to attack the Church meant finding out just what
was to be attacked. I already knew some of the Benedictines at Fort Augustus and from one of them sought information. He calmly presented me with St. Thomas
Aquinas' proofs for demonstrating the existence of God,
together with the whole set-up of Catholic philosophy.
That reason could enter into religion was a completely
new idea to me. I fought hard against accepting any such
possibility, but after a year of struggle and argument was
received into the Catholic Church on November 11, 1950—
St. Martin's day, the patron saint of the English parish
in which I had been born in Salisbury! So the book that
had intended to attack the Church, *Scotland of the Saints*,
was, when it appeared, the very opposite, a Catholic book,
with the Church's imprimatur.

Ireland lay across the narrow seas from Scotland, another Gaelic and Celtic country. To follow to Ireland the
Celtic Saints that I had studied in Scotland seemed the
obvious road, to Columba and Iona I really owed my conversion. So when the lease on the Fort Augustus house
was up, came a move to Ireland in the autumn of 1951,
and more books about the Celtic Saints, a companion to the
first Batsford one, *Scotland of the Saints*, namely, *Ireland
of the Saints*, and a study of the pilgrimages still made in
Ireland to the old monastic sites of the Irish saints, *Irish
Pilgrimage*, and finally, a deeper study of the thought and
prayer and spirituality of the Celtic saints,—not as something remote from us, but as something to make use of
today, the answer to our present problems. This last,
The Celtic Saints: Our Heritage (Macmillan), came out
in September, 1956. And because I had learned to love the
hills and to climb in Scotland, I scrambled on the Irish

mountains too, and wrote (in 1955) *The Mountains of Ireland,* the first full-length book ever to be written on the Irish hills.

Perhaps it was not strange that my early desire for truth brought me, now within the Church, to the Dominican Order, whose motto is *Veritas,* Truth. In 1952, in Galway's Claddagh, I was received into the Third Order of St. Dominic. I think I first came to the Dominicans through St. Thomas Aquinas, but an intense devotion to St. Dominic himself followed becoming a Tertiary.

At the end of 1955, the Irish Dominican Fathers asked me to write the history of the Irish Dominicans. Not since the Latin of De Burgo in the 1760's, had a history of the Order in Ireland been attempted. It is a fascinating story, of 700 years of Dominican and Irish and Catholic history, of the gracious medieval priories whose ruins still dot the countryside, of the long persecutions and the Penal laws, and finally of recovery and restoration. Nearly a hundred Irish Dominicans who died for the Faith are included in the official process for the beatification of the Irish martyrs. I followed their tracks, saw the places where they had died, the chalice belonging to Father Thaddeus Moriarty hanged in Killarney in 1653 and other precious relics still in Dominican possession. I looked at the Dominican Archives, at the faded pages of the account books kept by the friars in the days of the Penal laws in the eighteenth century; the regular tips they gave "ye Mayor's sergeants" (the police of that day) in Galway, so if there was a search for friars they would get warning; the food they ate, the different things that made up their small income, daily expenses—tinning a leaky kettle, buying a sieve, all these things are entered in these books. I went, too, up and down the country to the old sites where the friars had lived in cabins in Penal days, as near as they could to their old ruined medieval foundations, and asked the Irish people for the traditional stories of the friars.

Many of these still survive, though the older people who had the full tradition, are mostly dead. My book, *The Irish Dominicans,* was published in the spring of 1957 by Dominican Publications, Dublin.

So I seem to have come full circle, from the first desire to write and to know Truth, to be writing about the way the Truth was defended in Ireland, of the way the Catholic Church survived attack after attack, and of the Dominican Order's part in that survival and in the eternal defense of Truth.

REVEREND URBAN NAGLE, O.P.

ON THE TENTH OF SEPTEMBER, 1805, FATHER SAMUEL T. Wilson of the Order of Preachers—one of the four founders of the first American Province of Dominicans and its first Provincial Superior—arrived in the United States. One hundred years later to the day, I arrived. That is the end of that little story. There are no conclusions to be drawn from the interesting coincidence, but I've always wanted to see it in print.

Since Father Wilson is out of the narrative now, it doesn't matter where he arrived, but my independence was established in Providence, Rhode Island—the plantation which separated itself from England two months before the other twelve colonies.

My father, Edward John Nagle, and my mother, Mary Elizabeth Keefe, were born in Providence too, and went to the same parochial school, but all that happened a long time before my story begins. With striking originality,

they had me chirstened Edward John Nagle (they were
used to the name), so officially I was "Junior" until I
picked up "Urban" on joining the Dominicans. No one
made much of the "Junior" however, and I suppose it is
too late to start worrying about its recurrence now.

The only grandparent I remember was Mike Keefe, who
came to live with us, and when he told me that he had
fought on both sides in the War between the States (he
did come from Wilmington, Delaware, close to the border),
I knew there was a great capacity for impartiality and
understanding in the family, but I didn't know until later
that he was to be the prototype of some of the amazing
exploits of "Uncle Malachy."

A brief sojourn in Warren, Rhode Island, from my fourth
to my ninth year—the term of a five year lease that father
had on an iron foundry—introduced me to the bucolic joys
of a small New England town, marked my debut into
variety, and completely submerged the entire family in
Kirkman's soap.

Mother wanted some new furniture for the larger house,
but father made it clear that he had put all the money
he had and was able to borrow into the foundry. That
announcement didn't impress mother at all, although she
must have heard the words, because when father wanted
to make a point about money, he was inclined to roar.
She needed furniture, and the incidental fact that our
venture into capitalism left us very broke was a trifle.
So she resorted to wiles and asked father if she might get
some furniture with Kirkman's Soap wrappers, to which
even father had to agree. She forgot to say that she
hadn't bought the soap. We got the furniture, but for five
years and more every time one of us opened a closet door
we were deluged by an avalanche of hard, sharp-edged
cakes of brown soap without designating wrappers. It
was a clean house. We had much more soap than food.

My debut into the theatre—at the age of six—was a

moment of ecstatic joy followed by weeks of sadness and remorse. I was asked to sing at the parish catch-all or variety show, having been discovered by the music teacher at school. She and mother agreed that "Robin on a Tilting Bough" would be appropriate for one of my tender years performing under such pious auspices.

However, the piano player who was an old pro even to the cigarette that was glued to his lower lip, gave me a hasty education out of the side of his mouth. He said the second last spot was top billing and that Robin, no matter how loud I bellowed, would lay an egg. So for his edification I ran the underworld repertory of the average six-year old. Came the night, and as I sauntered onstage in my white Russian suit, really intending to sing about the tilting bough, he beat out the intro for Casey Jones and I went through the four verses and choruses as loud as I could. That the house came down was inevitable. It's a ridiculous picture even now. Then when I did a chain of encores that I didn't exactly understand, I was lifted up on the shoulders of stars of an hour before who had suddenly become merely the supporting cast. But when mother and father appeared in the wings, I was dropped on the floor. Mother was mortified and wept. Father roared. It was from him I got the voice. The reason I know that mother was mortified was because she said so about fifty times. I was never quite trusted theatrically again after that mortification, but I had my moment.

Father moved his foundry back to the suburbs of Providence and his family and what was left of the soap back to where we started from, and there I met the Sisters of Holy Name School. Little did I dream that I would one day be chaplain at a Motherhouse, nor did they, I presume, or I would have been singled out for an intensive and highly specialized education.

High School brought me the good fortune of having the Christian Brothers. In the good old days, before the State

told the Church how to run its schools, these specialists
offered erudition to their charges with all gentleness, but
if it was spurned, they pounded it in—and if you think
that's a metaphor, you're . . . well, you're young.

There was a bit of sheer luck in the fact that the class
of '22 contained an exceptional batch of bright or shrewd
young men who have, as my forebearers would have undoubtedly said, "gone far." It made for competition, and
to keep pace with the more literate and literary characters,
I read practically all the hogwash of the early twenties
just as they were beginning to roar. I don't begin to keep
up with the market now because those who write haven't
time to read.

It would be a display of erudition or a feat of memory
to list the authors, but you know the standard bearers of
the lost generation. They confused the world and they
confused me, but the futility was so obvious that it had
a salutary effect on some of us. We had to escape into
orthodoxy.

My romantic reaction toward security sought cold stone
cloisters and stained glass and this became concrete as the
Dominican Fathers opened Providence College. There was
a pull toward the priesthood and I was very friendly with
my uncle who was a pastor in the diocese, but he lived in
an ordinary rectory not too unlike our own house, and I
think I was going through the Miniver Cheevy stage.
Every seventeen year old in those dear dread days wanted
at times to be an anarchistic Communist (we called it
Bolshevik) or a Trappist.

There is a minor mystery about religious vocations—and
all vocations—in that one is attracted according to his
current stage or phase, and as the years pass, the reasons
which brought him into the place in which he finds himself are quite forgotten, but the call rings more deeply for
new and more fundamental reasons. After becoming a
Dominican, I learned that they were known as guardians

of theology. I didn't know that theology needed any guarding and I certainly wouldn't have chosen myself for the job.

My interest in white stone cloisters is certainly diminished in favor of steam heat and running water—but the Dominicans accepted me and the party for whom I can speak is very happy about it.

There isn't much that can be said about the quiet life and the years of wrestling with St. Thomas Aquinas in this brief space, except that in the long run St. Thomas usually wins, and that poetic thinking and fanciful writing usually get laced into syllogistic form, and that crisp, clipped Anglo-Saxon prose gets beaten down into cumbersome Latinisms. The seminarian has to do battle to keep from writing like every other seminarian.

By way of diversion, I wrote plays for the novices and students. For the benefit of collectors, may I suggest that none are extant, and that is the best thing that anyone could say about them. The first ambitious venture was *Barter* (which I can't pronounce, being a New Englander), and it won a national prize, so after achieving unexpected success as a playwright, I made an effort to learn how to write a play. The next comparable distinction came from the Christophers for *City of Kings*. So I am reconciled to winning a prize every twenty years. Watch out for 1968!

There was a detour in the quest of a degree in psychology in the days when I thought that this science would be a help to understanding people and their problems. But the degree has done no one any harm as I've never taught a single class in that mysterious subject.

Ordination brought its share of world conquering zeal, and it seemed that a new era was at hand (just for me) with the moving pictures and the radio. My tangential studies and aberrant accomplishments might be directed

to the more widespread dissemination of what I believed.
That was the drive in my contribution to The Blackfriars'
Guild. This latter enterprise, which consumed hours
that grew into years, was filled with joys and sorrows,
successes and failures, and all of these that I could capture
are packed into a book called *Behind the Masque*. Being
half told in some three hundred pages, it's too much to
tell here.

That was the exciting avocation and it brought me another world of vicarious living. But there were the bread
and butter jobs (I don't like butter, so I never eat it, and
it makes this sound foolish but you can't say "the bread
jobs") and so I taught for six years at Providence College
and edited the *Holy Name Journal* for six years. It seems
I did everything in terms of six years, like living in Washington, Providence, Manhattan, and Jersey City. That
decision wasn't in the bond but it always happens. And
that is one of the wonderful things about the religious
life. You make one decision and the poor superiors (in
the Irish meaning of the word "poor") have to make all
the others.

Radio and television held a fascination for me and
"Uncle George and Uncle Malachy" have been done in
both media on seventy to eighty network shows. (We use
the word "show" in deference to the commercial jargon.)

The perfect squelch caught me after the fourth talk—
at the end of the first series—in which George had to be
invented to be a foil for Malachy. There were about fifteen
people in the show, with a quartet and a string ensemble,
announcers, technicians, etc., and they all flew out to other
assignments between 11:59/30 and 12 m. I stood all alone
picking up my notes sure that no one loved me, until the
last of the four talks when a little man came out of the
control room and said, "That was the best series of talks
I ever heard." I filled up like a blowfish, so overwhelming

was my gratitude, so he continued. "You were twelve minutes on the nose every Sunday." He didn't know what language I was using.

Twenty years in what the current heresy of Communism calls "the transmission belt"—theatre, moving pictures, radio, television and journalism—many of them running concurrently made for a pin-wheel pace, and I began to think that my escape from the twenties was something of a boomerang.

But good things come to him who waits enough six year spells, and I was relieved and made chaplain of the Dominican Sisters' Motherhouse at St. Mary of the Springs in Columbus, Ohio.

It's a quiet existence and seemed startlingly different at first. The Sisters have some unendurable customs like "Early to bed and early to rise makes you healthy"—and that's all. I wrote most of my plays in the early morning hours, and now I'm getting up when I used to go to bed.

But the current production has a permanence. You don't strike the sets and say "Good Night" to the actors when they head for home in their street clothes. These people are real.

I think I've found my white stone cloister at last. Maybe I'll do a book about it. There is much inside the walls which the world should know—much of joy and hope, labor and sacrifice, and the sprinkling of sorrow needed for sanctity—and perhaps most of all the awareness of God.

EDITOR'S NOTE: Father Nagle's published plays include *Barter* (Longmans, 1929), *Catherine the Valiant* (id., 1931), Savonarola (in *Theatre for Tomorrow*, edited by Emmet Lavery; *id.*, 1940), *Lady of Fatima* (McMullen, 1948), and *City of Kings* (Christopher Press, Rochester, N. Y., 1949). Among his works, other than drama, are *Behind the Masque* (McMullen, 1951), *Uncle George and Uncle Malachy* (Bruce, 1946), and a number of pamphlets published by Our Sunday Visitor.

THOMAS P. NEILL

IF BIRTH AND EARLY CHILDHOOD HAVE A DETERMINING IN-
fluence on one's later life—as it is popularly held—then
I should have been born a writer of Western fiction. For
I was born in 1915 in a mining town on the continental
divide in Colorado. Not much later the prohibition amend-
ment became part of the law of the land, but apparently
not in Telluride, Colorado, because my earliest memories
are of busy places on Main Street which, I was told, were
"saloons," and of our neighbors having truckloads of grapes
delivered "to make jelly." These same neighbors, I remember, had the only effective remedy for the flu—
mysterious ingredients dissolved in a tall glass of hot wine.

I was the oldest of four children, and by the time I was
in the fourth grade, my parents decided to move to a more
"civilized" community where we could grow up in the
Faith. From Telluride I took certain impressions that
have never been erased—a rough, pagan society where

charity abounded, although the word was probably unknown, a society I have always contrasted to more
sophisticated communities to underscore the advantages
and the shortcomings of the latter. Through the next four
years we moved frequently. I attended something like a
dozen grade schools, public and parochial, and cannot remember any great differences among them except that in
some you stood up to recite and in others you sat down.
But I did learn some geography, and I came to know that
the Irish in South Chicago were quite different from the
Mormons in Utah.

Eventually our family settled in St. Louis, where I attended high school and college. These eight years were
the period of the Great Depression, which turned young
people's minds to social thought and inclined them to
believe that the industrialists who had built America had
somehow pulled a great hoax on the people. St. Louis
was—and is—a conservative city, not aggressive like Detroit or hurried like Chicago. St. Louisans find time to
read and to cultivate the vanishing art of conversation.
I therefore spent my years of study in a society that is
quietly cultured, where young people gather in each other's
homes rather than in clubs, where I frequently found myself discussing Plato with a friend's lawyer-father or St.
Thomas with a banker. In such surroundings it is natural
for a young man to turn to things academic and to want
to stay with them as long as possible before taking up
some pedestrian occupation.

Sometimes, I think, it is good to drift for a while.
Rushing to a destination is never good if the destination
is wrong, for one either ends up in the wrong place or
else spends several years retracing his steps. At any rate,
I kept open all the avenues I might follow—law, journalism,
civil service, personnel work, and I forget what others. A
scholarship to do master's work at Notre Dame presented
itself, and then a fellowship for doctoral work at St. Louis

University. In each case the work was its own reward, and eventually I found myself an instructor in modern European history with the opportunity of exploring with graduate students whatever realms of intellectual, cultural, and social history deserved exploration. I had drifted into the profession of reading, teaching, and writing.

A man is supposed to know what influences, in the form of books and men, whetted his appetite, formed his attitudes, and shaped his mind when he was growing up. I know the books I read, the men who taught me, and the fellow-students who influenced me one way or the other. But to isolate the contribution of each is impossible. "The Catholic Revival" was much talked about in those days; students almost had to read Chesterton, Belloc, Hollis, Gill, and the others, and then they had to wonder why there were not comparable American Catholic writers. I shall never know whether the teachers who stimulated me or those who repelled me were the more influential. As a whole, though, they opened up for me a centuries-old tradition of learning, the intellectual and cultural past of Christendom. It was natural for me to undertake independent explorations of this rich tradition and on occasion, as a citizen, to apply this wisdom to contemporary problems. It was also natural, in time, for me to make a few small contributions of my own to this stream of thought.

Somewhere along the line, I began to write for publication. Just when or how I do not remember. But I do remember writing small bits of high school news for the local newspapers. In college, ambitious students can write longer bits for the student newspaper—which I did—and even editorials when one has somehow acquired a reputation among undergraduates as a critical thinker. St. Louis University had a respectable literary quarterly when I was a student. It served as a vehicle for undergraduate literary effort, a testing ground for style, and an experimental plant for daring ideas. It also served to discover and develop the writing talents of several undergraduates. Here I published articles on various subjects and in varying veins. Here, too, I learned not to write satire unless the label "Satire" is put under the title. Some of these articles showed up as reprints, and each such occasion confirmed my suspicion that I might have that mysterious thing referred to in the writers' school advertisements as "talent."

These were lean but good years. Sitting around with fellow-students, arguing, discussing, settling world problems, ignoring the passage of time, this is the closest approach we Americans have to the academy of Athens and the scholars' club of more recent times. Wit sharpens in clash with other wits, thinking is refined, generalizations are qualified, and each disputant is driven to read the ancient masters and the modern experts in order to bring more ammunition to the next verbal battle. Out of such groups, I suspect, writers do emerge. But teaching and scholarly pursuits precluded any serious thought on my part of a writing career. Almost every article and book I have had published since 1939 was born in the classroom or on the lecture platform. They are all written versions of previously given lectures. This has its advantages and disadvantages. It makes for colloquial style, for a wordiness and looseness foreign to fine writing. But it helps one achieve what I consider the purpose of writing: the communication of one's knowledge and judgments to the reader, just as the speaker communicates to his listeners if he is a good speaker. It centers the writer's attention on the reader and the message rather than on style.

Writing, then, has been for me another form of teaching and of academic conversation. It is not a hobby because it is hard work and it is not rewarded, as oral communication is, by seeing how the reader is affected. It is not a hobby, moreover, because it is so closely connected with my professional work as a teacher that it can never

be done "on the side" or in my spare time. I see only two
reasons for enduring the drudgery of writing. The first
is to communicate one's convictions to a wider audience
than one can assemble in a classroom. The second is to
make money. A professor in a Catholic university obvi-
ously writes for both reasons.

Professors can write three kinds of books or articles
(excluding literature in the technical sense) : scholarly
works, popular works, and textbooks. All three are
legitimate, I submit; and all three are necessary. Scholarly
work is easy to do and it is absorbingly interesting.
Popularization is difficult, and it is generally badly done,
because it requires of the author both the knowledge of
the scholar and the human sensitivity of the politician.
Good textbooks are the hardest of all to do well, and they
are the most poorly done because there are so few men
or women who combine scholarly knowledge and pedagog-
ical skill with the ability to write accurately and interest-
ingly. I have tried all three kinds of writing—and only
the reader knows with what degree of success or failure.

In 1941 I married Agnes Weber, of Denver, Colorado.
Few of my colleagues have been so fortunate in having a
wife who understands what a professor-writer must do
to make a mark in his profession, who are willing to give
so generously and ask nothing in return. We have nine
children, seven boys and two girls, who at this moment
are in five different schools. The modern world seems to
have conspired against large families and, despite their
teaching to the contrary, Catholic organizations are a
party to the conspiracy. If my wife and I had one or
two children, we could perhaps meet the demands made
upon us by fathers' and mothers' clubs, parish associations,
Boy Scouts, Cub Scouts, Young Ladies Sodalities, and a
host of other organizations, insistently demanding our
presence seven or more evenings each week. We find that
with nine children we must restrict ourselves to maintain-

ing a single organization, our family, which is in session twenty-four hours a day, run democratically on one occasion and dictatorially on another, but where we like to think that charity abounds and good fruit will be produced.

We consider ourselves fortunate to live in the years when the Church in America is achieving maturity. It was formerly the Church of the immigrants and it tried to minister to these foreign Americans and to see that they kept the Faith. It succeeded in this task because of the heroic work of our grandfathers, but in the process it developed an unhealthy minority complex which we of this generation must dissolve. The Church in America has moved from the social apostolate to the intellectual and spiritual apostolates, and my wife and I consider ourselves privileged to play a small role in developing these new apostolates. This, we think, will be done by the providential concomitance of many things: by dedicating to God and by raising in the Faith a large family; by prayer and by playing a part in directing parish activity in the right direction; by seeking the truth in one's professional work and by disseminating it, which in some small way leads to ultimate Truth and to the glory of God; and by doing what we can to spread through American society the Light which enkindles the world and is the sole source of hope that our children can honestly thank us for having brought them into the world and having done something to make it a habitable place for the children of God.

EDITOR'S NOTE: Dr. Neill's books include *Weapons for Peace* (Bruce, 1945), *Makers of the Modern Mind* (id., 1949), *They Lived the Faith* (id., 1951), *Religion and Culture* (id., 1952), *The Rise and Decline of Liberalism* (id., 1953), and, in collaboration with Dr. Raymond Schmandt, *History of the Church* (id., 1957).

REVEREND PIUS PARSCH, C.R.S.A.

NORTHERN MORAVIA, TODAY A PART OF CZECHOSLOVAKIA, IS the homeland of my forebears. I can trace my lineage back to the sixteenth century. The first seven of my identified ancestors were farmers, thereafter they were townspeople and artisans. My father was a small businessman in the city of Olmutz in Moravia. All my ancestors, both on my father's and my mother's side, were German; they were practicing Catholics; were sound and healthy people; and most of them reached a ripe old age. They were not rich, neither were they paupers, but honest, solid folk.

My birthplace was in a little village near Olmutz called Neustift. I was born on May 18, 1884, the second child of my parents, and was baptized on May 25, 1884. Two uncles, priests, took part in the ceremony; one as minister, the other as sponsor. My baptismal name was John (the Evangelist) Bruno. I was a good, quiet child of whom my mother used always to boast, saying I was very diligent.

Though somewhat delicate, I was always healthy, and had no serious illness; I did suffer a lot from headaches, however. In the city of Olmutz where the family had settled I attended first the kindergarten and then the primary school. After the fourth grade I was ready for the "exchange," that is, a year spent in a Czech village in order to learn Bohemian. After completing the fifth grade in the primary school, I entered the classical "gymnasium" for eight years. We had Latin from the first year on, and Greek from the third. Except for one year, I was always an excellent student, even though I was not particularly gifted and, specifically, had no talent for languages. Nevertheless, I was diligent and ambitious, a student who took his studies seriously. Already as a schoolboy I had some hobbies, favorite subjects which are unusual for that age: I took an interest in genealogy and later, Egyptology.

I was always religious. At home there reigned a pious spirit, the more so as there were priests on both my father's and my mother's side. One especially strong influence came from my father's brother, a priest, with whom we two brothers always spent our holidays. In his rectory we used to play at being priests and had our complete equipment for Mass there. Certainly it was there that my future vocation to the priesthood was awakened and developed. Indeed, I felt in me the call to the priesthood from childhood. Neither in the family nor outside it was I ever urged to it. But at home it was taken for granted: Hans will be a priest, Rudi (my brother) would be an officer.

I cannot say that, otherwise, in my time at the "gymnasium," any man or priest exerted a great spiritual or religious influence upon me. There was no student club or religious society. My fellow students were mostly indifferent to religion, and the townspeople very liberal. At school I was considered an outsider, and went my own way. A very close bond existed between my father and

me. I loved him dearly. He was a fine man, and a good
father. And although he possessed only a little schooling,
he was mentally keen. He had a preference for historical
subjects, was a coin collector, and was city archivist. As
a self-taught man, he had to acquire his linguistic and
historical knowledge laboriously. So, as a student at the
"gymnasium," I was able to help him in many things. I
took an interest in his work too. My parents' family life
was a model one and close. Alas! my father died quite early
in 1902, in his forty-seventh year. I was barely eighteen
years old. After graduating with distinction, I at once
entered the monastery at Klosterneuburg near Vienna as
a novice, and on August 28, 1904, I was clothed with the
habit. Thus began my clerical life.

I might now indicate how, at the very beginning of my
vocation to the cloister, the first signs of my later life's
work, the Bible and the Liturgy, became evident. I brought
with me from the world little religious science; of the
liturgy and the Bible I had no idea. But even in the
cloister I discovered no enthusiasm whatever for the liturgy. The cultivation of liturgical worship in the monastery was likewise by no means extraordinarily vigorous.
Yet my first encounter with the liturgy made a deep impression upon me. I remember that right after the first
few days I asked for a commentary on the psalms from
the library, because it was intolerable for me to say the
psalms without understanding them. Thus a particular
fondness for the breviary took hold of me at once. In the
course of my theological studies this fondness increased so
much that I formed the resolve to write a commentary
on the breviary, since I found none in all the liturgical
literature. I also began to read the Bible zealously and
became very fond of it.

After my priestly ordination (1909), I immediately went
to a parish in the capital, and remained for four years as
assistant pastor at Maria Treu in Vienna. At that time I

was completely the parish priest, spending long hours daily in the confessional, devoting myself to parish societies, and organizing a student club. Meanwhile, I had received my doctorate in theology. My liturgical preferences were put entirely in the background. In those first four years of my priesthood I did not learn how to direct a single activity which could awaken an interest in the liturgy. I was exclusively a parish priest.

When obedience called me back to the cloister after four years, I had the choice between the chair of pastoral theology and that of the New Testament in our theological school. Because I liked parish work, I chose pastoral theology. Along with that, I was expected to help in the training of the novices. Once more my old love for the liturgy awoke. In the novices' classes I occupied myself chiefly with the explanation of the psalms and the breviary.

This activity did not last long, for the first World War broke out. It did not keep me at home however; I volunteered for chaplain duty at the front. My wish was granted in May, 1915. I went to a front line regiment and remained with it until the end of the war. It was a particularly instructive period for me. In my association with officers and men I acquired a knowledge of man; I learned to know the mind of the ordinary individual and his need for religion. Pre-war parish life had been weak and soft. Mankind was too little understood. My own ideas matured in caring for souls during the war. Man needs, I thought, stronger fare than that which the often sugary piety of pre-war days could offer him. Thus was the way paved for the new ideas which are joined to the two well-springs, the Bible and the Liturgy.

But in the field I also came into direct contact with the Bible and the liturgy. It happened this way. After the first year, when there were so many troop-movements, my regiment took up a position in the Carpathians, where we encamped for the winter. Thus I had plenty of free time.

One day the thought that I knew nothing at all of the life
of Our Lord and Savior was weighing heavily on my mind.
At once I had a commentary on the Gospels sent to me
from home, and then I began with avidity to investigate
the life of Jesus. A harmony of the Gospels hung before
me, and so through study I came closer to the Gospels.
I said to myself: something is lacking in priests and in
the people when they know and understand so little of the
Holy Scriptures.

Again my love for the breviary and the psalms appeared.
Just at that time the new Psalter of Pope Pius X had
been introduced. I now began a commentary on it, a
liturgical explanation of the psalms of each of the hours.

And then a third interest arose. I often said Mass for
the soldiers, at times for the whole division, as well as for
a small group, and for the sick and wounded. I found it
distressing that the soldiers understood nothing of the
Mass. On the other hand, I had learned about the collaboration of the faithful of the Greek rite in Galicia and
Bukovina. Thereupon another idea came to me which, of
course, matured only after several years: the active participation of the laity in divine worship. The war came
to an inglorious end, but I brought back with me a rich
booty, the two goals of my life's work which are of far-
reaching importance for the entire Catholic Church: to
make the Bible a book of the people, and to guide Catholics
to an active participation in the liturgy.

In the middle of November, 1918, I returned to my
cloister. I was not given much time to adjust myself.
Again I took over the task of teaching pastoral theology
and instructing the novices. I also soon found a meeting
of minds. With the novices I at once conducted a Bible
class on the life of Jesus, and then a class on the explanation of the breviary, especially the psalter. Thus I was
enabled to make the clear observation that the simple Bible
class by far gave the young men the greatest pleasure.

Then I started a Bible class for the laity too, dwelling particularly on the life of Jesus, and soon after began an explanation of the Mass.

It was about this time that I heard of a *missa cantata* which was held in student circles. I decided to hold, with my lay group, the first Mass with the active participation of the whole congregation. It was near the feast of the Ascension in 1922. The day before, I assembled the group in St. Gertrude's, the little church which was destined to become the cradle of the lay liturgical movement, and explained the action and meaning of the congregational Mass (we called it the liturgical Mass then). On that occasion a difference of opinion arose. Many a Catholic in the group, recruited in other circumstances, from that moment broke off from our association. The congregational Mass was, frankly, still very primitive. The Kyrie, Sanctus and Agnus Dei were sung in German; Professor Goller had prepared simple, hymn-like melodies for us. The Proper parts, and the Gloria and Credo were recited by the faithful in chorus. The leader read the lessons and prayers. We had an Offertory procession, and even the kiss of peace was signified through charity. That was the first lay liturgical celebration of the Mass in German-speaking territory. Since that time, such "liturgical" Masses were often celebrated and were by degrees perfected. It now set up for me years of liturgical missionary work. In some twenty churches of Vienna I held liturgical weeks, in which I explained the Mass and at the close conducted the congregational Mass.

Now the so-called lay liturgical movement began, of which I can be called the originator. I must explain briefly, then, what are its goals. The liturgy, the public worship of the Church, which in early times set the rhythm of Christian devotion, was, in the Middle Ages, put further and further in the background in favor of private and lay devotion. Hence subjectivism and individualism in the religious life of Catholics came strongly to the forefront. All too much leeway was given to human action in opposition to the operation of divine grace. So liturgical worship languished more and more and finally became a function of the priest, at which the people, during the liturgy and in place of it, gave themselves to private devotions.

Pius X, the great pope of the liturgical reform, was the first to take cognizance of this anomalous situation. He is the father of the liturgical revival which set in after the war. The movement first caught fire in Belgium. In Germany it was the abbeys of Maria Laach and Beuron which ardently took up the idea. They turned first to the academicians and intellectuals, for whom a whole new world was unfolded and made accessible by it.

Up to that time, however, the movement had one weakness: it was still very intellectual, that is, it confined itself to explaining the movement. Cultured Catholics were indoctrinated in the spirit of the liturgy, they learned to understand the text, and were qualified to assist at the solemn rites of the abbeys, without themselves, however, being permitted to participate.

Forth from Klosterneuburg came the second impulse. The people, the ordinary people ought likewise to be included in the movement. And then was a most important axiom, which the abbeys had left completely out of account, inscribed upon our banner: the active participation of the laity in the liturgy. The faithful should be present at worship not "like dumb listeners," but should actively enter into the liturgy and play the role in it that was meant for them. That is the particular aspect of the liturgical revival as it went forth from Klosterneuburg.

The lay liturgical movement has concerned itself first of all with the Mass, and it looks for all the possible ways of bringing the laity into its celebration. The laity must realize then that much in the Mass has become set and fossilized. The movement recognizes the fact that the instruction part of the Fore-Mass has almost completely lost its purpose of bringing the word of God to the hearer. It realizes that the laity were left almost entirely out of consideration, and were represented by the choir and the ministers. It even had to wage a campaign so that the Offertory-meal might be distributed to the faithful *in* the Mass. The lay liturgical movement then came to three types of congregational Masses: the Mass recited in unison (gesprochene Chormesse), the Mass sung in unison (Betsingmesse), and the Solemn Mass sung by the congregation (Volkschoralamt). The Mass sung in unison is the popular type, which should be the parish Mass of the people; the solemn congregational Mass doubtless comes close to the classic liturgy.

Yet, not only the Mass has been included in the movement, but also the ecclesiastical year with season and feast, with procession and custom; the parish, the church with its altar, organ, baptismal font; the sacraments, the canonical hours with their psalms and lessons—all these have been brought within the compass of the movement. Indeed, a new type of piety has been developed which goes back again to the early Church. The Middle Ages and modern times preferred impetratory devotion and the fear of sin; the early Church lived in devotion proceeding from grace, in that common worship for which our movement stands. Thus we believe, and our work will extend in ever widening circles in the Church and, also, will erect a bridge of agreement with our separated brethren.

For this lay liturgical work, two organizations were established in Klosterneuburg which complement each other: the Lay Liturgical Apostolate and the Liturgical Society of St. Gertrude. The former is an institute that includes a publishing house and an advisory board for lay liturgical work. The latter organization is a Catholic association which endeavors to carry out the lay liturgical revival in a practical way. Theory and practice thus go together. The Apostolate studies the method, and provides texts and aids; the Society is the training school, as it were, which is expected to put into practice what the Apostolate teaches.

The lay liturgical Apostolate has grown from an insignificant beginning to become a noteworthy institute. Here are two proofs from our publishing house, two columns upon which it rests: the Mass leaflets and the Klosterneuburg liturgical calendar. The Mass leaflets are sixteen page booklets which contain the Mass of the day with both the proper and the common parts. Millions of these leaflets were distributed in the past twenty years and have helped countless Catholics to understand the Mass and the ecclesiastical year.

The liturgical calendar, *Jahr des Heiles*, is a sign-post through the ecclesiastical year. In 1923 it appeared as a small directory; since then it has gone out year after year in ever larger editions and in ever greater size. Finally, it became a perpetual calendar which ran through all the phases of the Church's year and drew from every liturgical source. Upwards of 200,000 copies of this work have been distributed. The book is a daily companion for unnumbered priests and lay people. Bishops state that it lies upon their prie-dieu for daily meditation. Convents use it for table reading. To the missionaries in pagan lands it is a book of consolation. It has been translated into many languages. It is the only book of its kind in the world.

The publishing house has endeavored furthermore to disseminate all the liturgical texts—the Mass, the breviary, the ritual, and the pontifical—in inexpensive, popular editions.

The cradle of the lay liturgical movement is the small, eight hundred year old chapel of St. Gertrude, where, since 1922, the liturgical society has held its services. There, all that the lay liturgical Apostolate has striven for has been tried out. There, on all the Sundays and Holydays, divine worship has been celebrated with the active participation of the laity. There, the canonical hours have been said with the people. There, Holy Week and the other feasts, and the Easter services have been carried out liturgically. From all the corners of the globe have come priests and laymen to study there the possibility of the liturgy for the laity. This beautiful development was broken up in 1938 by National Socialism. In 1941 the monastery of Klosterneuburg was seized by the despots of the Third Reich and expropriated. We choir-monks had to go into exile. The publishing work had to be given up, and the modern printing presses were destroyed. I went into a workers' parish in Vienna (Florisdorf) where I remained for five years and worked for the parish. When the bombs fell on Vienna, the industrial district of Florisdorf was badly hit. My own house was demolished. For a year and a half I lived in the tower of the church. In September, 1946, I returned to our monastery, which had been restored to us. Now once again I can resume my literary and liturgical work. If God grants me life, I want to work on for these two blessings of the Catholic laity: the Bible and the liturgy.

EDITOR'S NOTE: Dr. Parsch died at Klosterneuburg in 1954. His autobiographical chapter, written expressly for *The Book of Catholic Authors*, was translated from the original German by Father Paul Day, C.M., professor at St. Joseph's College, Princeton, N. J.

English translations of some of Dr. Parsch's works are *The Liturgy of the Mass* (Herder, 1940), *The Breviary Explained* (id., 1952), *Know and Live the Mass* (Catholic Book Pub. Co., 1952), *The Church's Year of Grace* (Liturgical Press, 1953), and *Sermons on the Liturgy for Sundays and Feast Days* (Bruce, 1953).

HERTHA ERNESTINE PAULI

MOST OF THE BOOKS I HAVE WRITTEN IN THIS COUNTRY
deal with people, things, and ideas that are at home in
America but came from abroad, as I did. I was born in
Vienna, Austria, in 1909. My father was a scientist, my
mother a journalist, and as soon as I could write, I became
a dramatist: my plays based on children's classics from
all over the world, were performed before mothers and
aunts, with myself, of course, as producer, director, and
star. At seventeen I ran away from college to become
an actress, made my stage debut as Juliet, and later joined
Max Reinhardt's famous theater in Berlin, remaining until
Hitler came to power and Reinhardt left for America.
Then I went home to Vienna, quit the stage, and began
to write for a living.

I wanted to create characters of my own, instead of
acting out parts written by others, and from the beginning
I wrote about people whose lives I would have liked to live.

The hero of my first novel was Ferdinand Raimund, an actor who became a leading poet and playwright in the Vienna of Beethoven and Schubert (*Toni: ein frauenleben fuer Raimond*. Zsolnay, Wien, 1936). Publication of a second novel, about a great Austrian woman writer and fighter for peace, Baroness Bertha von Suttner, was halted by the Nazi seizure of Austria. My book (*Nur eine Frau*. Zeitbild, Wien, 1938) was banned, and I had to leave my homeland on the day of Hitler's entry.

From 1938 to 1940 I lived in Paris, working on a novel about an Austrian refugee girl in France. When the German armies entered Paris, I escaped on foot—always just a step ahead of the swastika columns and frequently strafed by the swastika planes—to southern France. One of my writer friends in that mass flight was Franz Werfel. Like Werfel, I passed through Lourdes, the town of St. Bernadette, and both of us remained grateful to her for the miracle of our rescue.

Brought to the United States in 1940 on an "emergency rescue visa" with the same group of writers, I did secretarial work in New York, then spent a year at scenario writing in Hollywood. I was glad to return to New York in 1942, when my first book in English was published. It was a biography of *Alfred Nobel* (L. B. Fischer, 1942), the "dynamite king" and founder of the Nobel Prizes. These awards for science, literature and peace had always been a subject of intense interest in our family, long before my brother Wolfgang received the 1945 Nobel Prize in Physics.

As a boy, Wolfgang had played "Stille Nacht" on the piano for us, each Holy Eve—and it was like a greeting from home when I heard the beloved carol ring out from Rockefeller Center at my first American Christmastime. But my friends here amazed me by calling "Silent Night" an American song; they did not know about its Austrian

origin, nor about its charming story.   I tried to write the
story for a magazine, but wherever I sent the article it
was turned down.   Sadly I related my discouraging experience at a Christmas party.   Among the guests was a
juvenile editor.   "Why don't you make a children's book
out of it?" she said.

I tried that, and found that I liked writing for children,
because there are no frontiers in the children's world, and
because they believe, as I do, in the conquest of reality and
in realization of dreams.   *Silent Night, Holy Night:* the
story of a song, was published by Knopf in 1943—and then,
to my joy and surprise, the *Reader's Digest* condensed it
as an article.

As for me, I continued to write for children and about
my favorite holiday.   My next two juveniles told the *Story
of the Christmas Tree* (Houghton, 1944) and of *St. Nicho-
las Travels* (*id.*, 1946).   In the publisher's office they called
me "the Christmas girl."   But I wanted to go on with adult
books as well.

A shining symbol was always before my eyes: the Statue
of Liberty, which had come here from abroad and had
greeted on my arrival like a familiar friend.   Looking
up its story, I found it a deeply human one, but one so
intertwined with American history that I hesitated to
undertake the job alone.   I found a collaborator in E. B.
Ashton (Ernst Basch), who had translated and edited my
Nobel book.   For five years we worked together on *I Lift
My Lamp* (Appleton, 1948), and after its publication we
decided that he would remain my "better English."   We
were married and settled down on Long Island, in a hun-
dred-year-old farmhouse behind a twenty-foot privet hedge
that encloses a fine playground for our dogs.

Since we have no children of our own, my first readings
of my stories are usually the children of our friends.   And
as they want to know about my grown-up books, too, I

turned our Statue of Liberty story into a juvenile, *The Golden Door* (Knopf, 1949), and am now writing the life of Alfred Nobel once more, this time for teen-agers.

Eventually, in *Lincoln's Little Correspondent,* I also did a story without any foreign background—but this was no sooner published than I returned to Europe for the first time since my flight. The visit was short and exciting, and to me its most touching encounter was with a red-headed little girl. Her father was an American flyer who had secretly married a German girl just before he was sent to the Pacific. His bride had died in giving birth to a child, who was raised by a hide-bound German grandmother while she dreamed only of her lost American father. And now, with the help of an American girl friend of mine, the little red-head had her dream come true.

After my return I knew that I had to tell this story to American children—not only because it fascinated me and because I loved the child, but above all because throughout this country there are now more and more such children, born in ruins abroad and come here to a new life and a home they never had.

Three is a Family (Washburne, 1955), as I called my story, was just finished when I received an invitation to contribute to the Vision Book series. I welcomed this challenge to write for children about Saints and their way of communicating visions to the world; to project an inner image has always seemed to me the highest of goals. And yet I was afraid that I might find no suitable theme for a Vision Book. I could think only of St. Bernadette who had seemed almost tangibly close to us at Lourdes—but her story, I felt sure, was too well known. But I was amazed to discover that there was as yet no children's book about Bernadette, who was herself a child at the time of her visions.

In writing *Bernadette and the Lady* (Farrar, 1956) I had a strange experience. I had trouble with the ending;

there were several ways of handling it, but none of them seemed quite right. Having done my best, and feeling not quite happy with the result, I left with a friend for a week's vacation on Cape Cod. Hot and tired from the long ride, we had just stopped to rest up in a small village when my friend cried, "Our Lady of Lourdes!", pointing at the door of a tiny church in front of us. We went in—and saw little Bernadette beside the altar, kneeling before her Lady as though alive! Then and there I knew how my story had to end.

My next Vision Book, *Christmas and the Saints* (Farrar), took me back to the Holy Night. I was astonished to discover how many Saints are connected with the story of the Nativity: they brought the vision of the Child in the manger from Bethlehem to us, passing it from hand to hand, as it were, from land to land, from generation to generation. Our thanks for the Christmas we know is due to the Saints, men and women and children, who devoted their earthly lives to the heavenly message of peace to all men of good will.

The message of peace was also the theme of my next adult book, published in the spring of 1957. This is another novel, a new version of the one that was halted by the Anschluss in 1938, about the life of the Austrian countess, novelist, and Nobel Peace Prize winner, Bertha von Suttner. The German edition appeared in Vienna in 1956. Here it is entitled *Cry of the Heart*. It is a book very close to my own heart, like a handclasp between my old and my new homes.

JOSEPHINE PHELAN

BORN IN HAMILTON, ONTARIO, CANADA, I RECEIVED MY EDU-
cation at the Loretto Academy, in Guelph, Ontario, where
my father moved when I was four years old. After high
school I attended the University of Toronto, continuing as
far as an M.A. degree in Canadian History and acquiring a
lasting interest in that subject. I have been a school
teacher, a publisher's assistant, and am now a librarian in
the Toronto Public Library.

After unsuccessful attempts at short story writing, I
turned to my first interest, history. I chose as a subject
Thomas D'Arcy McGee, a young Irish immigrant, a poet
and journalist, who rose to the rank of a minister of the
Crown in the Canadian government, but died in 1868 by
an assassin's bullet because of his opposition to the Fenians
who were raiding the Canadian borders.

This biography, *The Ardent Exile* (Macmillan of Canada,
1951), won me several awards including the Governor Gen-

eral's medal and the University of British Columbia medal for biography. Looking for other historical themes in the Canadian West, I found the material I was gathering for another biography turning into a boy's story of the days of the fur traders and the buffalo hunts. This story, *The Boy Who Ran Away* (Macmillan of Canada, 1954), had among its characters a very attractive historical personality, Father Albert Lacombe, the Oblate missionary. He became the subject of my new biography, *The Bold Heart* (Macmillan of Canada, 1956). I hope that this happy chain reaction will produce more historical subjects to write about.

My interests are books, writing, Canada, and many friends who with all their variety share one or the other of these interests.

I have always lived in Canada, except for a brief residence at the University of Wisconsin. My travelling has been in Canada and the United States, with the result that, to date, my books have travelled more widely than their author; reviews have turned up from as far afield as South Africa.

REVEREND GODFREY POAGE, C.P.

WHEN MY FRIENDS ASK HOW I STARTED WRITING, ALL I CAN do is smile. For my first published articles were travelogues and love-lorn columns in the Sunday magazine section of the Des Moines, Iowa, *Register and Tribune*.

All this began back in June of 1937. I had just finished a year of college at the Passionist Seminary in St. Louis, Missouri, and was looking for a summer job. The local newspaper needed filler-copy, and I volunteered to furnish it.

In the bales of manuscript that I turned out the first week, the editors selected one little three-hundred word article. But it was enough. I saw my name in print. There in a newspaper with half a million readers was a thought that had passed from my brain to a sheet of paper and through the medium of type to thousands of people. Something happened to me in that moment and some of the printer's ink must have passed into my blood. From then on I wanted to write.

Now, years later, I look back on those hours in the newspaper office as the most valuable technical training I ever
received. There I had to meet deadlines. There my material had to be tailored to a certain amount of space. Always my subject had to be concrete, definite, and clearly
presented.

As the weeks went by, the feature editor took more of
my articles and I gained more of his attention. Time and
time again I heard him groan as he worked over one of my
long, rambling articles: "Keep your sentences short; the
shorter, the better. Keep your paragraphs short; the
shorter, the better. Use plenty of periods!"

This advice kept my thoughts from bogging down in the
middle, and I learned that any time a reader has to go over
a sentence twice to get its meaning, I had misfired.

The following year I was elected to the editorship of the
Prepannual, the seminary publication. In my sophomorish
enthusiasm I thought that the editor was the one who
wrote the whole magazine. In consequence, I tried to rewrite most of the contributions, until the moderator, Father Emmanuel Sprigler, C.P., straightened me out. "Give
the others a chance," he ordered. "They have to learn
too."

When I headed for the Passionist Novitiate in St. Paul,
Kansas, in the summer of 1939, I carried along my love for
writing. It seemed to me that the apostolate of the pen
was the most fascinating possible. But in the novitiate
there was little time for writing. If I got half an hour a
day, I was doing well. I used most of this time to tran-
scribe the instructions and meditations given by Father
Malcolm LaVelle, C.P. These were the richest possible material for later conferences and retreats of my own, and
were always exquisitely worded and to the point.

The year following my novitiate, I was sent to St. Paul's
College, Detroit, for further studies. There I wrote my
first two popular vocational booklets, *Follow Me,* and *Fol-*

low Him. Most of the matter in these works I had given
many times over in talks to boys and girls. When it came
to actually publishing the material, I first mimeographed
copies of the proposed manuscripts and submitted them to
seventh and eighth grade teachers in the neighboring
parochial schools. Their students were asked to delete
any word or scratch out any section that did not appeal to
them.

When the manuscripts were returned, I correlated all
the corrections and criticisms. Practically every manuscript, for example, had the word "extraordinary" crossed
out. It finally dawned on me that this was too big a word
for most of the youngsters to read. They knew its meaning,
but simply skipped it in a text. I substituted "unusual"
and the sentence was easier to read. Now after fifteen
years of circulation, the sale of these two booklets has
topped three million.

In the years that followed I wrote other vocational pamphlets, but none has ever enjoyed the circulation of these
first two—with the exception of my latest, *Many Are
Called.* This is a booklet on answering parental objections
to religious vocations. It had an initial run of one hundred
thousand. Now the sales are getting close to a quarter
million.

After ordination, I was invited by the Central Office of
the Sodality to handle the vocation classes at the Summer
School of Catholic Action. There I came under the influence of the late Father Daniel A. Lord, S.J., and from
him I learned the importance of letter-writing. In the five
summers I spent with him I could not begin to calculate
the number of letters he wrote. I recall how once he
worked all day on letters as we travelled together across
the country in a Pullman. At the station I mailed about
forty letters for him and thought he was through for the
day. Later that evening he came to my hotel room and

inquired: "Do you know where there is a mailbox?" In his hand were seventeen more letters.

When I commented on this writing, he said "Letters are my favorite form of expression. For to me the task of writing is really the pleasure of a one-sided conversation. I fancy that across the table from me sits someone in whom I am interested, and to that person I pour out the ideas that seem important."

Another time Father Lord confided: "If you wait for inspiration, you will seldom if ever write. Writing is a craft. Learn your craft and exercise it as any other crafts- man does. When you have something to say, sit down at your typewriter and let go. Rarely in life does the genius produce the work of genius. Generally he is content with good craftsmanship."

I have quoted Father Lord at some length because I know of no other person with whom I have spent more time in my priesthood or who has influenced me more in writing.

However, it was not Father Lord, but the late Father Joseph Husslein, S.J., who induced me to bring out my first book. Father Husslein had been watching for young writers for his Science and Culture series, and thought he found a contributor in me. After attending some lectures I gave at St. Louis University in 1948, he asked me to put them into book form. The result was *Recruiting for Christ,* which was published by Bruce in the Fall of 1950.

During these years I was also doing a number of articles for various Catholic publications and continuing my pam- phlet writing. In 1952 I published *Catholic Religious Vo- cations* for the Vocational Guidance Manuals of New York, and in 1955 another guidance book for Bruce, entitled *For More Vocations*.

This brings me up to date. And all I need to add is that I have yet to write anything without putting at the top of

my paper the motto, "B.V.M." It is not that what I write
will contribute much to the glory of Our Blessed Mother,
but I do ask her help in putting the message over. I look
upon writing as an apostolate and to be truly and lastingly
effective it must have the blessing of God . . . and the smile
of Our Lady.

REVEREND JOHN F. T. PRINCE

MY EARLIEST RECOLLECTION IS THAT OF BEING SMACKED. The smacking was remarkable only in that it was a cheerful augury both of more to come and of my life-long immunity to the moral effect of smacks. As far as I can recollect, it had no effect at all and I went on doing it (whatever it was) : and I cannot even remember the name of the smacker. The latter is largely due to the fact that she was succeeded in her office (she was my nurse) by another, one Nurse Benham, who came to the family when I was three and stayed till I was nearly nine. She was an outstanding character, so much so that she obliterated all others in my infant memory. I was broken-hearted when she left; but though she herself departed, her influence remained: her standards were those to be adhered to, her judgments mine, and I verily believe they still are!

Her judgment was, on the whole, as sound as her intuition, and she had lots of commonsense. She had also a

more important virtue, and that was her extraordinary fidelity. Her loyalties were staunch and unchangeable as
far as people were concerned: once a friend, always a
friend; and she stuck by her friends through thick and
thin. Opprobrium on their account was nothing to her.
"Old friends," she would say, "are better than new." "Always?" I enquired. "Always," she said, and that was that.
Her opinions were almost as much sinecures as her friends.
This is not necessarily a virtue and may be quite the re-
verse like the terrifying unchangeableness of Miss Murd-
stone and her irrevocable judgments. Nurse Benham, however, did in one instance alter entirely her judgment and
way of life; that was when she became a Catholic.

Well I remember that outstanding event! My parents
were Anglicans of the High Church variety. But for many
years (longer, he used to aver, than he cared to say), my
father had been fully convinced of the truth of Roman
claims. But he procrastinated, salving his conscience by
making of himself a sort of signpost to Rome. And one
of the people he put on the right road was Nurse Benham.
He was a first-class apologist: a convincing and attractive
talker as well as a student. So that in the case of my nurse
not a long time elapsed between her speaking to him of her
religious difficulties and her arriving (already more than
half-instructed) at the door of the Oratory seeking admission to the Catholic Church. That was, so to speak, the
beginning of the end: my father had started sending his
own household before him into the Church: and now he
could no longer evade the issue. One evening in the spring
of 1914 I awoke from sleep (seven o'clock was bedtime) to
find my mother in the room half crying. She was talking
to my nurse and this is what I heard:

"I suppose you knew all this was coming, nurse?"

"I guessed."

"Won't he ever change his mind?"

"I think not."

"Or come back?"

"I'm sure he won't."

There was a fearful rift at first; then unreluctantly my mother followed my father and we all "came in."

That is how I come to be a Catholic and a convert. Entirely without personal credit in the matter. How did I become a priest?

I was never what is called "a religious child." We were sent (while still Protestants) to church on Sunday—to the country parish church nearby, whereas my father and mother attended an Anglo-Catholic church in the town some miles away. Nurse took us to church which was Evangelical, or Low Church; and I remained throughout the service on a mute condition bordering on terror. The vicar wore an apostolic halo of white hair (in fact, at one time I thought he *was* an apostle or at least intimately associated with the angels and saints) and having the gift of repetition, preached sermons which were both terrifying and interminable. I knelt down morning and night, by my bedside, but prayed (if I prayed at all) without devotion. When we became Catholics religion became at least colourful. That I came to regard it as much more than that was due, in the first instance, to my being sent unavoidably for a period (with Nurse Benham) to my maternal grandparents. They were ardent Protestants and no doubt considered it their duty to prove it to their seven year old Papist grandson and his nurse. They lived in a gloomy, rambling house in a small Midland town— everything was redolent of solid Victorian Protestantism except the nearby Catholic church, and that was out of bounds. I need not recount the details of persecution which followed the usual pattern. But I remember the hours which my grandmother devoted to railing against Popery. Her three brothers were clergymen in the Church of England and one of them, black-browed and bearded was a thousand times more terrible than the vicar at home.

From him, I fancy, did my grandmother (for she was really a religious and charitable woman) get her ammunition for the onslaught. Anyway, the effect, of course, was to develop an immense reverence for the Papacy and love of the Church which, please God, I may never lose. I loved the Church first when I first saw her hated and with that love came a pity for the folk that hated, and a great yearning somehow to help in the work of getting them to *see* so that they could no longer *hate*—any more than they could hate our Lord. There (if anywhere) was the beginning of a vocation: not in any conscious love of the church's liturgy nor in her external beauty nor in admiration of this or that priest or missioner, though later all these things were to be experienced. Through childhood and youth, through joys and sorrows (and of the latter, one stands out casting the long shadow of a mountain against the setting sun), the desire for the apostolate survived. I was ordained in 1931 at the age of twenty-four, after doing my studies at Fribourg University.

And how did I come to write? Or rather, why have I written such a lot—saying (so it seems to me) much the same thing over and over again?

I must admit that I wrote a great deal (even before I became a priest) without saying anything in particular. I also drew and painted pictures and continued to do so until my sight gave out. And my pictures (like my poetry and stories and fantasies, and even an operetta) sold. That was because, like most people, I needed money and the only way to get it in my case was to work for it.

I also travelled and had a great many adventures and met many people who had nothing at all to do with the Catholic Church or any other church. And the more people I met, the more like they seemed to be to the people that Nurse Benham talked about and even took me to see on her days out. It is true that the highlights of her world were a flour mill, complete with its miller, a lovely old

farmhouse, squalidly respectable streets which could however contain veterans of the Indian Mutiny and Balaclava
and many sad or sick or angry people who were friends of
hers. These, however, were just the people I was to meet
later, though one of them was a world-famous artist and
another a communist commissar. And though the 1914-
1918 war changed much, it had not changed human nature,
and the code by which one knew it. That code was Nurse
Benham's and through the use of it I arrived at certain
conclusions. There was, for instance, the great postwar
challenge of communism. I saw it from the angle not
only of the artist and the commissar and my own superiors,
but also through the eyes of the sick and sad and angry
friends of my old nurse. I recognized the same tired and
hungry faces, and God knows there were enough of them
in the 1920's and 1930's. I recognized also the same flash
in desperate eyes—and I knew that it was from fire that
could not be put out. Indeed, I began to see that it was
not desirable that it should be put out. "I am come to cast
fire upon the earth" and I found a formula for it. I started
to write articles and books about it and at the suggestion
of the late Father Bede Jarrett, O.P., I called it *Creative
Revolution*. That was the name of my first real book. It
was published in the United States, with a good preface
by the late Father Joseph Husslein, S.J., and was a Catholic Book Club selection.

For *Creative Revolution* was not an acidulous arraign-
ment of Bolshevik errors nor a documental calendar of
atrocities. These shock but do not convert. It was a demand that Christians conduct their lives so that by the
very force of example, the millions of disciples who acknowledge Christ as their leader, remake the world of today as He and His "chosen few" repatterned the Roman
Empire. "We shall then achieve the true revolution. For
we must rid ourselves of the delusion that in opposing
Bolshevism the Church falls into line with those who op-

pose it because it seeks to subvert the present wretched economic order. What the Church opposes is the materialistic philosophy of communism, negating all the true worth of man." Alas! we must admit that materialism is not peculiar to the Soviet. What the world needs is a revolution which would have the power to make Christianity fully effective as the best means of completely reforming modern society. The revolt of the twentieth century is an outstanding indictment of neglectful Christians, and only when Capital and Labour will revolt against Mammon with the same energy that Bolsheviks have revolted against God can we hope for light. The best antidote for the failure of modern society is the Christian (that is, Creative) Revolution!

Today all this, of course, sounds pretty obvious but it was not so twenty five years ago and there was a whole lot of hammering to be done before the nail got really driven home. It is, in short, the *constructive* approach that is needed. But people find destruction so much easier. (It was more fun, wasn't it, until we were taught better, to knock our bricks about when we were children?) So with communism. I believe, for instance, that there can be nothing more futile and more dangerous than the belief that communism can be destroyed by military warfare, that you can fight to the finish (in the spiritual arena) with anything but spiritual weapons. Foster this illusion (as the enemy would have you do) and you will make sure of a victorious communism rising, rank and prolific out of the rubble and the carnage.

To Father Bede I once quoted Longfellow's pathetic lines:

> "Poor sad humanity
> Through all the dust and heat
> Turns back with bleeding feet
> By the weary round it came

> Unto the simple thought
> By the great Master taught."

"When will that be?" I queried with a sigh. And Father Bede answered, "Perhaps not today, but for certain tomorrow." God grant he was right!

EDITOR'S NOTE: Father Prince, a priest of the diocese of Plymouth, England, is a frequent contributor to *Blackfriars, The Month, Clergy Review, Irish Ecclesiastical Record, Catholic Herald, The Tablet, Punch*, etc. His books include *The Death of Iris* (Curtis, Switzerland, 1928), *Creative Revolution* (Bruce, 1937), *A Christian in Revolt* (Douglas Organ, London, 1946), *A Guide to Pacifism* (Shelton & Murray, England, 1956), *Peter the Ludicrous*, an operetta (1925), as well as poems and carols.

MARY PURCELL

SOMETIMES I AM CROSS-EXAMINED BY PEOPLE WHO WANT to know why I have, up to the present, written only four books, while my brother has five to his credit. Remembering that I am almost ten—and probably look twenty—years older than Paddy, I try to apolozige for myself. But the interrogation usually goes a step further. I am asked what saint did I write about in my first book. I apologize again and abjectly explain that *The Pilgrim Came Late* was a book about a murderer. After that, naturally, conversation lags a bit. Before I've made up my mind to wax confidential about the dancing—and similar diversions—that took up a lot of spare time in my twenties, or to mention the card-playing—and similar diversions— that absorbed a lot of time and money during my thirties, someone has passed the inevitable, if fatuous, remark that life begins at forty. I agree, shake hands all around, and take to my heels.

I was born all of fifty-one years ago, on May 28, 1906,
"by the banks of the Suir that flows down by Mooncoin."
Our particular perch on the Suirside was named Moonveen,
a townland marked only on Ordnance Survey maps. It
was a quiet and lovely place with a wood where The Hunt
came, a river bend round which the fishermen rowed, and
wonderful characters like Ned Mack Doyle, Billy the Boll,
Big Henry and Lizzie Mistletoe, and Biddy-Bean-Bhocht.

My parents taught in Carrigeen school. When I was
four we moved to Carrigeen village and I lived there for
the next ten years, attending my mother's school and going every Saturday to the Mercy Convent, Waterford, for
lessons in Irish, step-dancing, violin, piano, painting, and
heaven-known-what-else. My next five years were spent
in St. Louis Convent, Monaghan, and from 1926 to 1928 I
was in Carysfort Training College for Teachers. From
1928 to 1935 I taught in Dunmore School, just outside
Kilkenny. Since 1935 I have taught in Dublin city, first
in Marino, and for the past fifteen years in St. Joseph's, a
school on the Quays, just across the Liffey from Guinness's.

I wrote a crime novel in 1946 and, simultaneously, began
writing feature articles for a juvenile paper—mostly potted
biographies of heroic characters likely to appeal to young
people. In 1947 I got the idea of writing about St. Joan
and began research work in earnest, trying to fit as much
French and history study as possible into fairly full days.
Later that year, I began to work as assistant editor of *The
Pioneer,* the organ of the Pioneer Total Abstinence Association of the Sacred Heart, a reparation society num-
bering almost half a million Irish people.

I had a bit of bad luck that year when, on my first visit
to France in connection with my studies, I was unmerci-
fully bitten by relay squads of mosquitoes and got a blood-
poisoning that necessitated my taking the first available
plane back. Aer Lingus was booked up for weeks, so, after
a nightmare twenty-four hour wait at le Gare des Invalides,

I got transport on an America-bound plane that was touching down at Shannon. I had to be rushed to Barrington's Hospital where I spent the remaining weeks of my summer holidays!

I do not find that teaching school all day, and switching over to writing—either for *The Pioneer* or my own books —in the evenings, makes me over-tired. In fact, one occupation acts as a foil to the other. Being with the little ones—four to eight years are the ages in our school—has the effect of making me not quite equal to adult company for several hours after school; but an hour of intensive study pulls me right back among the grown-ups again. Similarly, after an evening spent in concentrating on writing or reading or study, when I am likely to arrive in the classroom in a particularly exalted or abstracted state of mind, I have those about me who can be guaranteed to bring me to earth again speedily.

Only the other morning I decided to improve the shining hour by telling, in simplified form, an anecdote I had come across in some reading the previous night. In the middle of my tale, I nabbed two "whisperers" in the back desk. The chief culprit was told to stand up and shout out for the benefit of all the subject under discussion. It was myself, not my story. And the gist of the confab was that "Joe on'y said the teacher's hair was gettin' very grey." See what I mean!

Writing does not come easily to me. It took me more than four years to write *The Halo on the Sword*, a story of St. Joan. Frequently I have to rewrite a paragraph many times before it satisfies me. If I see a play or read a new poem that appeals to me, I can then write with great speed and ease, going on far into the night. But such poems and plays are rare, and if you want to know what appealed to me most in recent years, the play I liked best was Bryan Mac Mahon's *Bugle in the Blood;* while Padraic Fallon's poem "The Countryman" and the Gaelic poems of Seumas

O h-Aodha and Seumas O'Neill struck some responsive chord in me.

I can go for several weeks without any recreation. Then I go on a 'thriller-binge,' reading a cross-section of all the latest in murders. Not cleverly-constructed problems in detection, but just murder stories. I often promise myself that, if ever I have spare time again, I will write another murder story. I spend my time during bus rides and traffic-jams in thinking up murder. Indeed, I have four perfectly fool-proof ways of doing away with the Awful People who giggle at the wrong lines and times in Abbey, Gate, and Longford plays. But, alas! even mayhem isn't quite what it used to be. As the Cost of Living goes up the Murder Business deteriorates. So, for the moment, I have foresworn my evil designs and am cleaving to the saints.

EDITOR'S NOTE: Books by Miss Purcell include *The Pilgrim Came Late* (Clonmore, 1948), *The Halo on the Sword:* St. Joan of Arc (Newman, 1952), *Don Francisco:* the story of St. Francis Xavier (Newman, 1954), and *Matt Talbot and His Times* (Neman, 1955).

CORINNE ROCHELEAU
ROULEAU

MRS. WILFRID ROULEAU—CORINNE EVANGELINE ROCHELEAU
—was born (1881) and brought up in Worcester, Massachusetts, where her parents and grandparents on both sides of the family have been established for nearly a hundred years. She had a normal and happy childhood, among her brothers and sisters, four of whom are still living. In her ninth year, deafness developed, progressed swiftly, and soon grew almost complete. In spite of the best medical care, prolonged for years, deafness has remained practically total.

There followed a period of schooling in American and Canadian convents, the most fruitful years being the four spent at a school for deaf girls conducted by the Sisters of Providence in Montreal, where she received private lessons from two expert teachers, one for French and one for English, while a third taught her to regain her lost voice and to become an expert lip-reader, which soon followed. Then

she was sent for a year to a private school with hearing
pupils, and to the Art Museum of Worcester for classes in
drawing. Later, there was a year of travel and study in
Europe. From which it can be seen that her education was
not entirely academic. But it fostered in her a great taste
for study, an appreciation of fine things, and the feeling
that, lacking a college degree, she should go on studying
and learning practically forever, which has been her schedule ever since.

It might be pertinent to add here that her mother, a
church organist, had given her piano lessons very early, so
that, when deafness closed down on Corinne permanently,
she had had four years of precious initiation in musical
"primaries," so to speak. Although this made the first few
years of deafness doubly hard to bear, eventually it made
matters easier and pleasanter for her, since she could understand, without looking too blank, what people meant
when musical matters were mentioned. Her excellent
memory carries to this day a collection of airs, old songs,
and hymns held over from childhood days.

While still in her teens, she lost both father and mother.
She and her four sisters kept house together; a married
brother occupied the other half of the family home. Two
sisters having married and gone, Corinne for the next seven
years, acted as housekeeper, counselor and first friend to
her two youngest sisters, still at school. After which she
decided to fend for herself. She attended a business college for a refresher course, then presented herself for Civil
Service examinations. Having passed, she was appointed
clerk in the research department of the Census Bureau in
Washington, D. C., where she stayed for two years. The
climate of the Capital not agreeing with her health, she
reluctantly resigned and left work and a city which had
altogether satisfied her. Returning to Worcester, her
brother (H. Oscar Rocheleau, later and for twelve years
high sheriff of Worcester County, the first and only Cath-

olic sheriff that old Yankee bailiwick has had since Co-
lonial times), asked her to take over the office of one of the
several clothing stores owned by the Rocheleau family in
New England. This she did without much enthusiasm,
but there she remained, nevertheless—and soon as a full
partner—for seventeen years, or until the recession and
depression which swept the country in 1928-29 also swept
that store from the street where it had held open foors for
nearly half a century.

Now pretty well cleaned out as to money, but still un-
daunted, although in her forties, she went back to her
Montreal convent school for another refresher course, this
time in rest and meditation on ways and means. This
convent school has played an important part in her life.
She had returned to it year after year for a sort of continuation course in voice culture, since it is necessary for
people totally deaf (and she has never used a hearing aid)
to give continued care and much attention to the speaking
voice, if they want to acquire and retain a normal one.
Her old teachers always received her with open arms, and
the pupils looked up to her with a sisterly curiosity, while
she willingly shared with them the experiences of her own
life "outside," in a more worldly and strenuous area.

Last but not least, she found in Montreal her best guide
and wisest mentor in the person of a former chaplain of
the school, then auxiliary bishop of the Canadian metropolis, Mgr. Alphonse Deschamps. Himself an excellent ed-
ucator, he had directed her in her studies and also encouraged her to do research work along educational lines,
especially about the deaf-blind—those little known but very
numerous "Helen Keller cases," as they are sometimes
called. This had already led to her writing an extensive
biographical study of one such case, a peculiarly difficult
one, successfully dealt with at the Montreal school. This
story of little Ludivine Lachance, titled *Hors de sa Prison,*

was published in Montreal in 1927 and crowned by the French Academy the following year.

Back in Montreal for a sabbatical year imposed by the depression, she put the finishing touches to another work, done in collaboration with Miss Rebecca Mack, of Cincinnati, a woman who had long specialized in work for the blind. This volume, intended primarily for teachers of the deaf and blind, was titled *Those in the Dark Silence* (Volta Bureau, Washington, D. C., 1930). In the same month of July, 1930, Miss Rocheleau addressed a meeting of the American Association of Teachers of the Deaf, in conference at Milwaukee.

Then she decided she had done about enough social work, and had better get around to living a normal family life at last, her tastes having always been domestic anyhow. The following month, August, 1930, she married Wilfrid Rouleau, a retired chief examiner for French and Spanish work in the Government Printing Office, Washington, D. C., where they returned to live.

The years in Washington were the happiest in her life. And there was still time for a few of the old interests: as chairman of a committee of the Volta Bureau; as translator and proof-reader for publications of the Department of the Interior and the Pan American Union (now the Bureau of American Republics) ; for longish articles written on various subjects; for lectures before educational bodies in New York, Philadelphia and Washington. But always there was the glad return home.

But some things are too perfect to last. Death took her husband in 1940, and she returned to the Montreal convent school, where the Sisters also maintain a sort of French style "pension" as an annex. There she spends much of her time, varied by stays in the United States.

And there is always work to do. At the request of the school authorities, she gave a three-year course of lectures in the teacher-training department. This course has been mimeographed for future use. She also revised, brought up-to-date and translated into English her *Hors de sa Prison*. In 1947 she was asked to speak before the century-old Société Historique de Montréal, the meeting being presided over by the president of the University of Montreal, Mgr. Olivier Maurault; and her address was later published in the *Bulletin* of the Franco-American Historical Society of Boston. For the sum total of her works she was presented with the Grand Medal of Honor of this Society in November, 1947.

In 1948 Longmans of Toronto published her first novel, *Laurentian Heritage*. It is a story of the peaceful and picturesque way of life led by the well-to-do French Canadian country folk before the turn of the present century, and which remains even today much the same in its essentials; a way of life familiar to the author, the sixth generation of whose relatives still own and cultivate the land they bought from the Indians in the 1700's.

And so, most of the time, straight down the long years it has been working, studying, reading, writing,—with a quiet zone for meditation. All of that has brought her a deeper, more sympathetic understanding of human nature, fine contacts, some precious friendships, much generous appreciation from various sources, and the intimate feeling that her own life has not been useless. This makes for contentment, since it seems to her that these, with the Faith that lights and warms them all, are the main ingredients of what we call happiness in this world.

FRANK SCULLY

THE AUTHOR OF TWO GREAT UNPUBLISHED WORKS: THAT
(1) children should be seen and not heard but authors
should be neither seen or heard, they should be *read*, and
(2) that governments should pay authors for ploughing
under every third idea and pay publishers ninety per cent
of parity for all remainders, I often wonder why no one
ever suggested that I run for higher office than ringmaster
of the Scully Circus and its Trained Fleas from Heaven.

I have survived the wounds of living for sixty years and
know that my number is up. This is a pity, because writers
don't really begin to know how to write until they have
been trying for at least forty years. By then the millions
of words they have put together and somehow got into
print are really contrapuntal exercises. Only last week I
wrote my first piece worth preserving. It was a Prayer
for Writers. I wrote it on the eve of attending a Retreat
for Married Couples at El Cajon, California. The retreat

master was Bishop Charles F. Buddy of San Diego.   He
has a diocese that sprawls behind the smog, fog, grog and
hog-eat-hog that has become the City of Los Angeles, now
the third largest in the country, and quite sure that in ten
years it will be the largest.   If it achieves that goal, it will
be the largest city in the world to gas itself to death.

I am, if nothing else, an authority on survival.   I was
born in Steinway, a minor note in the symphony of Greater
New York, on April 28, 1892.   I was educated in a high
school named after William Cullen Bryant, a poet who
once edited the New York *Post*.   I overdid in athletics and
was injured so badly I was carted off to my first hospital
with osteomyelitis of the femur, a couple of expensive
words meaning an abscess in the thigh bone.   Between
operations I managed to attend the School of Journalism
of Columbia University and work on *The Sun* evenings.
I ended college with a profit of $385, all medical bills paid.

I then added tuberculosis of my lungs to my osteomyelitis
of the femur, and from there on began adding maladies as
if I were decorating a Christmas tree.   For the next twenty
years I wrote my way out of thirty hospitals in seven
countries, chasing an elusive cure.   Without these troubles,
it is doubtful that I would ever have got out of New York.
With them I saw much of America and Europe, half the
time from a horizontal position.

By 1927 I was up enough to become publicity and advertising director of Metro-Goldwyn-Mayer productions in
Nice, France.   I found the Riviera to be like Tucson, Arizona, except that it was on a tideless blue sea instead of
on the great American desert. I began meeting notables
until they could be rated a dime a dozen.   I was even
elected president of a motion picture producing company,
which was doing fine until the invasion of Hollywood pictures equipped with a sound track blitzed us out of business.

Between times, I made my calls on hospitals, hoping that
one final operation would kill or cure me.   They always

ended by doing neither. On one occasion, however, infection had spread so far that it appeared that only an amputation of my leg would save my life—if it didn't kill me.

It was about this time in my life that love entered it. I had met a Norwegian mother and her two daughters at a *pension* in Nice. We all became great friends, and the youngest of the group would run errands for me. She finally took a job as secretary of sorts until it was time for the family to return to Oslo. We parted in Paris, a sweet place for such a sorrow.

The girl's name was Alice Mellbye Pihl. Her great-grandfather was Norway's foremost historian. Her mother was a fine pianist and painter. Alice was about nineteen. I was thirty-seven. We were secretly engaged when she left for Oslo and I left for London. I doubt that either of us thought that anything would come of the engagement. After all, Paris is a very romantic place. Besides, I was a cradle Catholic and she was a cradle Lutheran.

But when word reached Norway that I was dying in the south of France, her mother saw in her little *pike's* eyes something mothers see even before those in love see. So she went out, bought a ticket for her little Alice from Oslo to Nice, got her some new clothes and a new hat and sent her to save my life if it were at all possible.

She arrived shortly after I was removed from the operating room, and for the next three months fought harder for my life than I did myself. It was not the glossy sort of fight one reads about in women's magazines. She slugged, washed sheets, floors, sterilized dressings, and made up for the deficiencies of the hospital and staff. She was the most beautiful nurse I have ever seen, and by that time I had seen hundreds.

Before this crisis had brought us together again, I had knocked off a ghosting job that was quite a success. It went out under the title of *My Reminiscences As a Cowboy* by Frank Harris. It sold 40,000 copies in America, which

was good for 1930, and about 12,000 in England. It had
one flaw, however, which should interest writers. I wrote
my own contract and was told that it would be invalid if
it did not contain a time clause. I put one in for five years.
Later the book was sold to Hollywood for motion pictures.
But I got no part of this, for in writing the contract I had
bilked myself out of all rights after five years!

My next plunge into the book world was *Fun in Bed*. I
suppose many people bought it never suspecting that it was
a handbook for convalescents. It became a best-seller and
hung on for years. Being in the middle between the
surgeon and the undertaker, how could I lose! I wrote six
of these books. They are still around. The last one was
the cream of them all and was called *The Best of Fun in
Bed*.

After *Fun in Bed*, now down to one lung, one leg and
hardly more than one idea, I wrote another best-seller.
This too was a ghosting job. It was Frank Harris's *Life
of Bernard Shaw*. I turned out about three books a year
for a while, besides writing a weekly column for *Variety*,
the bible of show business, and some magazine articles and
short stories.

Somehow, in between all these literary activities, Alice
and I were married civilly in Paris and in a chapel in Nice.
It was a mixed marriage. Our first child, a son, was born
in Paris. Our home was in a villa on a hill overlooking
Nice, but the hospitals were better in Paris.

Everybody who was anybody (and who isn't *somebody?*)
seemed to come to that villa. Many of them came on a
downbeat in their lives, and among these were Jimmy
Walker and Betty Compton. It was after he had been
bounced or resigned as mayor of New York. I was asked
to write their story and all sorts of fantastic offers came
pouring in, as this was before magazines like *Confidential*
came along to foul up still further the fouled up private
lives of notables.

In all this, Alice was quietly edging her way into the Catholic fold and in the spring of 1933 she was baptized by Abbe Van den Daele. Privately, I thought that this was a cross I was being asked to bear, because I had looked on most converts as rather humorless and driving people, and I was down to a slow t.b. tread. She insists to this day that it was my precept and example that turned her from a Lutheran to a Catholic, though I still can't believe I was ever for a moment *that* good.

In the summer of 1933, we left for New York to see old friends and for Alice to give birth to another baby. We planned to return to our villa in Nice in the fall. We never went back. Instead, we were lured to Hollywood on a picture contract. Ordered to rush out by plane, we took a steamer by way of the Panama Canal instead. I insisted that I was not well enough to work in a studio and was permitted to work at home. But I was told that this could not be further east than Pasadena. It seems that William Faulkner had asked for a similar privilege and when the producer called his hotel to find out how his script was progressing learned that Faulkner had returned to Mississippi. When he said home, he meant *home!*

Though I can seemingly do as much writing in a given year as most professionals, I am not cut out for clock-punching. My health fails me for long stretches at a time. So when my studio contract expired, I was glad to take the money and go back to my old way of nursing myself along between literary labors.

We took the money and built a house on a hill that overlooked Hollywood and Los Angeles. In those days we could see the sea at our right. Our home looked down into the schoolyard of the Blessed Sacrament parish. We could even see if our children were playing hookey. Our home was called Bedside Manor and there I worked with the hope of being interrupted.

By then heavy industry began moving into the Los Angeles basin, and from our hilltop we could see the small beginnings of smog far to the south of us. Little by little it crept north, east, south and west. So we looked around, as the military say, to retreat to a previously prepared position.

We found it ninety miles east of Los Angeles. After the success of *Behind the Flying Saucers,* we bought a ranch at Desert Springs (Alt. 4100 feet. Pop. 191), and the first task we put ourselves to was converting a bunkhouse into a chapel. By 1957 it had been in its sixth year. It is called Our Lady of the Desert and is the only house of worship of any kind within many miles. It was built to house fourteen people but we rarely have less than twenty five for Sunday Mass, the porch takes care of the overflow. The Blessed Sacrament is there from spring to autumn.

Winters we repair to Palm Springs ninety miles to the south, because the school problem is not very easy to solve in Desert Springs, whereas in Palm Springs anyone who can walk a mile for a Camel can walk to a parochial school. It was in Desert Springs that I wrote *Blessed Mother Goose,* a Catholic version of the old nursery rhymes. I removed all the meanness and beatings and British propaganda from the classic.

In Palm Springs I wrote the first half of my autobiography. It was called *Cross My Heart* and was a Catholic Digest book club choice for December, 1955. I should get around to the sequel in a year or two.

Meanwhile, every week I contribute "Scully's Scrapbook" to *Variety* and every month for seven years have been contributing a piece called "Just a Moment" to *The Way of St. Francis.* I am paid in Hail Marys by the *Way.* There was talk of increasing these, but, fearing that this would only be contributing to the general inflation, the editors decided against it.

Two of our children were married in 1956, a third was in nurse's training school at Mercy Hospital, San Diego, and two younger ones were in parochial school, the last starting in the fall of 1956. Whether there will be anymore is not in the hands of the disciples of Margaret Sanger but in the hands of God.

My chief non-literary interest is searching for a cure for muscular dystrophy. I am president of the California foundation of this work. Our executive director is Martha McGeein, a Catholic and a victim herself. We have a project at the U.C.L.A. Medical Center, and anyone who really believes that he can't take it with him and wants to give it to us can send his check to her (Los Angeles 19) or to me at 2096 Calle Felicia, Palm Springs, California (End of the Commercial).

Pax et Bonum, as we Franciscan Tertiaries say.

EDITOR'S NOTE: Mr. Scully was Knighted by Pope Pius XII, in the Order of St. Gregory the Great, in December of 1956. He is a past president of the Catholic Interracial Council of Hollywood. His books include *Blessed Mother Goose* (House-Warven, 1951, and Greenberg, 1954), and *Cross My Heart* (Greenberg, 1955).

JAMES GERARD SHAW

WRITING IS A DISEASE, A TRADE, AND AN ART. I HAVE THE disease, work at the trade, and am as fascinated by the art as a lunatic with the moon.

The disease set in early. When I was about ten and living in Scotland I showed a "poem" to my Irish mother who gave me a one-sentence criticism that says everything that need be said about all the verse I have ever written: "It may be the God's truth, Jimmy, but it's no poetry."

Much later, when my head was crammed with knowledge I was sure no one had ever possessed before, I burned to write something the world would not willingly let die. Nothing but the best would do and I scorned to lower myself to the level of the popular professional writer. My superior knowledge and my undoubted genius could not be wasted on the commonplace, could not be prostituted for a byline or a buck. I would starve in an attic and write, really write. I was drunk with words like "scholarship," "art," "truth" and "beauty." I talked endlessly about them . . . and wrote nothing.

I told myself that I was a perfectionist, an absolutist, and it took more years than I care to remember before I realized that there was another word for it. I was a coward. I was afraid of the challenge, afraid of defeat.

By the same token, I was lazy, shrinking from the hard work of compelling thought to words. For writing is the hardest of hard work. Any excuse will do to turn away from that blank page in the typewriter. One time, after I had found that attic and all the freedom in the world to write, I shut myself up with the typewriter and swore that I would not open the door for three days. I sat down, put in a fresh sheet of paper and stared at it for half-an-hour. Then I started looking hopefully around to see if I had forgotten to lay in cigarettes or sausages or bread or anything that would give me an excuse to go out. But everything was unhappily there. I sat down again and stared some more. My eyes fell on the rough, bare boards of the floor. I said to myself, "Shaw, this is a disgrace! Here you have been in this place for six weeks and have done no more than swish a mop a few times over this floor." So I got up, pushed the typewriter aside, found a scrubbing brush and a pail of hot water, got down on my hands and knees and scrubbed that floor thoroughly to its fartherest corners.

Anything but write.

I was an egoist then and I am an egoist now. The only difference is that I know more about my ego. I know that I have some things that I want to express and a certain urge to find words for them. I know that the higher the thing I want to express, the more my words will fail me. But I also know, in the words of a real writer, "For want of me the world's work will not die."

This is not of itself a happy knowledge. But it brings

freedom, freedom to be myself, freedom to satisfy my urge to write by working at the trade of writing with whatever skill I acquired in studying the art.

Journalism helped set me free. It gave me a deadline, the necessity of putting something down and letting it go. To my surprise (and my humiliation) I found that some pieces I had ripped off as fast as I could make my fingers move read much better than things I had labored over for weeks. I lost all self-consciousness about seeing myself in print. I learned that the only difference between a writer and a person who is not a writer is that the writer writes.

A young lady, without knowing it, pushed me into finishing my first book after years of stalling. She hit me between the eyes with a French saying which means, "Getting the thing done is part of art."

Writing that book brought me one of those rare illuminations that come from sudden and personal realization of an obvious truth. I discovered all by myself that if you write one page at a time the pages will actually pile up until there are enough of them for a book. Up to then I had written in mad bursts, sometimes all through the night. If it couldn't be done at once, I felt, it couldn't be done at all. I had learned the lesson of the tortoise and the hare.

The trade of being a Catholic writer, at which I keep working, is not a profitable one materially. But it has its rewards. There is more satisfaction in having told two thousand people how the Middle Ages made the rosary than there can be in having told ten million how Marilyn Monroe makes her bed. A trade is not only a means of earning a living. It is also a way of spending your life.

Writing is still hard work for me (I put this article off for two months on the pretext of thinking it over and finally sat down with only the faintest idea of what I was going to say), but I am rather glad of that. I believe it was Mauriac who said that writing is hard and hateful because the writer knows he has to wring out his heart's blood. When words come easily it is usually because they mean nothing to you. And they are likely to mean exactly as much to the reader.

I do both kinds of writing. I am reasonably content to be a bridge between the people I would like to be and the people who do not yet know those other people, a ladder between the knowledge within my reach and minds that need a ladder to get to it. That much purpose I have kept.

But I must be honest and admit that I still hope that practice of the craft does not forbid achievement in the art. I still have hankerings after immortality. I should like to write before I die one single sentence that will be worth the time spent in reading it.

By way of autobiography: I was born in London, England, May 20, 1909, got out of there at three, and finished high school in Scotland at fifteen, having spent three months of every year till then in my mother's County Donegal. I went to sea and worked for three years before going to Loyola College, Montreal. Since then I have commuted between the United States and Canada as student, teacher, journalist, editor, and free-lance writer. I am unmarried and work where circumstances take me.

I have probably been most widely read in some verses called "Our Lady of the Broom," most frequently read in a column "Among Ourselves," and derived most writing satisfaction from putting years of research into a book called *The Story of the Rosary*.

At the moment I am doing what I would like to be doing for the rest of my life: gathering material for one book, writing another, and waiting for the last one to come off the press.

EDITOR'S NOTE: Books by Mr. Shaw are *The Story of the Rosary* (Bruce, 1954), *Our Lady of the Cape* (Palm Publishers, 1954), *Edwin*

Vincent O'Hara: an American Prelate (Farrar, 1957); he collaborated on *English Voices* (Sadlier, 1946) and *Born Catholics* (Sheed, 1954), and he is writing a life of St. Columcille for Farrar, Straus & Cudahy's Vision Books series.

REVEREND PAUL SIWEK,
S.J.

WITH THE EXCEPTION OF MY APOLOGETICAL LECTURES DE-
livered in Paris, and later published under the title *In
Search of God,* all my works have been of a scientific nature. From my youth, science has seemed to me the highest
ideal after God. With my entrance into the Society of
Jesus (in my native Poland, at the age of fifteen), this
belief has lost none of its force with me. On the contrary,
it has been strengthened. For I see in science one of the
most powerful weapons in the apostolate for God and the
salvation of souls. Indeed, how otherwise can we reach
non-Catholic intellectuals and move them to give up their
atheism, materialism, freudianism, or other abberations?
They will never put a foot in our churches. They will
never read a publication written for the faithful. The only
way to reach them is through books of a scientific nature.
These they will read if only to try to refute us, and in
reading them they will, in spite of themselves, learn much

that they need to know; they will get a better idea of the
Catholic religion, and thereby surely many of them will
return to God. Hence, one should not be surprised that
Popes Pius XI and Pius XII insisted so strongly on "the
apostolate of science" in their allocutions to the professors
and students of the Roman colleges. Nor that of all the
forms of the modern apostolate of the Jesuits, the present
General of the Society did not hesitate to give precedence
to science.

The science to which I devoted myself was philosophy,
and the problems which particularly interested me were
those commonly called metaphysical psychology. Its object is the existence of the soul and its nature,—its spirituality, immortality, free will, affections, tendencies, and
so on. Experimental psychology, which I studied in the
Psychological Institute in Paris, was also of great help to
me in solving these problems.

My first researches were on the relation between soul
and body. The results are contained in my three theses;
the first, *The Psychological Parallelism According to Spinoza,* was presented to the Gregorian University in Rome
for my degree of Aggregate Professor; the other two were
published in Paris in the Collection des Grands Philosophes,
and were entitled *L'âme et le corps d'après Spinoza,* and
La psychophysique humaine d'après Aristote. Through
them I won the degree of Doctor of Philosophy (Docteur
ès Lettres) of the French State after a defense of my
theses which lasted for five consecutive hours. In all kindness, may I take the liberty here of warning our students
against the "doctorat de la Sorbonne," commonly called
"the little doctorate." It is lightly regarded in France and
abroad is scornfully called "the export doctorate."   ⟨

In my theses on Spinoza, I tried to prove the nullity of
the monistpantheist solution of psychological problems,
that is, of the problems which concern the mutual relations
of soul and body. In the thesis of Aristotle I gave the solu-

tion which alone satisfies all the requirements of reason
and experience.

From 1921 to 1930, I taught at the Gregorian University.
To encourage my students to study Aristotle (in my opinion, the world's greatest philosopher), I translated his
psychological work, *Peri Psyches,* from the Greek into
Latin. To my translation, I added the Greek text and a
commentary. This had necessitated my studying all the
Greek manuscripts which included any Aristotelian psychology, and thus I was able to emend the Greek classical
text and to clarify certain passages which had hitherto
remained obscure. The result was my *Aristotelis De Anima
libri tres,* which was published by the Gregorian University.

For the same reason, I undertook the study of all the
Greek manuscripts of the Aristotelian work generally
known as the *Parva Naturalia,* dealing with sensation,
memory, dreams, longevity, life, and death. This study
covered a hundred and ten manuscripts and required ten
years of assiduous labor in the libraries of Rome, Florence,
Venice, Milan, Naples, Udine, Paris, Oxford, Madrid,
Escoriale, Vienna, Munich, Berne, and Constantinople.
This long and costly research was made possible by the
generosity of the pre-World War II Polish government.

To Spinoza, besides the two books previously mentioned,
I devoted two other works. The first of these, *Spinoza et
le panthéisme religieux,* was honored by a letter of con-
gratulations from Pope Pius XI sent me through his secretary of State, Cardinal Eugenio Pacelli. The second appeared under the title *Au coeur du Spinozisme.* In both of
these works I explained and criticized the foundations of
Spinoza's philosophy, which still exerts a great influence
on philosophers. It forms the basis of almost all the
modern pantheistic systems, while the Communists, on the
other hand, see in Spinoza their true "father."

In 1934, Cardinal Hlond invited me to address the Thomist Congress at Poznan on the theory of the reincarnation of souls (metempsychosis), the basic dogma of Theosophy, Anthroposophy, Latin Spiritualism, Brahamanism, Buddhism, and other systems. It is very popular in many countries of Europe, America and Asia; and it constitutes a serious menace to true religious faith.

My series of studies in this field were collected and published in Polish, French, Spanish, and Portuguese, and later in English under the title of *The Enigma of the Hereafter*. It refuted in advance, so to speak, the theories of Mr. Bernstein's unfortunately popular book, *The Search for Bridey Murphy*. His arguments in favor of the reincarnation of souls have no validity, as I proved in my review of his book in the May, 1956, issue of *The Priest*.

On June 10, 1940, Mussolini declared war on the Allies. As my name was on the German black list, I was forced to flee from Rome as soon as possible. After many hazardous experiences, I eventually succeeded in reaching Rio de Janeiro, Brazil. There I was invited to deliver a series of public lectures sponsored by the Centro Don Vital. For my subject, I chose the eternal problem of evil, which was then taking a particularly tragic form in the atrocities being perpetrated by the Nazis on their innocent victims. I had to show how evil could be reconciled with the idea of a just and infinitely good God. These lectures were published in French and Spanish. The English edition, *The Philosophy of Evil*, included only the first part of the lectures, that which treats of the finality of evil in the existence of living creatures, especially in that of man. The second part, which deals directly with the relation of God to evil, the publisher omitted as being "too theological." Some of it, however, has appeared recently as articles in various scholarly reviews, and I hope to have it published soon in book form.

I come now to my "opus vitae." It is entitled *The Riddle of Konnersreuth,* and contains the results of my investigations of the phenomena which made a simple country girl a world celebrity.

Once when I was invited to deliver a series of lectures on the Catholic faith, the name of Theresa Neumann was on everyone's lips. Could I not—I asked myself—make her the subject of one of these lectures? Today people demand "concrete proofs of experimental criteria" instead of the abstruse arguments of metaphysics. And such proofs are certainly clear in the marvellous facts of Konnersreuth, —that the arm of God has not been shortened in our time!

Moved by these reflections, I began my study of the case. Unfortunately, most of the works on the subject were limited to the personal impressions of their authors. Even the excellent collections of historical facts made by L. Witt and by M. Gerlich did not include any scientific criticism. Being expert in neither theology or modern science—in particular, psychology—they simply attributed the amazing phenomena in question to miracle.

This mental attitude alarmed the hierarchy, for it exposed the Faith to the contempt of unbelievers. There was need for a scientific work on the Catholic doctrine of such subjects as ecstasy, visions, stigmatism, and prolonged fasting.

My researches were conducted in this spirit, and my book was welcomed by eminent theologians and scientists. In his preface to the work, Archbishop Carinci, Secretary of the Sacred Congregation of Rites, called it "a model of its kind" and "a precious contribution to the study of analogous cases." He added that "Through this work your Reverence has earned the gratitude of Science, of the Church, and in a particular manner, of the Sacred Congregation of Rites."

Just recently, I received from Rome the fifth edition of my *Psychologia Metaphysica*. It is the official textbook of the Gregorian University as well as of many other Catholic faculties throughout the world. From its initial appear-

ance in 1939, I have been urged to have it translated into
English. The same suggestion has often been made in regard to my works on Spinoza. Alas, my material circumstances do not allow me to even think of it. On this point,
may I be permitted a personal observation. Only one who
is rich can seriously cultivate science, said Aristotle. (He
was fortunate in Alexandria the Great without whose generous help most of his books could not have been published!) The Aristotelian aphorism is particularly poign-
ant in the matter of publishing scientific Catholic books in
a Protestant country. After years of research in various
archives and libraries, the author completes his manuscript and submits it to a publisher who, if he is to continue
to publish, must endeavor to get not only a confirmation of
its calibre but also an estimate of its potential market.
Being Catholic, it will likely be bought only by Catholics;
and being scientific, it will probably be bought only by
those Catholics interested in the particular problem treated.
And so he has often to conclude that he can publish it only
if the author bears a large part of its production costs.

But where can the author get the money? Catholic universities are usually so pressed in meeting their own expenses that they cannot help him. If he gets into some
lucrative work to raise the money he risks losing his capacity for the intellectual apostolate, or he may become
discouraged and abandon it. We often hear of the dearth
of American Catholic scientific productions. Certainly the
circumstances I have mentioned are an integral part of the
problem. Only one who is rich, said Aristotle, can seriously cultivate science. Should that be so in our country
and in our time?

EDITOR'S NOTE: Father Siwek was a professor of philosophy at Fordham from 1946 to 1949 and has been a research professor there since
1949. He became an American citizen in 1952. His works are *The
Philosophy of Evil* (1951), *The Enigma of the Hereafter* (1952),

The Riddle of Konnersreuth (1953), *La psychophysique humaine
d'après Aristote* (1930), *L'âme et le corps d'après Spinoza* (1930),
Spinoza et le panthéisme religieux (2. ed '50), *Le problème du mal*
(1942), *La réincarnation des esprits* (1942), *Une stigmatisée de nos
jours* (1951), *Psychologia Metaphysica* (5. ed '56), *Aristotelis De
Anima libri tres* (5. ed '52); as well as works in Polish, Portuguese,
and Spanish.

EDITH STEIN
(Sister Benedicta Teresia, O.C.D.)
(1891-1942)
by
Margaret Deveraux Conway

IN AN AGE WHEN WOMEN FUNCTION ABLY IN ALL TYPES OF positions, the great Jewish Carmelite of Germany may seem lost in the shadows of her own vocation. She was, however, both singular and wonderful; a woman of true wisdom, an intellectual whose mind was turned toward God, and a martyr to one of the destructive political fungi of our day.

The facts of her life have the simplicity and chiaroscuro of a fine etching. She was born in Breslau in 1891. Her father died when she was quite small; she and her six brothers and sisters were reared by a matriarchial Jewish mother, who observed all the exacting ritual of Orthodox Jewish life with the loving fidelity of a servant of God. Her father's death, however, in a sense also took her mother from her; for the care of the lumber business fell upon Frau Stein, and Edith was chiefly the concern of her older sister Erna. She was, even as a child, bright and ambitious. When she left preparatory school her natural brilliance was such that the headmaster said of her: "Strike a stone (stein), and out gushes wisdom."

Her mother's exact conformity to ritual held no attraction for her quick mind and—especially after she entered the University of Breslau—she drifted toward atheism. Her scholastic pre-eminence was such that in due course, if she stayed on at Breslau to write her doctorate in psychology as originally planned, she would have been one of the leading atheistic professors of the school. Fortunately, a book intervened to change her destiny.

It was a learned tome by Edmund Husserl entitled *Logical Investigations*. The book was a critique of the German philosophers of the nineteenth century: Hegel, Kant, Fichte, Nietzche, and others.

The bright-eyed Jewish girl, on the basis of this book, changed her field of interest and went for the summer term to the University of Gottengen, where Husserl taught. This transfer from one school to another was permissible and encouraged in the German universities of that day. Edith fully intended to return to Breslau for her degree; but events and interests kept her at Gottingen, where she wrote her doctorate under Husserl and obtained her degree in 1921. She stayed on after that to become her teacher's assistant, aiding him in preparing his new book, tutoring for his classes those candidates who were not yet prepared to understand him. To her sorrow, while she went onward to the fulness of Thomistic reason, she saw her much loved teacher, in the new book she was aiding him to prepare, revert to a modified form of subjective philosophy.

During these days in Gottingen two other impulses toward the Church were given her. It is a wry comment on the limitations of the curriculum of a secular university that the first time Edith Stein read anything avowedly Christian was during a literature class studying Gothic Old High German, when she encountered the "Our Father."

During the latter part of her student days the war came to Germany. She left temporarily to serve in the hospitals of the German Red Cross. One of her tutors who, with his wife, was also a friend of hers volunteered for army service and died on the field in 1917. Edith hastened back to Gottingen to comfort Frau Reinach in what she felt would be the widow's inconsolable despair. Instead, she found her calm and resigned to her loss. Edith afterwards said: "It was then I first encountered the Cross and the divine strength it inspires in those who bear it ... It was the moment in which my unbelief was shattered, Judaism paled, and Christ streamed out at me; Christ in the mystery of the Cross. Therefore," she added simply to a priest shortly before her death, "at my clothing I could express no other desire than that of being called Sister Benedicta 'of the Cross.' " And so she was called, for her full name in Carmel was Sister Benedicta Teresia a Cruce.

Her actual conversion was occasioned by the reading of another book, *The Life of St. Teresa of Avila, Written by Herself*. Edith read it through in one night; when dawn broke she closed it saying: "That is the truth." That very morning she bought a missal and a prayerbook. When she had mastered them she went to the pastor of the little parish church in the town where she was staying, to ask for baptism. More study, however, was required of her, and it was only on New Year's day, 1922, that the sacrament was administered. She took the name of Teresia, after the great saint. She rejoiced in Christ, but her joy was clouded in pain, the pain of telling her mother. In her eyes, to leave Judaism for Christ was to betray callously the millenia of suffering the race had endured for its fidelity to the only God. Judaism was the perfect theocracy, and to leave it rendered one a traitor as well as a blasphemer.

Edith came and knelt before her mother and said very simply: "Mother, I am a Catholic." She expected recrimi-

nation—and met a torrent of tears. She stayed with her
mother for several months, reorientating her own life,
softening the blow upon her family. She joined with her
mother on the Day of Atonement at the synagogue, confusing the old woman utterly because she prayed the
psalms from a Catholic breviary while the rabbi read them
from the Jewish religious books. And when the rabbi read
out the words: "Hear, O Israel, thy God is one," Edith's
mother bent to her in distress and uncomprehending love
to complain: "Do you hear? Thy God is but one!" And
Edith had to be silent, for it was not given to her mother
to have faith in the Trinity.

Edith's first impulse was to give herself completely to
God in the religious life. The priest who was directing her
forbade this and sent her to fulfill her vocation in God in
the very work she had been doing. She settled down to
teach—for ten years in a *Hochschule* conducted by the
Dominican nuns at Speyer, to write her philosophical works,
and to learn the science of prayer in the peaceful enclosure
of the convent. During that period, besides writing many
articles for learned reviews, and giving lectures for various
societies, she translated St. Thomas's *Questions Concerning Truth* into brilliant German. Towards the end of this
time, she also published her own work on *Potency and Act*.
This was in 1931.

The same year, she decided to return to the university
level of teaching and obtained a position as tutorial lecturer at the German Institute for Teaching, at Muenster.
Just as she was acclimating herself to her old and well-
loved atmosphere the campaign against the Jews in Germany became so stringent that she found herself forced to
cease lecturing on February 25, 1932, after but a year's
work and just at the point where she was preparing to
make public her proposal for an extensive reform of higher
grade teaching in Germany.

She was not too dismayed, for she felt this calamity was

a dispensation from Providence to give her the opportunity to follow the vocation to Carmel that she had cherished so many years. She went to Cologne and had an interview with the Mother Superior, explaining simply that she felt that God was keeping something for her in Carmel which she could find only there. The novice mistress pointed out gently that she would have to give up her work and the acclaim of her career, to which she replied: "It is not human activity that can help us, but the Passion of Christ. It is a share in that, that I desire." Already she seemed fully cognizant that she was to honor God through her prayer in Carmel for the salvation of herself, her people, and her country. Perhaps she even had a premonition of her death.

The Carmel agreed to accept her, and she went home for a long vacation before the entry day. She found it even more painful to tell her mother of her vocation than she had of her conversion. She deferred it from day to day, until one afternoon as they sat knitting, she was asked what she planned to do with the nuns in Cologne.

"Live with them," she replied gently.

Her mother was dumbfounded, unable to do or say anything further that day. But before Edith left home, she addressed one more piteous appeal to her:

"Is it possible for a Jew to be pious?"

"Certainly . . . if one has learned nothing more."

The old woman cried out: "Why have you learned more? I don't want to say anything against Him. He may have been a very good man. But why did he have to make Himself God?"

Edith fitted into the life of prayer at Carmel, but into little else, for she was awkward in the extreme at both housework and sewing, the two chief activities of Carmelites outside of their life of prayer. The nuns, who knew nothing of her background, must have wondered why she was among them. But she was gentle and took her own imperfections humbly. Because of her mother's age, Edith had permission to write a letter to Breslau every Friday. She heard faithfully in return from her sister Rosa; but not until after her clothing, from her mother. Then the eighty-four-year-old woman went out alone to visit the new Carmel in Breslau. She was received courteously and kindly and allowed to discover just what her daughter was about. She never wrote directly to Edith, but thereafter she always sent her greetings and her love.

After Edith's profession and reception of the veil in 1938, the Father Provincial of the German Carmelites ordered her to return to her writing. She rewrote and completed the enormous manuscript she had begun years before, *Finite and Eternal Being*. She had the joy of seeing the first volume published, but corrected proofs of the second volume were returned by the publisher with a note of regret saying that he was forbidden by law to publish the books of non-Aryans. That, together with a visit made by the local election officials to the Carmel to know why she did not vote, and the Mother Superior's admission that Sister Benedicta was registered as non-Aryan and had no voting rights, convinced the Superior that Sister Benedicta should leave the country for her own safety. The Carmel in Echt, Holland, welcomed her. There, in a short while, her sister Rosa, who had become a Catholic, joined her, living as a lay person at the convent and performing outside tasks for the nuns.

At Echt, Sister Benedicta continued to write, completing the last page of her book *Science of the Cross* on the very day she was led away to her death. Even in Echt she was not safe. When the Nazis conquered Holland, they began to put in effect there the same non-Aryan laws they had enforced in Germany. Her Sisters in Christ in Echt, fearing for Edith, as her Carmelite Sisters in Cologne had previously feared, obtained permission from a Carmel near Freiburg, Switzerland, to have her come there, but the

necessary legal and official permissions dragged out pain-
fully. Sister Benedicta had a holy indifference to the outcome, but by dint of such perseverance on everyone's part,
the Swiss entry papers were obtained and all that remained
was to get an exit visa from the Germans.

Tragic events intervened. The Catholic and Protestant
Churches of the Netherlands had been protesting the German treatment of the Jews.

Retaliation was swift and simple. On Sunday, August
2, 1942, two S.S. men appeared at the Carmel at Echt.
Thinking that they had brought the exit visa, Sister Benedicta went to meet them. When she greeted them, one of
them said harshly: "Get your things together. You have
five minutes to get ready. We are taking you away."

At the Superior's request, the time was extended to ten
minutes and the nuns bustled about to get the few things
that Sister Benedicta was allowed to take with her: a
blanket, some food, a few toilet articles. Still in her habit,
she left the enclosure and, with her sister Rosa, was taken
to the temporary concentration camp at Amersfoort. There
she joined about twelve hundred Dutch Jews including
other Jewish Catholic religious. On their habits—Dominican, Franciscan, Trappist, Carmelite—the yellow star of
David was hastily sewn.

Sometime on the night of the sixth of August, most of
them were suddenly taken away. It is known in general
that a large number of them died in the gas chambers of
Auschwitz (in Silesia, near Edith's home), but where and
when specific individuals died is impossible of proof.
Edith's last known message, given at the railroad station
in Schifferstadt to a young woman who had been her pupil
was "Give my love to the Sisters . . . I am on my way to the
East."

So Edith Stein disappeared, into the unknown so far as
human knowledge is concerned. But behind her, as a
guidepost, she leaves the simple facts of her life out of

which her double adventure was built, that of a mind seeking truth and a heart seeking love. Each way was hard. In a field which few women trod, she, as she stated it, "lived at the edge of the abyss" where philosophical ideas can so easily turn into the destructive perversions of error, and she not only found the truth, but shone in it as shines the morning star, linked through and with the Davidic star of her Hebraic heritage. And her heart found God, not in the quick onrush of young love which is the grace of her sister in Carmel, the Little Flower, but with the slow, steady, mature love that spreads its protective shade as the plane-tree by the roadside. Her mind, her hands, and her heart knew every crisis of our century and with God's grace brought all to perfection. She has undoubtedly won the reward that was promised by her great Jewish brother, the Apostle Paul, and has gone into that region where she may know as she also is known, in the triune God.

Out of such strength is a valiant woman of our century made.

EDITOR'S NOTE: Through the courtesy of *The Magnificat*, Miss Conway's chapter on Edith Stein is presented here. Among the available works of Edith Stein are her *Writings* (Newman, 1956), selected and translated by Hilda Graef, q.v.; *Endliches uns Ewiges Sein* (Herder, Freiburg, 1950), *Kreuzeswissenschaft:* studie ueber Joannes a Cruce (Nauwelaerts, Louvain, 1950); *Des hl. Thomas von Aquino untersuchungen ueber die wahrheit, Quaestio I-XIII* (id., 1953), and *Teresia von Jesus* (Kanisius verlag, Freiburg, Schw., 1952).

NEVILE HUNTER WATTS

I DON'T KNOW WHAT INTEREST MY LIFE SHOULD HAVE FOR anyone else, sufficient to make it worth while to describe it or anyone else's to read. But, after all, every individual life has something unique in it, something which, could it be communicated, would contribute to the sum of man's knowledge of his race. I'm just one of the human crowd, most human in my failings and my self-importance; but in the sight of my Maker I have a peculiar value and a special import. There's a pigeon-hole in heaven where my papers are docketed. And it isn't everyone who has been undeservedly lucky enough to find a Way of Life—a way that makes life add up and come close to a reasonable result, as I have. Everyone's life is different, but some lives are more different than others.

I was one of the large family of an Anglican clergyman, and I was brought up to be "good, like father," who, in my eyes, could do no wrong. To be good meant to be like Jesus

Christ, to be obedient and gentle and honest, not to pull my sisters' hair, and not to play with my toys (except Noah's Ark) on Sundays. On my walks with my mother or nurse, I would occasionally meet a Catholic priest (generally fat and rather shabby) or a pair of nuns, and, on enquiry about them, I would be told that they bowed down to images, worshipped the Virgin Mary, and devoted their efforts to "getting hold" of simple Protestants, especially rich ones.

Throughout my boyhood and adolescence I was, by my mother's influence and prayers (for which I have never ceased gratefully to bless her memory) preserved from the grosser sins. Twice I was swept emotionally off my feet by religious spasms: once after Confirmation, when in the presence of my embarrassed family I went to my knees and burst into tears in the dining-room; once, at the age of seventeen, when a celebrated revivalist preacher conducted a week's mission in my father's church. But these were both transient and, in my second year at Cambridge, I avowed myself as an agnostic, and for the next seven years I never, except to comply with college rules or to conform to my family when I was at home, entered any place of worship.

After graduating I applied for and obtained the post of Classical master at Downside, a celebrated English Catholic school. My parents, who had expected that my lapse into irreligion would prove as transient as my earlier phases of religiosity, had not resigned the hope that I would enter the Anglican ministry, and were strongly opposed to my connecting myself with a Papist institution; crucifixes in all the class-rooms, my father urged, would surely be most distasteful to me. But I pointed out that, having refused to swallow anything, I was secure from the fate of being tempted to swallow everything, and that my choice of the post was due merely to its being situated in a part of England which I had known and loved in walking-tours.

The school was run by Benedictine monks, and among them, and among my pupils, I soon found friends. I taught Latin and Greek, I played cricket, I walked in the beautiful countryside, and I was supremely happy. But, though I soon outgrew my prejudices against the Catholic Church, I drew no nearer to her. I invented a nature-religion of my own, whose high priests were Wordsworth and Shelley. One evening, in converse with a Catholic lay colleague, I threw out some ill-considered and probably ill-mannered jibe at the Church. My friend, with perfect firmness and perfect good humour, proceeded to dress me down until I was no more than a limp rag. I was humiliated, but my humiliation germinated within me and slowly, in the year that followed, grew into a realization of the meaning of the Church. I fought against this, even to the extent of breaking off my engagement to a Catholic girl on the ground that our religious differences amounted to an incompatibility which would make married happiness impossible. She became a nun, and I have no doubt that it was her prayers that broke down my resistance to the light and brought the truth into clear focus. I put myself under instruction, and after six months was received into the Church.

My Protestant relatives, deeply resentful at my defection, were at pains to represent my 'lapse' into 'Romanism' as the reaction of a weak and malleable nature to its environment; it was just a case of protective assimilation to background. The first World War wrenched me away from this background and probably gave my family to hope that my delusions would succumb to an alien and possibly hostile milieu. And it might well have proved so, but for the grace of God. Sunday Mass was intermittent, chaplains were rare birds, and the only other Catholic officer in my battalion had given up the practice of his religion and was a man of low, indeed of no, morals.

On my return from the war, I resumed my teaching

routine, trying to infect my pupils with my own passion
for the literature, and above all for the poetry, of the two
languages commonly known as 'dead'—the two most alive
languages in humanity—Greek and Latin. Out of these
has grown the literature of the English-speaking races,
and my love for this grew with and out of my love for
the former. I spent a summer holiday in making a
selection of English medieval religious poetry, which Burns
and Oates published in 1924, under the title *Love Songs of
Sion*. I worked at two volumes of translations of Cicero's
speeches for the Loeb Library. In 1937 Burns and Oates
brought out a small collection of my verses, *Pedant Poems*,
as to the value of which I am under no illusion. More
important and more formative than these was my taking
up lecturing in 1926 for the Workers' Educational Association. This organization, non-political and non-sectarian,
provides for adults in scores of towns and villages all over
England evening courses in a wide variety of subjects,
the only limitation being that the instruction shall be non-
vocational,—education for life, not for livelihood. I threw
myself into this work with avidity, travelling distances up
to thirty miles or more after my day's work in school,
often three evenings in the week. My audience would
number sometimes sixty, sometimes six. I would talk as
a low-brow to low-brows. By this I mean that I was not
interested, and made it no part of my business to interest
my class, in the snob-values of literature,—its use as a
means of social or vocational advancement. I tried to
present literature, and above all poetry, to them as a means
to fuller and deeper life for themselves because it would
help them, paradoxically, to live not in and for themselves
but in and for others, to care more about more things.
"Christianity taught us to care. Caring is the great thing,
caring matters most," wrote von Huegel on his death-bed.
Great literature, too, teaches us to care, and so can be a
handmaid to religion.

During more than twenty years of this work, members of my classes had from time to time told me that they would like to have some record of my talks. So in 1946, I sent a selection of them to a publisher—a Catholic publisher, as I was confident that my angle on literature had been a Catholic angle. The book was accepted by Sheed and Ward, published under the title *The Vision Splendid,* and has found a fair number of readers on both sides of the Atlantic.

Such has been my brief and spasmodic literary output. If it has any import at all, it may be summed up in lines which perhaps contain more truth and value than all else that I have written put together:

> To set thy heart a harp to every breeze;
> To greet life's grandeur on adoring knees;
> To see the world as pitying Godhead sees,
> One-souled, one-hearted with "the least of these"—
> This is the end of all philosophies.

REVEREND FRANCIS XA-
VIER WEISER, S.J.

BEING A COLLEGE PROFESSOR BY DUTY AND HABIT, I SHALL
probably write this sketch as I would give a lecture in
class. However, at times even a college class may turn out
to be interesting and enjoyable.

I was born in Vienna, Austria, in 1901. At that time
the city was still the gay capital of a famous empire.
Furthermore, it was, and still is, the great metropolis of
music and song. You might say that we grew up to the
tunes of Haydn, Beethoven, Mozart, Schubert, and Strauss.
I have a vague feeling that this atmosphere of culture,
music, and art, had much to do with my desire to write.
At the age of eight or nine, while still a little boy in
grammar school, I used to ask God daily in my evening
prayer to "let me write books."

According to the Austrian system of education, I started
the study of Latin at the age of eleven, and Greek when
I was fourteen. For good measure, there was added a

three-year course in Italian; also religion, literature, history, geography, mathematics, physics, chemistry, biology, drawing, music, art appreciation, and singing. All these subjects, topped by a two-year course in fundamental philosophy, constituted the secondary schooling (Gymnasium). After that, at the age of nineteen, we were ready for the university.

However, instead of proceeding directly from the gymnasium to the university, I entered the novitiate of the Jesuit Order. In 1924 I started the seven-year course at the University of Innsbruck in the Tyrol. The fruits of these studies, at least the recorded ones, are academic degrees in philosophy, theology, and education. The unrecorded fruit (which is more important), is supposed to have become a part of my personality, and is known only to God.

After ordination in 1930, I came to the United States for a year of special studies. From 1932 to 1938, I was stationed at Vienna as editor of a youth magazine and national moderator of the student sodalities. When the Nazis occupied Austria in 1938, Catholic youth work was made wellnigh impossible. I "returned" to the United States that same year and have remained here ever since, first as a parish assistant in Buffalo and Boston, then, from 1943 to 1950, as pastor of Holy Trinity Church in Boston, and since 1950 as a teacher at Emmanuel College in Boston.

The desire and urge for writing never left me. My superiors prudently encouraged this trend even during my years as a student. From 1928 to 1953, I wrote sixteen books in German: novels, biographies, and six plays. Some of these works are still "going the rounds" in new printings. Since the first of them appeared twenty-eight years ago, many parents in Europe who had read my books as youngsters and whose children read them now, think of me as either dead and buried, or as a very, very old

man. Who can blame them! I greatly enjoyed their
startled looks when I met many of them in Europe last
year. It does flatter your ego to surprise people by being
younger than they thought you were.

But let us talk about my books in English. First, I
am often told that my style is somewhat accomplished,
clear, and pleasantly attractive to the American reader.
Allow me to tell you a secret. I never had the benefit
of "studying" English; never had a teacher or any formal
instruction in this language. All the English I know,
was—to use a popular expression—just "picked up"
by reading good English books. (The word "good" refers
to both English and books.) That is the reason why I am
now so keenly and sadly aware of the incredible harm
which the atrocious language and spelling of our comic
books must cause to the minds of children. If reading
"good English" books gave me my knowledge of the
language, what kind of language habits will the comics
produce in our children?

How did I come to write these books? When I arrived
in this country in 1931 and again in 1938, I was deeply
impressed by many aspects of American life. Among them
was the charming sight of the popular Christmas celebration. This tradition had been molded into one unit out
of the best national Christmas lore of various immigrant
groups. It was only during the second half of the last
century that our American Christmas observance came to
be established.

Soon I discovered that most people have no clear notion
of the origin, background, and true meaning of these customs which they observe in their homes. Since the great
majority of our Christmas, Easter, Thanksgiving, and other
observances actually go back to the inspiration of liturgical
thought and symbolism, I judged it a worthwhile subject
to explain. Also a priestly subject; for, given the fact
that our popular customs contain the radiation of the

liturgy, the understanding of this radiation would make the
celebration of our Christian feasts within the family
warmer, holier, and more truly joyful. At the same time,
a better grasp of the religious meaning and message of our
family customs would give parents valuable help for the
religious training of their little ones.

It took me six years of research, which I did hobby-
fashion, besides and between my many other duties. (Here
comes the college professor again, looking at you over the
rim of his glasses, raising his finger, and telling you that
much can be accomplished in the course of years by using
spare minutes.) I extended my studies over the span of
the whole ecclesiastical year, its feasts and seasons, including both the liturgical observance and the traditional
folklore.

At times, of course, I felt very much like abandoning
the project altogether, especially when repeated efforts at
clearing up a particular point remained fruitless. Once I
tried for weeks to find authentic information about the
traditional pictures imprinted on a certain kind of European Christmas pastry. In vain I searched the pertinent
encyclopedias and other literature in various languages at
the greater libraries of Boston. Finally, when on the point
of dropping the matter completely and leaving it out of
the book, I happened to be told by a family that they had
an old Christmas pastry pan in the attic. Immediately
I went and looked at it. Hidden beneath the dust of years,
I found a mold pattern of fifty pictures—exactly the ones
I had been looking for.

The books appeared at intervals of two years: *The
Christmas Book* in 1952, *The Easter Book* in 1954, and
The Holyday Book in 1956. In the summer of 1956 I
wrote a booklet of about a hundred pages on *Religious
Customs in the Family* which was published by the Liturgical Press at the end of the year. My plans for future
writing hold as the next item a Handbook of Christian

Feasts and Customs, and after that—well, I'd better not look too far ahead.

I have not discussed the publication of books with other authors, so I really do not know much about the problems, disappointments, and frustrations to which writers might be subject, except from occasional hearsay. If you should infer from this remark that I am personally free from such annoyances, you have conjectured correctly. It is a pleasure, almost amounting to a duty, to publicly acknowledge the courteous and cordial spirit of cooperation exercised by my publishers, Harcourt, Brace and Company, and by all the members of the firm who had anything to do with my publications.

Autobiographical sketches are sometimes a nuisance for both writer and reader. In this case, however, it is different, at least on my side of the printing press. I did enjoy writing these lines; and since genuine joy is contagious, I hope and pray that my readers will not have wasted their time in perusing what I have written. God bless you all!

ANTONIA WHITE

I SUPPOSE IT IS NATURAL FOR AN ONLY CHILD MUCH AD-
dicted to reading to take early to writing. I think I was
five when I first began to 'compose' on my own, using very
pompous language copied from the Victorian children's
books on my grandmother's shelves. Like all children, I
found it difficult to finish the works so enthusiastically
begun. However, when I was seven, I found a most satis-
factory solution to this problem: I discovered the blurb.
So instead of laboriously composing books, I took to writing
highly flattering reviews of works by myself. Nothing of
these existed but their titles, but I got as much satisfaction
out of the self-written reviews as if I had actually produced
the volumes I attributed to my 'versatile pen.' Now, fifty
years later, it still gives me a curiously unreal feeling to
read press-notices of my own novels. I think I find it hard
to realize that the book really exists and is not just a fig-
ment of my imagination.

I was born in 1899 and baptized a Protestant. In 1906, my father, who was a schoolmaster, became a Catholic and thereby prevented himself from ever becoming a head-master of any of the English Public Schools. My mother was converted along with him. It is her maiden name of White that I use as a writer. Her brother, Victor White, emigrated to the United States and became a naturalized American citizen. The portrait of my great-great grand-father by Sir Thomas Lawrence now hangs in the Art Gallery of Omaha, Nebraska, and, if ever I visit the United States, I shall go and look at that portrait which I re-member so well from my childhood. I was received into the Church at seven. At nine, I went to a convent school and it was there on my fifteenth birthday, that something happened that affected my whole writing life. It was one of those tragi-comic misunderstandings, but it gave me a shock from which I have never quite recovered. Up to that day, I had thoroughly enjoyed writing. I was monotonously 'top in composition' in class and, on free-study afternoons, I would write stories and poems for the sheer pleasure of it. These would often be carefully copied into exercise books and presented to my parents and grand-parents. When I was fourteen, I planned something really ambitious months ahead as a surprise for my father's birthday,—nothing less than a full-length novel. My father was the person I most loved and feared in the whole world, and I planned my novel to astonish and de-light him by being highly edifying as well as sensational. My characters were to begin by being dreadfully wicked and worldly and, after a series of exciting adventures, to end up by being dramatically converted. The worst of all was to finish up as a saintly Trappist. I had written about five chapters of the wicked and worldly part. Being very innocent, I did not know how to make my future Trappist wicked enough so I merely said he 'indulged in nameless vices'... a phrase I had read somewhere and which seemed an excellent blanket. Unfortunately, I yielded to author's vanity and let a school friend see these opening chapters. She rashly read them in study-time and a nun confiscated the manuscript. The next thing I knew was that my parents were sent for and I was virtually expelled. I was too paralyzed to explain to my outraged father that I had meant no harm and that all my characters were to end up paragons of virtue. He remained so convinced that I must have a precociously corrupted mind that it was not till long after his death that I ever attempted to write another novel. I put that absurd, yet agonizing, episode into the first novel I ever published, *Frost in May* (Viking Press). But that was not till 1934 ... twenty years after it occurred.

From the time I left school, apart from a brief period of being a deservedly unsuccessful actress, I did, however, earn my living by writing in one form or another. I wrote magazine stories and articles; I wrote free-lance advertising for five years and spent nine as a copy-writer in a big London agency. But, apart from two or three short stories, I wrote nothing 'serious.' I felt safe only writing things to order. I was obsessed with the idea that if I wrote anything of my own, something wicked and corrupt would creep into it and I would be faced again with horrified disapprobation.

Frost in May was written almost by accident and, once again, to please someone I loved. I was turning out some old papers and found some totally forgotten pages I had written while still at my convent school. My husband read them and said "You must finish this and make it into a novel. I want a chapter every Saturday night read aloud to me." I obeyed. The book was finished, quickly accepted, and is still being sold. Because a loved person had approved of it, I thought the 'curse' on my novel-writing had been lifted forever. Far from it. After I had written a few chapters of my next novel, my husband left me. It must have seemed to my unconscious mind that writing drove away affection and all the old sense of guilt returned. I pegged on with articles and advertising copy to order and it was not till a breakdown landed me in nearly four years of psychoanalytical treatment that I slowly and laboriously resumed my interrupted novel. Even so, it was fifteen years in all between the writing of the first and the last chapters of *The Lost Traveller* (Viking Press), which was published in 1950.

Since then, I have had published two more novels: *The Sugar House* (Eyre, 1952) and *Beyond the Glass* (Regnery, 1954). But, though I can now force myself to write, it is never a pleasure. The old terrors always return and often, with them, a feeling of such paralyzing lack of self-confidence that I have to take earlier books of mine off their shelf just to prove to myself that I actually wrote them and they were actually printed, bound, and read. I find that numbers of writers experience these same miseries over their work and do not, as is so often supposed, enjoy the process. "Creative joy" is something I haven't felt since I was fourteen and don't expect to feel again. I have just had to learn to peg on without this pleasurable sensation. There is, however, a definite satisfaction in finishing a novel, though it is apt to disappear when the proofs arrive. And there is a more solid comfort in occasionally finding in an old book passages that give one quite a pleasant surprise.

Though bad reviews can wound a lot, good ones do not always inflate one as much as they might. So often the flattering remarks seem to bear no relation to the novel one has actually written, so that one feels rather like a cat that has been awarded a prize in a dog-show. What is far more heartening than even the kindest review is the letter from the stranger who has read the book and taken the trouble to write a personal appreciation. Best of all is the stranger who finds something in what one has written that corresponds to their own experience of life or even illuminates it. One such letter from a stranger in New Jersey (she is now a friend of many years' standing) gave me courage to tackle a difficult theme ... that of insanity. It is to this Catholic woman doctor that I dedicated my last novel, *Beyond the Glass*.

My novels and short stories are mainly about ordinary people who become involved in rather extraordinary situations. I do not mean in sensational adventures but in rather odd and difficult personal relationships largely due to their family background and their incomplete understanding of their own natures. I use both Catholic and non-Catholic characters and am particularly interested in the conflicts that arise between them and in the influences they have on each other. The fact that I lapsed from both faith and practice for fifteen years is naturally something I bitterly regret. Nevertheless, I think that it has given me a real understanding of those outside of the Church and of problems for Catholics themselves which those who have been spared 'doubts' do not always appreciate. Since I was fortunate enough to recover my faith in 1940, every year has given me a deeper conviction of its truth. If anything I have written or may write one day could reduce some of the misunderstandings between Catholics and non-Catholics, I would be more than rewarded for all the qualms and miseries I have every time I embark on the seemingly impossible task of writing another novel.

EDITOR'S NOTE: Miss White is also distinguished as a translator from the French. In 1949 her version of Guy de Maupassant's *Une vie* was awarded the Denyce Clairouin Prize; and since then she has turned into English Henri Bordeaux's *A Pathway to Heaven* (1952), Dr. Alexis Carrel's *Reflections on Life* (1953), and Paul André Lesort's *The Wind Bloweth Where It Listeth* (1955).